Also by Stanley Cohen

The Game They Played
The Man in the Crowd
Dodgers! The First One Hundred Years
Willie's Game (with Willie Mosconi)
Tough Talk (with Martin Garbus)
The Wrong Men: America's Epidemic of Wrongful
Death Row Convictions
The Execution of Officer Becker: The Murder of a Gambler, the Trial
of a Cop, and the Brith of Organized Crime

A Magic SUMMER

THE AMAZIN' STORY OF THE 1969 NEW YORK METS

Stanley Cohen

Skyhorse Publishing

To my three oldest friends, in order of appearance:
Donald Feldman, Martin Morgenstern, Martin Pops
and
in memory of two others: Howard Shaw and Harvey Matusow

Skyhorse Publishing books may be purchased in bulk at special discounts for
sales promotion, corporate gifts, fund-raising, or educational purposes. Special
editions can also be created to specifications. For details, contact the Special
Sales Department, Skyhorse Publishing, 555 Eighth Avenue, Suite 903, New
York, NY 10018 or info@skyhorsepublishing.com.

www.skyhorsepublishing.com

10 9 8 7 6 5 4 3 2 1

Library of Congress Cataloging-in-Publication Data is available on file.
ISBN: 978-1-60239-679-1

Printed in the United States of America

CONTENTS

INTRODUCTION

IT WAS A FITTING ENDING TO A DECADE WHOSE images, forty years later, continue to endure in a shared imagination. Mention the sixties, and anyone who lived through them will conjure visions of cities burning, college campuses under siege, national leaders felled by assassins' bullets, and the grim choreography of a war that tore at our souls from a distance of 10,000 miles. There was, at the time, the uneasy sense that the fabric that held our lives together was coming apart. Something special was needed to turn the mood of the country, a miracle of sorts, and there were two on the horizon.

In July of 1969, we watched the flickering, black-and-white images of men walking on the moon. It was an achievement that transformed reverie to reality, but it was, at its heart, a triumph of technology, the fulfillment of a nation's promise made by a president eight years earlier. But another "miracle" was just three months away. On a sunlit October afternoon, a scruffy baseball team with few brand names on its roster was going to win one for the rest of us. The New York Mets, underdogs of 100-1 in pre-season computations, were about to win the World Series all by themselves. Without government financing or the benedictions of science, they were about to carve their name in the indelible clay of baseball history as the "Miracle Mets."

Now, viewed through the prism of time, the Mets' achievement seems even more distinctive, for the game has been changing dramatically, and miracles would soon be harder to come by. Technology has come to the ballpark, and an avalanche of statistics produced by computers explains why events unwound as they did; it is all right there in the numbers. The intuition that used to challenge the odds has been outsourced to the microchip. There is no longer much of a difference in the way a game is conducted, as every manager has become prisoner to the percentages, apparently unaware of the adage that percentage players also die broke. Somewhere along the way, technology seems to have exposed the sleight-of-hand magic that had once gone unseen, and in the process our capacity for wonder has been compressed. What were looked upon as miracles in the past are now comprehended in the charts and tables that have replaced myth with calculation.

Today, a pitcher's effectiveness is modified by the number of pitches he is allowed to throw. When the '69 Mets were sculpting truth from the stuff of daydreams, there were no setup men or closers; a pitcher was expected to complete the game he started. No one had ever heard of pitch counts. Batting gloves were not yet the fashion, which meant that batters did not step out of the box after every pitch to readjust them, which meant that games ended in far less than four hours. The World Series was played beneath the crystal sunlight of October skies rather than after dark in temperatures that hovered near freezing. There were no wild card teams in the playoffs; in fact, 1969 was the first year that there were any playoffs at all, just one best-of-five series in each league, and that was considered revolutionary. No one knew what a DH was; pitchers batted when their turn came. Only doctors had heard of steroids.

In 1969, there were no luxury suites in Shea Stadium, but there were general admission seats that were actually within sight of the playing field, and you could usually get one on the day of the game. The scoreboard was in fact a scoreboard and showed the scores of out-of-town games; it was not a message board that told you when to cheer and how loud. Music was piped from the public address system only to suit a particular occasion, and came through at decibel levels that did not approach the sound barrier. On the field, the home team always wore white uniforms and the visiting team was dressed in gray; the colorful jerseys worn in softball beer leagues had not yet become the vogue. Players' salaries in 1969—except for a handful of superstars—were not much higher than those earned by many of the fans who paid to watch them play. They worked at other jobs in the off-season—jobs they often returned to when they retired from the game.

Some twenty years later, when I made my way across the country to interview them, almost all the players who put the magic in the '69 season were working full time. Art Shamsky was a real estate consultant and part-owner of a restaurant in lower Manhattan; Tug McGraw hosted a TV talk show called *Ya Gotta Believe* and ran a marketing firm called Tug McGraw Resources in a suburb of Philadelphia; Jerry Koosman and Wayne Garrett were involved in overnight courier services; Ed Kranepool owned a firm that manufactured marketing displays; Cleon Jones was in the roofing business in Alabama; I met with Jerry Grote in his real estate office in San Antonio, Texas; Gary Gentry also was in the real estate business; Ron Swoboda was sports director at a TV station in Phoenix, Arizona; Ken Boswell was sales manager for an auto dealer in Austin, Texas.

A few of the players were still in baseball. Tom Seaver, in the twilight of his career, was pitching for the Chicago White Sox and Nolan Ryan, in the Houston Astros uniform, was striking out batters; Bud Harrelson was the third-base coach of the 1986 Mets who were on their way to another World Series title. Ron Taylor was the team physician for the Toronto Blue Jays and director of the S.C. Cooper Sports Medicine Clinic at a Toronto hospital.

Now, forty years after the fact, Ryan is president of the Texas Rangers; Harrelson is senior vice president and first-base coach for the Long Island Ducks, an unaffiliated minor-league team. Seaver, who worked for many years as a TV color commentator, is a vintner in Calistoga, California, rising as early as 6 A.M. to tend to his grapes. Most of the other players have since retired. Five have passed on at relatively early ages: Cal Koonce, in 1993 at the age of fifty-two; Tommie Agee, 2001, at fifty-three; Tug McGraw, 2004, fifty-nine; Donn Clendenon, 2005, seventy; and Don Cardwell, 2008, seventy-two.

In retrospect, the '69 Mets seem to have inhabited another time; baseball was still a game, then. The fields smelled fresher, the sun shone brighter, and the nights were softer. And the players, yes, the players, they played harder then, didn't they? Weren't they tougher then, with wads of chewin' tobacco bulging from their cheeks? Now they chew bubble gum and blow bubbles as they circle the bases. But wasn't everything better then? Didn't the days pass more slowly, filled as they were with the texture of moments and events that could not be anticipated?

Of course the author is forty years older too now, and time has a way of embellishing the trophies of memory. There is a prime in the life of a fan just as there is in the career of a player, and those years can never be recaptured. They remain as treasures to be visited upon occasion, to be resurrected in the fullness of time, perhaps polished a bit, and then replaced in the storehouse of the past.

Yet we know that today is the prime of another generation. Our grandchildren are steeped in wonder as Jose Reyes steals a base, or Carlos Beltran runs down a drive into the gap, or David Wright launches one high and far into the late night air. Doubtless, they will look back on these seasons of their life and find the magic at some turning. Somewhere, at some time, their own Cinderella will find that the slipper fit; once again some band of losers will be feted with champagne and wrapped in blue ribbons.

Miracles, after all, are what we make them; they come when we need them most. So it is left for each generation to fashion its own as the occasion demands. The clock keeps ticking. Memory stalks time across the years and for those of us who remember it, the '69 season of the New York Mets is our path back to a time when our dreams, filled with promise and fed by the conviction that reality was ours to shape, were beckoning from a horizon that was well within the measure of our reach.

P R O L O G U E

THE ARITHMETIC SAYS IT WAS
easy. In 1969, the New York Mets won their division championship by eight games. They won the National League
pennant in three straight and the World Series four in a row
after losing the opener.

But the numbers alone do not tell the story. The measure of that season must be taken against the context of the
past. In their first seven years, the Mets finished last five times
and next to last twice. During that time, they trailed the division leader by an average of more than forty-one games a
season. In 1968, they lost sixteen more games than they won
and finished twenty-four games out of first place. In the spring
of 1969, the Las Vegas odds were 100-to-1 against the Mets'
winning the National League pennant.

But what appeared impossible in April, improbable in
August, and unlikely as late as September had, by the middle
of October, taken on the aspect of predestination.

The perspective of time makes sages of us all. Viewed
through the prism of the past two decades, the triumph of
the 1969 Mets seems to have had about it the taut inevitability of classical drama. Now, each event in that memorable
season reveals itself as both cause and effect, every pivot of

1

fortune the product of forces greater than chance. Together they weave themselves into a tapestry so neatly formed as to suggest that the outcome could not have been other than it was. That, of course, is a picture framed against a distant backdrop. At the time, it seemed as though magic were loose in the land.

Taken individually, the '69 Mets were not a remarkable team. Their roster was not crowded with names likely to be inscribed on plaques in Cooperstown. Only two members of the team—Cleon Jones and Tommie Agee—came to bat more than four hundred times that season. Most of the others were part-time players whose appearance in the lineup depended upon whether the opposing pitcher was right- or left-handed. They were, in short, a team that relied on exceptional pitching and an instinct to seize the moment when chance fell to its favor.

Yet they are one of the very few teams that have survived the years with an identity all their own, remembered and defined by the year in which they won. "The '69 Mets" is a phrase that lives alongside such others as the '27 Yankees, the '34 Cardinals, the '51 Giants, and the '55 Brooklyn Dodgers. Each is recalled in a special pocket of memory that is held apart from the teams that preceded it or those that followed. Some teams are remembered for the way they dominated all opposition, others for their late-season comebacks. Within such company, the Mets alone won their place in history because their triumph seemed to draw its breath from circumstances that ran counter to their nature.

The Mets were, after all, a team of modest breeding, heirs to a legacy of defeat unlike any other in sports. Born in 1962, baseball's first year of expansion, the Mets right from the start had embossed the act of losing with a stamp all their own. It was their special genius, it seemed, to devise strategies for defeat that challenged the imagination. They brought to their efforts a lovable futility that endeared them to New

York, the world's first sanctuary for frail dreams and fading causes. They were taken to the heart, embraced without question.

In their first season, they lost 120 ballgames, a number unequalled in all the years baseball had been played. In subsequent seasons, it often appeared as if they were trying to exceed their own record but failed also at that. Even their heroes were not of the conventional stripe—batters who produced runs and pitchers who got the critical out. They were, instead, much in the literary fashion of the sixties, antiheroes who slipped and stumbled, who tried but failed, whose every vision was clouded by a hostile reality. They performed with a heroic pathos that perhaps struck a familiar chord in those who watched and cheered them. The Mets greeted each day with a relentless persistence that locked eyes with defeat but refused to blink.

During those early years, it was suggested that someday the Mets would rise to the level of mediocrity and forfeit the devotion of their fans. But they surprised everyone. They bypassed mediocrity entirely. In the summer of 1969 they simply took a deep breath and sprinted to the top. Now, they told their followers, watch closely and you will see that anything is possible.

They won a total of 107 games that season, including the playoffs and World Series. In the next fifteen years, only five teams won more games than the Mets of '69. Theirs was not a victory taken by default. Trailing the Chicago Cubs by nine and a half games in mid-August, they proceeded to win thirty-eight of their last forty-nine ballgames, including runs of nine and ten in a row. They took seven of their last ten games with the Cubs. They won their season series from every team in the league except the Houston Astros. In postseason play, they dominated the Braves with their bats and then choked off the Orioles with their pitching. They won going to the lead when they could and coming from behind when they had to. And yet, when all the returns were in and the Mets were champions tried and proven, their victory was deemed a miracle. History is more easily written than emended, and if the Yankees of '27 will forever be known as Murderers' Row, the Mets of '69 will be remembered always as the Miracle Mets.

It is a subtle slander if taken literally, and the members of that team, virtually to a man, regard it with benign resentment.

"There was nothing miraculous about it," says Bud Harrelson, the shortstop. "We went out each day with the idea of winning, and most of the time we won. We were not a great offensive team, but we got the hits when we needed them. We had outstanding pitching and we played very tight defense. That's fundamental baseball, not a miracle."

But miracles are mostly a state of mind. They depend on the willingness, perhaps even the need, to believe that one's fortunes are held in hands more certain than one's own. And so the Met championship, to the players truly a product of hard work, skill, and dedication, was nonetheless a miracle to their followers. Met fans with seven years' longevity viewed the entire season through the lens of the team's disenchanted past. For them, what occurred in 1969 could not adequately be explained in the routine tabulations common to baseball. The Met championship was christened a miracle because the mood of the times called for one—and when it comes to miracles, timing is everything.

The sixties, of course, had been a windstorm of a decade, a period that seemed to have fallen out of time and breathed a life of its own. But now that decade was drawing to a close. In late July, America landed a spaceship on the moon, and two of its passengers turned myth into wonder by setting foot in its dust. The imagination was wakened to new possibilities. "If men can walk on the moon. . . ."

At the time of the moon landing, the 1969 baseball season was at its midpoint. The three-day All-Star break had begun. The Mets watched the moon walk in an otherwise empty passenger terminal in Montreal's airport. They had just split a doubleheader with the Expos, and now, bound for New York, their charter flight had been grounded because of an equipment failure. They watched as Neil Armstrong moved about on the surface of the moon, and they watched with particular interest.

"People had always kidded us that there would be men on the moon before the Mets ever got to first place," said Ed Kranepool, the only player who had been a Met since the team's first season, "and they were right."

But not, as it turned out, by much. The Mets were indeed a legitimate contender at that point in the season, but there were few who honored their chances. They were judged by many to be impostors, a team that had been favored by fortune but could be trusted to revert to form when their luck ran out. Sooner or later, it was held, their past would reclaim them.

Most skeptical of all were the fans, for they had the longest memories. A team's followers always outlast its players and even its owners. They do not get sold or traded, they do not retire or become free agents, they do not sell out to conglomerates, and they rarely switch allegiance. They represent a team's truest continuity; they are the repository of its history. And Met fans, who for years had thrived on failed hopes and comic relief, were of a very special type.

They were called the New Breed, a species for whom victory was an afterthought. Good-humored and raucous, they flocked to the ballpark each day with a spirit immune to circumstance. Disappointment was foreign to their nature, for they sheltered no expectations. They reacted to every hit as if it were a run; every run scored was cheered as a victory;

and a victory—rare commodity that it was—was greeted with the unabashed glee usually reserved for the winning of a championship.

During one game in 1963 (the team's last season at the old Polo Grounds), with the Mets trailing by thirteen runs in the bottom of the ninth, two out and no one on base, the New Breed sent up a chant of "Let's go, Mets." With each new strike on the batter, the cry grew louder and more insistent. It was a battle cry that needed no battle; it betrayed neither a glimmer of hope nor the sneer of derision. It was a simple and joyous act of defiance, the declaration of a will that would not surrender to the inevitable.

The Mets and the New Breed formed the happiest of unions, a partnership in which even the most dismal failures of the one nourished the heart of the other. It was a bond that has been compared to that between the old Brooklyn Dodgers and their Flatbush Faithful, just as the Dodger teams of the late forties and early fifties have often been designated the forebears of the Mets. It is a sentimental analogy. The teams were vastly different in nature, and they appealed to instincts that were equally diverse.

The postwar Dodgers were a team rich in talent, arguably the best in the major leagues, which nonetheless ended each season with a new frustration. Always, it seemed, they were a step short or a minute late. Five times from 1946 to 1952, they lost a championship on the last day of their season. In 1946, the Cardinals beat them for the pennant in a playoff game. A year later, the Yankees edged them in the seventh game of the World Series. In 1950, Dick Sisler of the Phillies eliminated them with a home run on the season's last day. Then, in 1951, Dodger despair was given new definition with Bobby Thomson's ninth-inning home run. The following season, it was the Yankees again, snatching the sixth and seventh games of the World Series in Brooklyn's Ebbets Field. The Dodgers were the mortal embodiment of Sisyphus, pushing the boulder up the mountain to within a foot, an inch, of the peak, only to see it slip and roll back down, a burden to be taken up with new vigor the following season. "Wait 'til next year" became a slogan that resounded with the bittersweet blend of hopefulness and dread.

The Mets, by contrast, had never been close enough to muse upon the prospects of a subsequent season. At no point in their first seven years could they have aspired to anything more than the bare threads of respectability. For Met fans, "next year" always promised to be little more than a replay of the one just past. Then, suddenly it seemed, this team that had measured prosperity in small change and fragile wishes decided to tap the till and shoot for the moon. In one quick and unexpected burst, the Mets appeared to stretch the distance from Mudville to Wonderland.

The attentive observer, however, might have detected some hints of change along the way. In 1968, while barely escaping last place, the Mets won seventy-three games, twelve more than the previous season and the most in their history. They also finished sixteen and a half games closer to the lead than in 1967 and within three games of the two teams just ahead of them in the standings.

But the real indication of what was to come could be seen only in a close scrutiny of their roster. A gradual evolution in personnel had begun as early as 1965, and it continued right up through the start of the '69 season. Most of it was home-grown talent, signed by Met scouts and nurtured in the farm system. They took the place of used-up veterans and untried journeymen with whom the Mets began life as an expansion team, when their aim was more to attract fans than to win ballgames. Players like Duke Snider, Gil Hodges, Richie Ashburn, and Warren Spahn—now in the sunset of their careers—were eased into retirement, and young but unpromising hopefuls such as Choo-Choo Coleman, Rod Kanehl, and Marv Throneberry, who remains the prototype of

Met futility, were shuffled off to other teams or, more often, into new occupations.

Up from the minors in 1965 came Cleon Jones, Ron Swoboda, Bud Harrelson, and Tug McGraw. Soon to arrive would be Nolan Ryan, Ken Boswell, Tom Seaver, and Jerry Koosman. Casey Stengel, managing his last season in 1965, referred to them proudly as the Youth of America. They trickled onto the Met roster, played their way into the lineup, and soon blended together with other, more seasoned, players obtained in trades. Jerry Grote and Ron Taylor came over from the Astros, Ed Charles from Kansas City, and Don Cardwell from Pittsburgh. From the White Sox came Tommie Agee, Al Weis, and J. C. Martin; and from Cincinnati, Art Shamsky.

Though few possessed world-class talent, the rookies had youth and promise, and the veterans, still with some good years left in them, had poise, experience, and, in some instances, a taste of what it was like to play for a winner. Perhaps most important, they were unconnected to Met tradition. They did not know they were supposed to lose with good humor or treat victory as an unexpected gift. If any doubts lingered, these would soon be erased by the Mets' second-year manager, Gil Hodges, who had little patience for defeat and even less for a player ready to accept it.

So the Youth of America gathered in St. Petersburg, Florida, in the late winter of 1969, perhaps without great expectations, but certainly shorn of the legacy of despair. They would soon embark upon a season like no other. And now, nearly twenty years later, each looks back upon the summer of 1969 with that mellow mix of loss and wonder that is each man's private heirloom.

PART ONE

A New Look

CHAPTER

1

RIGHT FROM THE START, 1969 was a year that bristled with innovation and the portents of a new era. The structure of baseball, for so long immutable, had begun to suffer the incursions of change in the fifties. Franchises with roots sunk deep in the soil of tradition set out to open new frontiers. They pushed west, first to places like Milwaukee and Kansas City, then across the continent as the Giants and Dodgers moved to California. In the early sixties, the major leagues expanded for the first time in the twentieth century. The American League added two teams in 1961 and stretched the once-sacrosanct 154-game schedule by eight games. A year later, the National League followed suit, giving birth to the Mets along with the Houston team that would become their seven-year rivals for last place. Still, there was only one pennant race in each league and only one postseason competition: the World Series.

Now, in 1969—baseball's centennial year—the format was altered dramatically. Each league again adopted two new teams, and the leagues were split into Eastern and Western Divisions with six teams in each. Henceforward there would be four season-long pennant races of 162 games. The division winners in each would then meet in a best-of-five playoff to determine the World Series contestants. There was more than one reason for the change.

The addition of new franchises was a way of holding off the antitrust forces in Congress. Baseball enjoyed a limited exemption from the Sherman Antitrust Act, but in the activist decade of the sixties new threats seemed always to be on the horizon. A congressman with a mind to stir the waters could conceivably be placated if his state were granted a major league franchise.

There was also a more urgent motive. Baseball's claim to being the national pastime was never more at peril than it was at the end of the 1968 season. For ten years, the appeal of professional football had been growing, and by the midsixties NBA basketball too began to attract wider public attention. Both those sports seemed better suited to a decade that prized speed and power over the cadenced pace and often invisible subtleties of baseball. For added measure, football and basketball, with their action focused on a relatively small portion of the playing surface, were more amenable to the eye of television than was the vast panorama of the baseball field. Clearly, four separate pennant races, which could easily involve half or more of the teams in each league, would serve to whet the interest of the fans in those cities.

Of course, change had long been anathema to those who governed baseball. Any tampering with the rituals of the game, even the slightest fine-tuning of the mechanism, was deemed an offense equal to heresy. Like no other sport, baseball thrived on continuity and tradition. So if the case for shuffling the deck required clear and convincing evidence, the 1968 season provided all that was necessary.

Attendance in both leagues had dropped to near-record lows, and television ratings, rapidly becoming the financial spine of the sports industry, had fallen commensurately. At a time when scoring was at its peak in other sports, and the illusion of nonstop action was invested with the highest order of priority, offense had virtually disappeared from baseball. Pitchers had assumed control and command of the game as they had at no time since the pre-Ruthian era of the dead ball. It was as if a new species of pitcher had, undetected, bypassed the hitters on the scale of evolution.

For the first time in nearly four decades, a pitcher, Denny McLain of the Detroit Tigers, won more than thirty games in a season. Bob Gibson of the St. Louis Cardinals compiled an earned run average of 1.12, the lowest in more than half a century, then set a World Series record with thirty-five strike-outs in three games. Six other pitchers had ERAs under 2.00, a figure usually low enough to lead the league. The Dodgers' Don Drysdale pitched six straight shutouts and established a record of fifty-eight and two-thirds consecutive scoreless in-nings. Don Wilson of the Houston Astros struck out eighteen batters in a nine-inning game, and Luis Tiant of the Cleve-land Indians fanned nineteen in a ten-inning contest. Catfish Hunter pitched a perfect game for Oakland, only the elev-enth such game in the past century. Four other no-hitters were recorded during the season, two of them on consecutive days in San Francisco's Candlestick Park.

As for the hitters, Carl Yastrzemski led the American League by batting half a point over .300, the lowest mark ever to lead a league. In one game, the Mets and the Astros played twenty-three innings without scoring a run. Perhaps the most graphic demonstration of the manner in which pitching dominated in 1968 occurred in the All-Star Game, where the best hitters in baseball combined for a total of just eight hits, and the only run of the game was scored on a double-play ball.

It was, as baseball's management saw it, a recipe for ex-tinction. The new four-division format could be expected to sustain interest late into the season, but it would not ease the stranglehold that pitchers held on the hitters. Assuming that fans wanted more scoring, the owners voted to make two small but basic adjustments: the pitching mound was lowered from fifteen to ten inches, and the batter's strike zone was narrowed. The first would temper the speed of the pitcher's delivery, and the second would assure the batter better pitches to hit. In addition, experiments were begun on two even more fundamental changes. A designated hitter, who would take the pitcher's turn at bat, was used for the first time during spring training in 1969, and some of the exhibition games were played with a new ball, called the 1-X, which was 10 percent livelier than the one currently in use. Thus the start of the 1969 season offered baseball in somewhat new, spruced-up wrappings.

There were also, for those who could read them, forebodings of a more ominous turn, still a few years away, that would transform the sport in a manner not yet calculated. For when spring training camps opened in February, they had picket lines in front of them. Most of the players had gone on strike. It really was more a boycott than a strike, brief and unofficial, since the players were not contractually required to report to camp until March 1. Nonetheless, it was the first general labor action in baseball's history, and it offered a suggestion of what the future would hold.

The issue was the division of television revenues. As sports increasingly became a national network commodity, television contracts grew more lucrative, and the players felt they were not getting their fair share. In the previous three years, NBC had paid baseball $40 million for the Game of the Week, the World Series, and the All-Star Game. About $4 million of that was contributed each year to the players' pension fund. The athletes believed they were entitled to more. The Players' Association, which had been conducting negotiations since the end of the previous season, urged its members to refuse to sign their 1969 contracts until the dispute was settled. Most players complied. Pitchers and catchers were expected to report more than a week before the March 1 deadline. On most teams, few did.

The Mets, however, were a team composed chiefly of young players hopeful of making the team and a handful of marginal veterans looking to hold on for another few seasons. As a result, when their St. Petersburg camp opened on Friday, February 21, the Mets led both leagues in the number of players in uniform. Thirteen pitchers and catchers reported. Those observing the boycott were pitchers Tom Seaver, Jerry Koosman, Ron Taylor, Al Jackson, Danny Frisella, and Bob Hendley and catcher J. C. Martin. Ed Kranepool, the Mets' player representative, declared he would stay out until the strike was over. Shortstop Bud Harrelson and outfielder Ron Swoboda were inclined to stay out with them. However, thirty of the forty roster members said they would report on schedule whether the dispute was settled or not.

Despite their differences, there was little contention between the two groups. Even some of those observing the boycott did so reluctantly. A number of them held informal training sessions at a playground near the house rented by Seaver and his wife, Nancy. The conditioning camp, as it was called, was devoted mainly to calisthenics and games of pepper and catch, and the workouts were, as it turned out, short-lived. The dispute was settled on February 26, five days after the team camps had opened and three days before the official start of spring training. The three-year agreement called for $5.45 million to be placed in the pension fund annually; players would now qualify for a pension after four years of service instead of five.

Though the strike would have serious repercussions for some teams, there were no visible scars among the Mets. Johnny Murphy, the team's general manager, had handled the situation with uncommon grace and understanding. One of the first player representatives himself, Murphy had helped write the players' original pension plan in 1947. He was grateful that the players had agreed to make the plan retroactive to include those whose careers, like his own with the Yankees, had recently ended. Unlike officials from other teams, Murphy threatened no reprisals against those who stayed out, and he treated both sides with an even hand. As a consequence, the Mets began spring training in harmony with management and with a sense of unity among themselves.

Every small edge certainly would be welcome, for the Mets approached the 1969 season with aspirations of moving up in the standings. A championship, everyone agreed, was still beyond their grasp, but some improvement might be expected. The new format had placed the Cardinals, Cubs, Pirates, and Phillies in the Eastern Division along with the Mets and the expansion Montreal Expos. The Cardinals, who had won the pennant the two previous seasons, were generally conceded a third straight championship, with the only possible challenge provided by an improving Chicago team under Leo Durocher. But in 1968 the Mets had finished within three games of the Phillies and only seven behind the Pirates, and both were believed to be within reach. The Mets therefore considered themselves to be within wishing distance of third place. For certain, they would not have to concern themselves about finishing last, since expansion teams rarely escaped the cellar. So it was a reasonably optimistic Gil Hodges that greeted his squad on March 1 and began to survey the talent in the room.

It took little study to conclude that the club's strength would be its pitching. Tom Seaver, with sixteen wins in each of his first two seasons, was already acknowledged to be one of the best in the league. Playing the Sundance Kid to Seaver's Butch Cassidy would be Jerry Koosman, a second-year left-hander whose nineteen victories were the most ever recorded by a Met in a single season. The leading contenders

for the other starting positions were Nolan Ryan, Jim Mc-
Andrew, and Don Cardwell. Ryan was a flame-throwing power
pitcher in search of control who had started eighteen games
in 1968 before developing a sore elbow at the end of July.
McAndrew had been brought up in midseason, started twelve
times, and pitched brilliantly, allowing slightly more than two
earned runs a game although winning only four of eleven
decisions. Cardwell, a veteran obtained from Pittsburgh in
1967, would add experience to the fledgling staff and possibly compete for the fifth starting position with Gary Gentry,
a rookie right-hander out of Arizona State.

Principal bullpen duty would be entrusted to right-hander Ron Taylor, who had dined on championship fare with
the Cardinals in 1964 and apparently savored the taste of
pressure. Being considered for the role of his left-handed
counterpart was Tug McGraw, a cocky youngster out of California who, as a twenty-year-old rookie, had outpitched Sandy
Koufax in a 1965 game at Shea Stadium. McGraw had never
been anything but a starter, but his conversion to relief was
one of a handful of position moves being weighed by the
Mets.

Catching was the only position that appeared to be set,
with the tough, aggressive Jerry Grote backed up by J. C.
Martin. The pair had a total of fifteen years' major league
experience between them, a matter of some significance on a
team whose first four starting pitchers had only three full
seasons among them.

The infield, by contrast, was a jumble. Bud Harrelson
was the only full-time player and his availability was not entirely without question. He was coming off a knee operation
at the end of the '68 season, and even if he was completely
sound, he would be lost periodically to military reserve duty,
as would several others on the team. Ken Boswell, another
reservist, was granted title to second base, but it was recog-
nized that he would have to be spelled defensively on occa-

sion. That help would come from either Wayne Garrett, a rookie out of Sarasota, Florida, or Al Weis, a recent arrival from the Chicago White Sox.

The corners—first base and third—were considered to be there for the taking. Ed Kranepool, a left-handed power hitter, had held a monopoly on first base since the Mets' first season, but it had never been secure. Management contended that Kranepool needed more encouragement than most. Perhaps his desire had atrophied during his early years with the team. Whatever the cause, it was felt that being obliged to compete for his position would improve his performance. This year, the competition was expected to come from Art Shamsky, an outfielder by trade, and from Cleon Jones, the Mets' regular left fielder and a right-handed hitter. If Jones took to the new position, he and Kranepool might give the Mets a left-right platoon with considerable power. Ed Charles, who had played most of his career with Kansas City and who was now thirty-four years old, was conceded the inside track at third. He would be challenged there by Garrett; by Kevin Collins, who had shuttled between the Mets and the minors over the last four seasons; and by the Mets' most promising rookie, Amos Otis, an outfielder with exceptional speed, who would be given a trial at the position.

The outfield was to be covered by Jones in left (when and if he was not at first base), Tommie Agee in center (coming off a poor 1968 season but Rookie of the Year for the White Sox in 1966), and Shamsky and Ron Swoboda in right. Swoboda, a Met since 1965, was a right-handed hitter with impressive power but an erratic presence in the field. Like Kranepool, he was believed to have potential that had not yet worked its way into his performance. Then there was Otis, being given a chance in the outfield as well as the infield, and another greyhound of a rookie named Rod Gaspar.

It was a cast that certainly could use help here and there, but that possessed, at the very least, the seeds of respectability. And they had another asset that was not to be overlooked and could not be overestimated. Gil Hodges had become manager of the Mets in 1968 and had, in that one season, imbued the team with a new attitude. He was a man of fundamental habits and beliefs—the type that might have been played by Gary Cooper in a John Ford western—and he imparted those fundamentals to his players in a matter-of-fact manner that left little to conjecture. He distilled to its most basic elements the spare wisdom that winning could become as routine as losing if one were willing to pay the price. The price was no different from that in any other line of work: attention to detail, discipline, good work habits, the desire to learn from one's mistakes.

Hodges had come to the Mets from the Washington Senators in what amounted to a trade for pitcher Bill Denehy and $100,000 in cash. It was not a trade the Senators wished to make. They had signed Hodges to a long-term contract, and during his four-year tenure the team had improved its position each year. Like the Mets, the Senators were the product of recent expansion. They were formed in 1961 to fill the void left when the original Washington franchise moved to Minnesota. After finishing last the first three seasons, the team responded to Hodges's quiet but inspired leadership. The Mets, who had been seeking a full-time manager since Wes Westrum retired late in the 1967 season, coveted the former Dodger star; and Hodges, who still made his home in Brooklyn, yearned to return. So the deal was closed, and Hodges returned to New York bearing the gift of his winning tradition.

He had never seen the Mets play a baseball game, and he set for himself the modest goal of seventy victories in 1968. That still left room for the losing of ninety-two ballgames, but nonetheless it would be the best season the team ever had. As it turned out, Hodges exceeded his aim by three, bringing the Mets up out of last place and improving their record by a full twelve games. It was not an easy season, however, and conceivably it cost him. On September 24, Hodges suffered a heart attack during a game in Atlanta. The seizure was described as a mild one, and the outlook was favorable. His doctors said he would be able to return to work the following season. The diagnosis was correct. Hodges was back at the Mets' training camp not quite five months after being stricken. He adopted a modest new health regimen, taking long morning walks, shedding about twenty pounds on a diet, and giving up his long-time cigarette habit. He betrayed no signs of weakness. He looked fit, he had lost none of his wry humor, and he remained optimistic even as the Mets came stumbling out of the gate at the start of the exhibition season.

CHAPTER

2

NEVER KNOWN AS QUICK START-
ers, the Mets dropped their first three preseason games. They
lost the opener to the Cardinals despite a good pitching effort by Jim McAndrew. The next game, a loss to the Houston
Astros, featured three hitless innings by Tug McGraw and,
as if by way of compensation, two errors by Ron Swoboda.
Swoboda, who had vowed to improve his uncertain fielding,
dropped a fly ball in the third inning and botched another
chance in the fifth. If it was pitching that showed promise in
the first two games, it was pitching that cost them the third.
Nineteen-year-old Jon Matlack, not yet ready for the major
league roster, gave up three home runs in the eighth inning
of a game against the Red Sox.

It took a meeting with a junior varsity to get the Mets
untracked. They swamped the Phillies B team 15–7, scoring
all their runs in the sixth and seventh innings. Cleon Jones
offered a preview of the kind of season he would have by
hitting for the cycle—single, double, triple, and home run—
all within four innings. Buoyed by their first victory, the Mets
promptly added another. They dismantled the world champion Detroit Tigers 12–0 with home runs by Jones and Art
Shamsky, and a grand slam by Gary Gentry, the rookie pitcher.

Detroit retaliated the next day, winning 7–4 in a game marked by the use of the new 1-X "super" ball. The Tigers pounced on the juiced-up ball for a double, a triple, and three home runs, hitting Don Cardwell especially hard. However, the ball did not seem so lively when Denny McLain was throwing it. Detroit's thirty-one-game-winner pitched four shutout innings, proving that even the liveliest ball will not travel far if the batters are unable to hit it squarely.

Keeping peace with their nature, the Mets appeared to prefer the old, deader ball to the new one. Having been held to four runs with the lively version after scoring fifteen and twelve in the previous two games, they welcomed the return of the traditional ball with a sixteen-run assault on the Cardinals. Amos Otis, Ken Singleton, and Al Weis hit homers, and the light-hitting Weis added a triple and a single. After a win the next day over the expansion Kansas City Royals, the Mets moved on to the Atlanta Braves' training site at West Palm Beach, where they found Paul Richards, the Braves' executive vice-president, of a mind to talk trade.

Richards, a conservative type who had had little patience for the player boycott, was bent on unloading Joe Torre, who had been active on the players' behalf. Torre, a catcher and first baseman, was a right-handed hitter with good power, exactly the kind of addition the Mets were seeking. The belief was that a player who could platoon with Kranepool at first would not only add punch from the right side of the plate but would also push Kranepool to the peak of his abilities. As an added fillip, Torre, a lifelong resident of Brooklyn, would bring home with him no small measure of crowd appeal. However, the deal foundered on Richards's asking price. In return for Torre he wanted Nolan Ryan's strong right arm; Jerry Grote, the first-string catcher; and the promising young rookie, Amos Otis. The Mets balked, and Richards rejected their counteroffer. Still eager to negotiate, the Mets declared Grote and Otis to be "untouchables," along with Seaver, Koosman, Swoboda, Jones, and Harrelson. Richards scoffed. "I never knew the Mets had so many untouchables," he said. "I'm surprised they didn't win the pennant." Before twenty-four hours had passed, he traded Torre to St. Louis for Orlando Cepeda.

The following day, Jim McAndrew, one of the players the Mets had offered for Torre, helped blank the Braves 3 – 0. The next day, Seaver, Ryan, and McGraw two-hit the Dodgers by the same score. The Met pitching staff now had twenty-five straight scoreless innings to its credit. Although the streak was snapped in the first inning of the next game, the Mets still managed to edge the Phillies 5 – 4.

But while young pitchers like McAndrew, Gentry, Ryan, and McGraw were looking impressive, the ace of the staff was having his troubles. It had been at best an indifferent spring for Tom Seaver. His worst outing came on March 22, barely two weeks before the opening of the regular season, when he was hit for nine runs in two innings by the White Sox in a game in which the Mets committed nine errors. To complicate matters further, McGraw injured his knee, and the initial forecast was that he might be out for more than a month.

As opening day drew closer, Hodges continued to shuffle his personnel. He was not only looking to determine who would stay and who would be farmed out for further seasoning, he was trying to fit players into particular roles. He was a manager who believed that all twenty-five players on the squad should have a function and that their contribution would be greatest if they knew what that function was and exactly what was expected of them.

On March 26, Hodges moved Wayne Garrett, who had been playing shortstop while Harrelson strengthened his knee, to second base, and the young redhead responded with two home runs. A day later, he tried Jones at first base and moved Rod Gaspar from left to right field. Gaspar, who was not expected to make the team, was hitting .304 in the exhibition season, not far below his .309 average with Memphis in 1968. Both moves worked, each in its own fashion. From the time Jones picked up a first baseman's mitt, Kranepool had gone 5 for 7. Jones, in turn, hit no matter where he played, and Gaspar continued hot at the plate, compiling a fourteen-game hitting streak by April 1.

The Mets finished their exhibition season with a respectable 14–10 record. When the roster was pared for the final time, it included eighteen players from the 1968 squad, an unusual degree of continuity for the Mets. The pitching, considered to be the backbone of the team at the start of spring training, looked even more auspicious at the end. Despite an indifferent spring, Seaver finished strong, allowing only two hits in eight innings of work against the Cardinals. Koosman, troubled by a sore arm during most of March, pitched five innings the week before opening day and said that his arm felt "perfect." McAndrew looked as good as he had at the end of the previous season, closing with seven shutout innings against Cincinnati for his fourth winning game of the spring. After giving up only three earned runs in twenty-nine innings, an ERA of 0.93, he was named to start the second game of the season, behind Seaver. Gary Gentry also had pitched his way into the starting rotation.

Nonetheless, some questions remained to be answered. Would Koosman's arm ailment resurface? Would Harrelson's knee hold up? Third base remained a problem, with Amos Otis, Ed Charles, Kevin Collins, and Wayne Garrett all to be given a chance there early in the season. In the outfield, center fielder Tommie Agee was coming off the worst season of his career, and right field was as open to competition as third base. Swoboda was considered untrustworthy in the field and was expected to do no more than platoon at the position. Who would the left-handed hitter be? Gaspar would start on opening day, but could he sustain the hitting pace he set in the spring? Shamsky, a proven left-handed batter with occasional power, would not be available for a while. Nursing a back injury, he had been left behind when the Mets broke camp in St. Petersburg. Four days before the start of the season, he was optioned to the Mets' minor league affiliate in Tidewater to work out and play himself into shape. Shamsky was not happy about it.

"I had a little bit of a problem with that," Shamsky recalls seventeen years later. "It had been a terrible spring training for me. I had been laid up in a hotel room in St. Petersburg for almost the whole time with an aching back, and then when I felt I was ready to play they decided to send me to Tidewater. Murphy, the general manager, and Hodges called me in and said, 'You missed all of spring training, you can't just start the season with the Mets.' I said, 'I don't need spring training to play for this team. I don't have to pick up a bat all winter and I can play on this team.' Well, they didn't appreciate that, but I was thinking, 'If you can't play for the Mets, then what are you doing in the big leagues?'

"So the season started out badly for me. I went down to Tidewater, and when I got there Whitey Herzog, who was the farm director, said, 'What are *you* doing here?' My first time at bat, against Syracuse, I think, I hit a grand-slam homer, and I thought, 'What *am* I doing here?' But I was recalled as soon as I came off the disabled list, and from then on it was a good year for me. I hit .300 and I got some big hits, and we became a real good ballclub."

Shamsky and I are chatting in his tastefully appointed apartment on Manhattan's East Side, near Sutton Place. It is early morning, and Shamsky is a gracious host. He puts on some fresh coffee, concerned that his brewing machine does not keep the coffee hot enough. He appears to be not very far from his playing shape. He is lean and trim, with movie-star looks, his forty-four years betrayed only by a slight thinning of his hair. He is dressed for work in a conservative business suit, with fitted white shirt and necktie. When the interview is over, he will head for his office at a real estate investment firm, where he works as a consultant.

Shamsky summons up the past as if his major league career were part of a previous life, an eight-year sequence that ended in 1972. Some of his memories of that period glisten with ornaments he will cherish always, but there are other recollections that litter the past like the broken toys of childhood. He was the property of five different teams during his brief career, and Shamsky gives indications of being a sensitive man who is less than casual about being sold and traded at the whims of others. He first came to the big leagues in 1965, with the Cincinnati Reds, a team that was building a wrecking crew that would become known as the Big Red Machine. He had worked his way through the minor league system with Pete Rose and Tony Perez. By 1966, he was playing with some regularity. He hit twenty-one homers for the Reds that season. Then, in 1967, he suffered an injury that required off-season surgery.

"I decided to have the operation in St. Louis, which was my home, instead of Cincinnati," Shamsky recalls. "I was just out of the hospital and feeling absolutely horrible when I got a call from Bob Howsam, our general manager. In my infinite wisdom, I thought he was calling to see how I was feeling. Before he could say a word, I said, 'Mr. Howsam, I feel terrific. I just want you to know that I'm looking forward to next year.' He said, 'I'm glad you're feeling well, because we traded you to the New York Mets this morning.' Now he's talking to a kid who's never been traded before, just came out of the hospital, and is feeling horrible. My first reaction was one of shock. But then it came to me: to the Mets! I was leaving a team that had some potential to win, and I was going to the Mets! I wasn't crazy about New York either. You know, you come to this big city and stay in a big hotel right in the middle of Manhattan, you go out to Shea and thousands of people are screaming at you and you don't understand what they're saying because you're from the Midwest, and you're going to be playing for a last-place team that had no chance of winning.

"Then Howsam says, 'Bing Devine will probably call soon to talk to you.' He was general manager of the Mets at the time. So I get off the phone, and a little later I get a call from Bing Devine. I had met him when I was a youngster growing up in St. Louis and he was with the Cardinals. Now he says, 'How are you doing? How are you feeling?' I told him, 'I'm feeling fine, just in a little bit of shock.' He says, 'Let me tell you something. New York is really a great place to play. You'll love it here.' Then he goes on for about ten or fifteen minutes telling me how great it is in New York, how great the Mets would be in a few years, how much he enjoys being in New York, and how he looks forward to having me on the Mets, that the Mets need a left-handed power hitter and that I'll fit right in over there.

"I said, 'Mr. Devine, I really feel a lot better now. You really made me feel terrific about coming to the Mets, and I want to thank you for your call.' He said, 'I'll call you in a few days and we'll talk about your contract. But in the meantime, just feel good about being with the Mets.' I said thank you and hung up. Two days later, I pick up the paper and read that Bing Devine quit the Mets and is going back to St. Louis as general manager. He tells me how great it is to be with the Mets, he makes a deal for me, and then he leaves. I said to myself, 'What's going on here? What's happening to my life?' But it turned out to be a blessing in disguise."

After a mediocre 1968 season, Shamsky had the best year of his career in 1969. He batted an even .300, hit fourteen home runs, and drove in forty-seven runs as the left-handed half of the right-field platoon. But it is not so much his personal achievements he recounts in looking back as it is having been part of the Mets' 1969 phenomenon.

"You could tell that something special was happening that summer," he says. "You could sense it all around you. I would see these huge crowds of people coming off the elevated trains on Roosevelt Avenue and rushing to the stadium, not wanting to miss the first pitch, as though if they missed even one pitch they would be missing something important. Then, during the playing of the national anthem, I would turn around and there was this awesome crowd, and I would feel a numbness come over me. You knew something special was happening and that you were a part of it. It was not just winning the championship. Not everyone remembers, but that was such a depressing time in America. The Vietnam War was going on. New York had all kinds of problems. For a short period of time, we made people forget about that. We made people feel good, not only in New York but all over America."

Shamsky recalls the events of that summer with a bittersweet nostalgia. Each thought seems to evoke a resonance of satisfaction, but there appears to be no kindling of joy. He looks off into the distance as if seeing it all unwind on an instant replay. He describes it like a man just wakened from a dream who remembers the details with precision but is not quite able to bring the total reality into focus. It was perhaps the time of his life that glows brightest in memory, yet it is banked against the brooding sense of missed chances. After a 1970 season that was virtually a carbon copy of the one before, it all seemed to come apart for Shamsky. He was injured during most of 1971, played in only sixty-eight games, was traded at the end of the year, and never played another full season. He retired at the age of thirty-one.

"I walked away from the game in 1972," Shamsky says. "It was a horrible year for me. I got moved three times that year. After the 1971 season, I was traded to St. Louis. Then we got caught up in the players' strike in the spring of '72, and the Cardinals released me. I signed with the Cubs for opening day, and in June I was sold to Oakland. I was there for about two months, and then someone got hurt and they didn't want to make a roster change, so they released me. At that point, I said I had enough of this. I was married at the time and it was creating all kinds of problems for me. It was demoralizing, and I was still having trouble with my back; the next year I said I don't want to go through this anymore, and I quit.

"Two or three years later, I thought maybe I made a mistake. The designated hitter rule came in 1973, and then salaries started to escalate, and looking back I thought I probably made a mistake. To this day I think I made a mistake, but I'm living with that now and doing all right."

Shamsky, who has the voice to go with his good looks, is a part-time sports broadcaster in New York.

"Broadcasting has kept me in the spotlight," he says, "even though it's a part-time job. It also keeps me in the world of sports, and I like that. But I like the business world too. I like the challenge of it. There are other aspects of life that can be just as challenging as sports. I'm doing well at it, and it helps to have been a member of the '69 Mets. In all candor, I play off that in business, I use it. I'd be crazy not to, especially here in New York. People still talk about that here. They recognize me on the streets. Cab drivers, bus drivers recognize me, and even with the Mets doing so well now, people still want to talk about 1969. There are so many things about that year that people remember. It meant so much to them, in so many ways. I still wear my World Series ring, and when people ask to see it I take it off and show it to them, and they look at it as if they were holding a million dollars in their hand. The '69 Mets were a symbol to them. We represented the distressed, the poor, all the down guys who all of a sudden felt they had a chance to make it, and it's touching that people related to it that way. To this day, it gives me an incredible high just to think about it."

Shamsky was, of course, a long way from that high during the spring of the year, and so were the Mets. On the eve of opening day he was wearing a minor league uniform, and the Mets were considered a long shot for, at best, third or fourth place. Tom Seaver, calling himself the supreme optimist, said he thought the Mets had a chance to finish second. "The only team we can't catch is St. Louis," he said. "The only other team we may have to fight off is Chicago. But we can beat Pittsburgh, Philadelphia, and Montreal."

Hodges, recovering from his heart attack, said he "never felt better," but he was reluctant to commit himself to so specific a forecast. The 1968 team had improved on its record of the previous year by twelve games, from sixty-one to seventy-three victories. Hodges, a man of moderation, set as his goal a similar improvement for 1969. He would be satisfied, he said, with eighty-five victories. It was, by all past reckoning, no modest estimate. And by the time the season was ten games old, it appeared as unduly optimistic as Seaver's.

PART TWO

Signs of Hope

CHAPTER

3

HIGH ON THE METS' LONG LIST
of unenviable statistics was their record on opening day. They
had played seven openers and lost them all. They had lost
them on the road and at home, on the East Coast and the
West, by large scores and small; they lost them early in the
game and they lost them late; they lost them to six different
teams and twice to the Cardinals. Now, it appeared, in 1969,
they were almost certain to reverse the trend. Coming off
their best season, they were opening at home against the
Montreal Expos, a team that had never played a game of
major league baseball. It was being handed to them this time,
wasn't it? The schedule-makers had decided enough was
enough. For the first time in eight seasons, the Mets were
favored to win on opening day. Acting the part of the gracious host, they invited Jean Drapeau, the mayor of Montreal, to throw out the first ball. A crowd of 44,541 turned
out on a raw, biting day in early spring to witness the first
international contest in baseball's history and to see the Mets
win an opener for the first time in theirs. They went home
half-fulfilled.

The Mets trailed by two runs before coming to bat. The
first of three errors by Ken Boswell and a base on balls set

the table for Bob Bailey, the Expos' catcher, who hit a Tom Seaver pitch for a double, chasing home the first two major league runs in Canadian history. In the second inning, the Mets retaliated. They took a 3–2 lead on a two-run double by Tommie Agee, and Jim (Mudcat) Grant, Montreal's starting pitcher, was replaced by Dan McGinn, a rookie from Notre Dame. McGinn turned out to be more trouble at bat than on the mound. After the Expos tied the game with a run in the third, McGinn drove a home run over the right-field fence an inning later to retrieve his team's one-run margin. In the bottom half of the inning, he returned it. With two out and two runners on, Gaspar and Boswell singled and Jones lined a double to right-center, and the Mets led 6–4. The scoring, however, was not yet half complete.

Seaver had thrown a great many pitches in the first five innings, and with a cold wind whipping through Shea Stadium, Hodges chose to bring in the seven-year veteran Cal Koonce to start the sixth. Koonce, who had not yielded a run all spring, surrendered two in the sixth and another in the seventh, and Montreal again led by a run, 7–6. It soon got worse. Al Jackson, an original Met who had been exiled to St. Louis for two years before returning to New York, came on in the eighth and pitched back to his roots. He gave a home run to Rusty Staub, then put two men on base before turning the ball over to Ron Taylor. Taylor did not fare any better. The first batter he faced, a rookie named Coco Laboy, reached him for a three-run homer, and the Expos led the game 11–6.

Now the Mets riffled through the files of their first seven years and dusted off an old and favored script. They forged their way back heroically but, as if unable to keep track of the score, they stopped one run short. There already were two out in the ninth when Jerry Grote singled with two men on to draw the Mets a run closer. Then Duffy Dyer, a third-string catcher who had played one game for the Mets in 1968, was sent up to pinch hit, and in his fourth major league at-bat, he hit one into the left-field bullpen for his first home run and first three runs batted in. The Mets trailed by one, and they still weren't finished. Amos Otis batted for the pitcher and singled. Agee walked, pushing the tying run into scoring position. That was as far as it got. A lanky right-hander named Carroll Sembera, who in three years with Houston had compiled a record of three wins and nine losses and would never win another big league game, rode in from the bullpen and struck out Rod Gaspar to end the game.

So the Expos had managed to do in their first season what the Mets had been unable to do in eight. They had won their first big league ballgame and owned a share of first place in the National League's Eastern Division. They might have been forgiven a degree of optimism when they returned to Shea the next afternoon. The Mets, however, picked up where they left off in the ninth inning of the previous game. They opened with a four-run spurt off Bill Stoneman on a couple of walks, a hit batter, and singles by Jones, Kranepool, and Grote. But the beneficiary of that flurry, Jim McAndrew, could not hold back the Expos, who answered with three runs of their own in the top of the second. Hodges called to the bullpen for Tug McGraw.

It was the beginning of the Mets' experiment with McGraw as a relief pitcher. The exuberant left-hander had started sixteen of the nineteen games he had pitched in since his rookie season. His relief efforts had been chiefly of the mop-up variety. But given his cockiness, good control, better-than-average speed, and wicked screwball, he appeared to have the tools essential to a bullpen stopper. His initial appearance could have been nothing less than encouraging. McGraw pitched six and one-third innings and gave up only one run before tiring with one out in the eighth, when Nolan Ryan came on and struck out two pinch hitters. The Mets, mean-while, had been padding their lead. They closed it out by a 9-to-5 margin, evening their season's record.

The next day they made it two in a row. Tommie Agee hit two home runs, one a towering drive that landed high in the upper deck of the left-field stands, and Gary Gentry, who had seen his first big league game on opening day, won his first start in the majors, 4 – 2. So the Mets now had a season's record of 2 and 1, a modest enough achievement for most teams but a milestone for the Mets. It marked only the second time in their history that they had won more games than they had lost. In 1966 they had made a similar start, winning two in a row after losing on opening day. Then they had stepped right into a five-game losing streak on their way to another dismal season. It was not much different in 1969. Having disposed of Montreal, they then lost four in a row and six of their next seven.

The first three defeats came against the Cardinals, who had started the defense of their National League title by los-ing their first three games. But they evened their record at the expense of the Mets, sweeping the three-game series by a total of only four runs. Joe Torre had three hits in the first game, helping his new team to a 6 – 5 decision. Then Dave Giusti beat Don Cardwell 1 – 0, and Bob Gibson outpitched Seaver 3 – 1, with the Mets leaving the bases loaded in the ninth inning.

The scores of the last two games were somewhat un-usual when measured against the early returns from around the league. An exceptionally large number of runs were scored during the first week of the season. Coming off the heels of the 1968 drought, it was an open invitation to the specula-tive. Rationalists were convinced that the lowered pitcher's mound and the tightened strike zone were taking effect as expected. Behaviorists contended that the conditioning of the pitchers had been retarded by the spring training boycott, giving the hitters an unaccustomed edge. The cynical mused that perhaps the souped-up 1-X baseball had not been discarded when the season began. The Mets might have wondered what all the speculation was about. In the seven games that followed the Montreal series, they would manage to score only eighteen times.

With their first homestand of the season complete, the Mets moved down the turnpike to Philadelphia, where Hodges began juggling his lineup. Looking for more production against left-handed pitching, he tried Cleon Jones at first base and Al Weis at second. Ed Charles, who had struck out three times against Gibson, was replaced at third by Amos Otis. It was not quite the right combination. The Mets split a pair of games with the Phillies, then went to Pittsburgh where they lost two straight.

In Pittsburgh their woes were not confined to the numbers on the scoreboard. Koosman's sore shoulder was acting up again. He started the first game but was unable to make it through the third inning, and Ryan was hit hard in relief. The next day they got a good starting effort from Don Cardwell, but the bullpen faltered again, and the offense continued to struggle. Cardwell, who had been shut out in his first start, yielded only one run and four hits through seven innings but again received no support. (Thirty-three years old and in his thirteenth major league season, he was learning what it was like to pitch for the Mets. In sixteen innings he had given up only two runs and ten hits, yet his record stood at 0 and 2.) Cal Koonce pitched the eighth and was tagged for three runs, and the Mets lost their sixth game in the last seven, 4–0.

Thus the Mets started the 1969 season by losing seven of their first ten games. They already were six games behind the first-place Cubs and ahead of only Montreal in the standings. Their pitching, which had been expected to carry them, was in a troubled state. Koosman's recurrent sore arm left each of his outings in question. McAndrew had been ineffective in his two starts, and Seaver had yet to win a game. Gentry owned the only two victories by a starter. McGraw, out of the bullpen, had the other. For added measure, the Mets had stopped hitting. In their last six defeats, they had been shut out twice and held to a single run on two other occasions. Hodges believed it was time to make some new lineup changes. He replaced Gaspar with Ron Swoboda in right field, installed Kevin Collins at third base, and moved Otis to his natural position in center field. He benched Tommie Agee. Agee, who had gotten off to a good start, had seen his average slip to .195, and conceivably the ghosts of the season past had begun to haunt him.

Nineteen sixty-eight had been a horrendous year for Agee. It began, as he saw it, with his being traded from the White Sox to the Mets. Chicago had finished only three games out of first place in 1967, which was thirty-seven and a half games closer than the Mets had managed. Although it had not been an especially good year for Agee, he perhaps harbored thoughts of playing back to his Rookie of the Year season in 1966, when he hit .273 with twenty-two home runs and eighty-six runs batted in. His first season seemed to justify the promise Agee had shown when he was signed by Cleveland in 1961 for what was then a substantial bonus of $65,000. He spent most of the next four years in the minor leagues, playing in just thirty-one games for the Indians and ten for the White Sox after being traded to Chicago in 1965. But in the following two seasons, he appeared in all but six of his team's games and was considered a pivotal player on a serious pennant contender. Then, two weeks before the end of 1967, he was traded to the Mets.

"I was kind of disappointed," he told Joseph Durso of *The New York Times.* "After all, the White Sox were contenders and the Mets were last. And I knew it would be difficult. I'd have a rough time getting adjusted to the National League."

In his first at-bat in spring training of 1968, Bob Gibson welcomed him to the National League with a fastball that exploded against his helmet and nearly took his head off. Agee crumpled to the ground and remained motionless for a worrisome period of time. Finally he stirred, was helped to his feet, and staggered off the field. X-rays proved negative, and Agee returned to the lineup in a few days, but the beaning set a pattern for much of his 1968 season. He opened well, with five hits in his first sixteen times at bat, but then he slumped, as he would a year later. He went 0 for 10 in a twenty-four-inning game at Houston and proceeded to go hitless as well in his next four games before being benched in favor of Don Bosch.

Agee's misgivings about playing in New York grew even stronger when his car was stolen on his first trip into Manhattan. For much of the remainder of the season, Agee, who while with the White Sox had been known to relish a good time, spent most of his free evenings in his motel room in Queens, not far from Shea Stadium. But if seclusion offered a sense of security, it did nothing to improve his hitting. Returned to the lineup after a brief spell, he continued to struggle at the plate. His batting average, already anemic, dipped to around .150 near the end of May. At one point he went hitless in thirty-four times at bat. Agee was in the doldrums, but he was also in the lineup. His batting slump did not affect his play in the field or his aggressive style on the bases when he did manage a hit or a walk. He had won the support of Hodges and his teammates, foremost among them his boyhood friend, Cleon Jones.

Agee and Jones were born within five days of one another in rural Alabama and grew up together in Mobile, neighbors of two other future major leaguers—Hank and

Tommie Aaron of the Atlanta Braves. They met for the first time in junior high school, and they played football together at the Mobile County Training High School. Jones played halfback and Agee was a wide receiver; during one season they worked the halfback option pass five times for touchdowns, and the team lost only one game in the three years they were teammates. They both attended Grambling College for a while, and if Jones appeared to be the better football prospect, Agee got higher marks for baseball. He hit home runs in his first four at-bats for Grambling and ended the 1961 season with a .533 batting average, the highest in the history of the Southwest Athletic Conference. On the strength of such a season, Agee was signed to a Cleveland contract at the age of nineteen. Jones transferred to Alabama A & M, and in 1962 he signed on with the Mets for just a shade over a thousand dollars. He made his major league debut a year after Agee made his, but in 1968, united again as teammates, their fortunes were on divergent paths. Jones was on his way to a prime season, but Agee doubtless felt that the shadow of the damned was dogging his steps.

He never managed to shake it. He hit only .217, with five home runs and an incredibly meager seventeen runs batted in, while appearing in all but thirty of the Mets' games. A year later, he recounted his agonies to two sportswriters from the *Times*.

"I can't describe how I felt that year," he told George Vecsey. "Sometimes it was so bad I felt like I was numb. I didn't know what to do, didn't know where to turn."

He told Joseph Durso what the off-season was like: "When I went home to Mobile," he said, "I wanted to explode. The Mets sent me to Florida to their instructional camp to work on my hitting, but after one week I told them I just had to go away. So I took about two dozen baseballs, went home to Alabama, and spent the winter thinking. Every day Cleon Jones and I would go out in a little boat and fish and talk about hitting. Then in the afternoons, Tommie Aaron of the Braves would come over and we'd go out to a playground and hit the two dozen balls around. And this spring in Florida, every time I'd bat, Cleon would tell me what I was doing wrong."

Apparently, Jones was a far better hitter than he was a batting instructor. For now, ten games into the season, Agee was on the bench, five points under the..200 mark. And Jones? Jones was hitting over .400 and leading the league.

On the second weekend of the season, the Mets took their 3-and-7 record to St. Louis, where Hodges unveiled his new lineup. Harrelson was moved from eighth in the batting order to Agee's leadoff spot, followed by second baseman Boswell. Otis, the new center fielder, batted third, ahead of Jones and Kranepool. Then came Swoboda, who was being tried in right field against both left- and right-handed pitching; Grote, behind the plate; and Collins, the Mets' third third baseman of the young season.

With Saturday's game rained out, Sunday matched Seaver and Gibson for the second time in a week. It was a confrontation along storybook lines: the Cy Young Award – winner at his vintage best against an emerging star nine years his junior. Both were right-handed power pitchers who went for the strikeout in tight situations, and neither was averse to throwing in close to a batter. They had the same fundamental approach to competition in general and to pitching in particular: the idea of playing was to win; a pitcher won by disposing of the batter; a batter who was relaxed and comfortable at the plate was a menace no pitcher should be quick to endure. Each was at his unrelenting best when the issue was in question. They were ready, if the need was there, to hold your head under water.

Their second encounter was as tightly contested as the first, but the outcome was different. The Mets won this one with a two-run flurry that Seaver himself began by drawing a walk. Harrelson bunted him to second, Boswell walked, and Jones and Kranepool settled the matter with back-to-back singles that gave the Mets a 2–1 victory.

The next day the score was 11 to 3, again in the Mets' favor. Collins, making his second start, hit a two-run homer as the Mets scored five times in the fifth inning. They split their next two games, losing 2–1 to the Phillies in eleven innings, then taking a 2–0 decision from Pittsburgh with Koosman, his arm free of pain this turn, pitching at the peak of his form.

It was still far too early in the season to describe any event as critical, but in winning three of their last four games the Mets had taken an important step forward. They had reversed a losing streak of some substance, squeezed past the Cardinals and Phillies in the standings, and moved to within four and a half games of first place behind Chicago and Pittsburgh. At similar junctures, in previous years, the Mets had never been able to right themselves. They would skid first out of range and then out of sight, as if each loss were an invitation to the next. Now, more than two weeks into the season, they were only two games under .500. Given their history, .500 baseball was an achievement of no small claim. But a sterner test was on the horizon. In the next ten days, they would play eight games with the Cubs—four at home, then four in Chicago.

It started out like old times for the Mets. Leo Durocher marched his team into Shea Stadium, and the Cubs won the first three games. After a Thursday rainout, Ferguson Jenkins beat Seaver 3–1. The Mets outhit the Cubs six to five, but three of Chicago's hits were home runs, by Jenkins, Don Kessinger, and Ron Santo. On Saturday, the Cubs assaulted Cardwell and piled up thirteen hits in a 9–3 victory, and the first game of Sunday's doubleheader was lost in vintage Met style. They led by three runs after seven innings and by two runs after eight, but then surrendered four runs in the ninth on two errors and a two-run home run by Randy Hundley. So desperate was Hodges to stop the bleeding in the ninth that he summoned Tom Seaver from the bullpen to get the last out. The Mets salvaged the second game when Mc-Andrew and McGraw combined for a shutout and Cleon Jones homered in the ninth with two men on. The hit raised Jones's league-leading average to a cool .443 and gave him an eleven-game hitting streak, during which he had driven home fourteen runs.

When the Cubs left town, the Mets packed for a three-day trip to Montreal before moving on to Chicago. They passed through Customs as a team tied for last place with the Expos and Cardinals, but in Canada their pitching asserted itself, and they won two of the three games. The series had begun amid rumors of a trade. The Mets, it was said, were ready to leave Ed Kranepool, their elder statesman in point of service, in Montreal in exchange for Donn Clendenon, a thirty-three-year-old first baseman with the right-handed power the Mets had been seeking since spring training. Kranepool, who had heard similar rumors in recent years, responded as he usually did. He hit a pair of home runs and accounted for the only scoring in a 2–0 win.

But the big news in Montreal was made by the Mets' pitchers, who had compiled a string of twenty-four straight shutout innings by the time the Expos crossed the plate in the second game. Seaver pitched a five-hitter. Cardwell pitched another strong game, although losing in the ninth. Nolan Ryan recorded four and two-thirds scoreless innings in relief, getting half of his outs on strikeouts. Not all of the news was good, however. Ryan had come on in behalf of Koosman, whose arm had "snapped like an elastic band" when he threw a fifth-inning pitch to John Bateman in the opening game. Koosman would miss his turn against the Cubs in Chicago. Also unavailable would be Jim McAndrew, who was bothered by a recurring blister on his pitching hand. Only Gentry and

Seaver from among the starting rotation would be ready for the Cubs, and Seaver would be pitching with only three days' rest. The Mets already were six games off Chicago's pace.

It was Friday, May 2, and the season was about to reach its first turning.

CHAPTER

4

BY ALL ACCOUNTS, WRIGLEY Field was the most beautiful ballpark in the country. It was the last of the old National League stadiums not yet condemned to the wrecker's ball and the only one whose roof was unadorned by floodlights. Located in the heart of Chicago's North Side, it offered the feel of rustic serenity banked against the hard-muscled pull of the working-class streets. Its red brick walls were covered with ivy in the outfield, and in dead center field were steeply sloped tiers of old-fashioned bleachers. Beyond the walls, beyond the bleachers, lay the big-shouldered city of Carl Sandburg and Theodore Dreiser. There the vista was unmistakably Chicago: slaughter house tough streets, lined with modest one-family houses and neighborhood bars that served a shot-and-a-beer more often than cognac on the stem.

From these streets and local taverns came the unconscribed army of Cub fans known as the Bleacher Bums. Their uniform, in the main, consisted of jeans, T-shirts, and yellow construction hats. Their reveille was blown by the lunch whistle, their weapon a collective voice that could curl the hide from an elephant's back. Their raucous presence gave little comfort to an opposing center fielder, but one would have to search with some diligence to find fans as unwavering in their devotion or as firm in their resolve.

Not since 1945, a wartime year when baseball was played chiefly by the aged and infirm, had the Cubs had a winner. Nor were they even close: in twenty-three seasons since the end of World War II, their best finish had been thirteen games out of first place. When suffering was measured by longevity, no one could touch a Chicago Cubs' fan; the Mets, by contrast, were neophytes. Now here were the '69 Cubs, under the driving stewardship of Leo Durocher (who knew all about finishing first and finishing last), atop their division since opening day, winners of sixteen of their first twenty-three games and opening ground on the field. The Mets, certainly, were not their main concern, and the Cubs opened the series in orderly fashion, winning the first two games 6−4 and 3−2.

Hodges, still maneuvering his lineup in search of the right combination, had restored Agee to center field; Agee, after two weeks on the bench, responded by going 4 for 4 with a home run in the opening game. But the next day, Saturday, the Mets lost more than the game. Nolan Ryan, making his first start of the season, pulled a groin muscle while throwing one of his smoking fastballs and was forced to leave in the seventh inning with a 2−1 lead. The lead did not survive the next inning. Cal Koonce walked in the winning run and lost his third straight decision in relief.

So the Mets now found themselves in a familiar position. They had lost three in a row, five of six to the Cubs. They were eight games out of first place, with only the presence of the Montreal Expos cushioning them from the cellar. It was Sunday, May 4, and Chicago had packed Wrigley Field to its seams for the doubleheader. They were standing in the aisles and sitting on the railings. They had come in rousing good cheer, buoyed by that sense of celebration that fuels the spirit when the outcome is no longer in doubt. The Mets, of course, had been this route before. Given the chance, they had always succumbed. This time the mood was different. The first signal came early.

In the second inning of the first game, Tom Seaver fired a fastball high and tight, and the Cub captain, Ron Santo, was sent spinning to the ground. An inning later, Bill Hands, the Chicago pitcher, nailed Seaver between the shoulder blades. In the fifth, Seaver retaliated, burying a pitch in Hands's midsection. The word was out now: the Mets were conceding nothing. Kranepool's fourth-inning home run had matched an earlier Cub score, and in the fifth, Boswell singled home a run and Swoboda lofted a sacrifice fly for another. The Cubs scored once more, but Seaver locked up with four shutout innings, and the Mets won it 3 to 2.

They took the second game by the same score. With Koosman and McAndrew unable to pitch, Tug McGraw was given his first starting assignment of the season. The Mets presented him with a two-run lead in their first at-bat, but McGraw allowed the Cubs to even it in the bottom half of the inning. Then he and Chicago's Dick Selma, who had spent the previous four seasons with the Mets, matched pitches for the next five innings. The Mets fashioned the winning run in the seventh when Swoboda rambled home all the way from second base on a wild pitch that Randy Hundley, the Cub catcher, was unable to locate in the grass behind home plate. For McGraw, it was his first complete game since 1966 and only the fourth of his career. He had begun life with the Mets as a starting pitcher in 1965; four days shy of his twenty-first birthday, he had earned a measure of attention by becoming the first Met pitcher to beat Sandy Koufax. How well does he remember the game?

"It was August 26, 1965," McGraw responds as if on cue. "The score was 5 to 2," he adds quickly. "I pitched the first six and two-thirds innings. Wes Parker hit a triple with a man on to make the score 3 to 2, and Jack Fisher was brought in to relieve me. Then, in the bottom of the eighth, Joe Christopher and Ron Swoboda hit back-to-back home runs to make the final score 5 to 2."

When interviewed by the press after the game, McGraw compared himself to the young gunslinger who rides into town and beats the old sheriff in a shootout.

"I was a little nervous about dealing with the press in those days," McGraw recalls. "I didn't like to get too serious, because it made me even more nervous. So I started using anecdotes to express my feelings, and it helped me to get along with the writers. I felt that I really didn't belong in the big leagues at that time. I had just gotten out of junior college, and I couldn't believe I could get there that fast. I knew something had to be wrong. The World's Fair was right across the street, Shea Stadium was practically brand new. . . . I had to pinch myself every day when I came to the ballpark. I lived at the Travelers Hotel across from LaGuardia Airport, and every time I drove to Shea Stadium, it reminded me of a huge birthday cake. Where the stadium was open in center field was where the first slice was cut out. When I got to the park each day I used to say, 'Happy birthday! This is unbelievable!' "

Even now, almost twenty years later, one has little difficulty imagining McGraw as a birthday celebrant. He bounds into a room as breezy and bright as if his eyes had just popped open on the first day of creation. He is a shade late for our appointment, and his arrival announces itself. Animation surrounds him. He retains the puppy-dog playfulness that stamped his playing days. One can still see him bouncing off the mound after the third out, heading for the dugout in quick, measured strides, his glove thumping a cadence against his right thigh.

It is just past eleven o'clock on a clear morning in early

May. We are meeting at the offices of Tug McGraw Resources, in Media, Pennsylvania, a suburban town a few miles south of Philadelphia. It is a firm that does some marketing and some public relations work, some of it for profit and some in the interest of charity. The offices, on the upper floor of a two-story building, are comfortable but unpretentious. The atmosphere, of course, is informal. Tug is dressed for work in khaki trousers, crewneck white sweater with the sleeves drawn up to his elbows, brown loafers, no socks. His shock of light brown hair is as unshorn as ever.

A structured set of questions has been carefully prepared, but the interview more nearly resembles a rambling reminiscence between old friends, even though this is our first meeting. It begins with a brunch in the coffee shop on the ground floor of the building and proceeds for about two hours in Tug's office. He is in no hurry. He greets each question as an invitation to elaborate, and he responds with the unsuppressed exuberance of youth. There are no hidden messages in what he tells you, no subtleties to be read between the lines. He comes at you live and unrehearsed. His name is Frank Edwin McGraw, but he is known to everyone as Tug. It has always been Tug. It should be.

"I never answered to any other name," he says. "My mother started calling me Tug when I was an infant because of the way I nursed. 'He's a real Tugger,' she said. My father's name is Frank and I'm a Frank, Jr. I have an older brother named Hank and an uncle Hank. I also have a cousin named Frank. When I was born there were lots of Hanks and Franks around. So when my mother referred to me as a little Tugger everyone picked up the nickname and started calling me Tug. It was the only name I knew as a kid.

"On my first day in kindergarten, the teacher called the roll and when she finished she said, 'Is there anyone whose name I didn't call?' I raised my hand. 'My name is Tug

McGraw,' I said. She looked at the roll and said, 'I have a Frank McGraw.' I said, 'No, that's my dad. He already went to kindergarten.' "

If it was circumstance that earned McGraw his nickname, chance also played its part in opening the door to his career in professional baseball. He was the incidental discovery of scouts who came to Vallejo, California, for a look at his brother Hank.

"Hank was one of the most sought-after athletes in Northern California," McGraw says. "He was a catcher, and when the scouts came to watch him catch, I used to pitch to him. But it was Hank they were interested in. He was six feet two, 210 pounds, and one of the greatest natural athletes I ever saw. He was eighteen months older than I was, and he was my hero."

Roy Partee, a scout for the Mets, signed Hank to a $15,000 contract and said he would give Tug a try when the younger McGraw completed his two-year course at Vallejo Junior College. But by the time Tug was graduated, in the spring of 1964, the Mets no longer were interested.

"I lost only one game during my two years in college," Tug says, "but there were no scouts and no offers. Hank called Partee, and Partee told him that at five-nine, 160 pounds, I didn't have the size to pitch in the majors. Hank said, 'If there isn't room in this game for my brother, then I don't want to play either.' He threatened to quit. The Mets weren't really pleased about it, but Hank was a good prospect, so they offered me a $7,000 bonus and sent me to their rookie league.

"The manager there was Ken Deal, and he wasn't the kind of guy you automatically took a liking to. In fact, you had to work real hard even to respect him. When I first got there, he gave me one of those talks: 'I didn't like your brother, I know I'm not going to like you, I know how you got here, and the first time you screw up you're going to pack your bags and go home.' He started me in the second game down there, and I ended up pitching a no-hitter in my first professional game. So right away, I went from a suspect to a prospect."

Ironically, Hank's career foundered. Plagued by injuries, he spent thirteen years in the minors and never played a major league game. Tug, in the meantime, was also having his problems. His victory over Sandy Koufax in 1965 accounted for half of his wins in nine decisions that season. The following spring he came up with a sore arm, was placed on the disabled list in May, and finished the season with a record of 2 – 9.

"I spent six months of the off-season with the Marine Reserves," McGraw says. "I came to spring training late and threw hard too soon. When my arm started to hurt, I was afraid to tell anyone because I felt I had to pitch well to make the team. Then in May, my arm blew and I was sent to Jacksonville for two months. When they brought me back up, my lack of experience began to catch up with me. I had a lousy spring in '67, and I spent most of that season and all of the next in triple-A."

During those early stages of his career, McGraw suffered through a confidence crisis.

"I was never sure," he says, "that my big-league dream was going to last, and I had no idea what I would do for a living if I didn't play baseball. So every off-season I tried something else. I went to insurance school and got an insurance license, I went to real estate school, I went to hotel restaurant and management school. Every year I tried something different."

One of the schools from which McGraw received a license was barbers' school, but that was after the fact. He already had been practicing that trade for many years.

"When I was a kid, my dad was having a hard time making ends meet. One way he could save some money was to cut our hair himself. Then one day when I was in high school, my father said he was going out to get a haircut. I said, 'Hold on a second. You've been giving us haircuts all these years; now it's my turn. I want to cut your hair.' He said, 'Sure, go ahead.' So I gave him a trim and he liked it; everybody liked it. I gave my big brother a haircut, he liked it. I gave my little brother a haircut, he liked it. I was a natural! Next thing you know, all the guys in school began giving me a quarter to give them a haircut. By the time I got to college, I was really good and I was charging a buck. When I got into pro ball, I gave my teammates haircuts, even with the Mets. I gave Casey haircuts, I gave Yogi haircuts, I gave all the guys haircuts.

"Finally they started writing about it in the papers, and one day I got a call from somebody with the barbers' union who said I was breaking the law. I didn't think I was breaking the law, but I was. You had to have a license. So I said, 'Okay, no problem.' I went down to Tri-City Barber College on the Bowery and Houston Streets in the off-season, and I got my barber's license. Okay, thank you very much, no problem."

McGraw's problem in 1969 was finding a place for himself on the Mets' roster. He had developed a screwball while pitching in the minors the past two seasons; when he unveiled it during spring training in '69, it took the batters by surprise.

"I had the most awesome spring I ever had," he recalls. "I didn't walk anybody, I struck out about two batters an inning, I only gave up about three or four hits the entire spring, maybe one or two runs, and it was all because no one had seen the screwball before. But the Mets didn't know what to do with me. On the last day of spring training, Gil called me into his office, and he said, 'Tug, I've got no room for you in the starting rotation.' I said, 'Well, I'll play first, I'll play center field, I'll do whatever I have to do to make the team.'

He said, 'What I need to do is fill in my bullpen. I need a long man.' I said, 'Hey, I'm your man, no problem.'

"In April and May, we were having some trouble with our starters and I got into a lot of games and I was doing really well. The only other pitcher in the league with a screwball was Jim Brewer of the Dodgers, so the hitters weren't used to seeing it. By June, I was still pitching well, and Gil called me into his office again. He said, 'Tug, I have three pieces of advice for you. One, I think you should think about staying in the bullpen permanently. You could be a great reliever and at best an average starter. Two, this team needs a late-inning stopper, and I want you to be my stopper. Three, I think you'll make a lot more money as a reliever than as a starter. Now it's up to you.' I said, 'Gil, if you think that's the way for me to go, I'm there already.' The rest is history."

History notes that McGraw went on to a big year in 1969 and that he remained a bullpen specialist for the next fifteen seasons—five more with the Mets and then ten with the Phillies. The year for which he is best remembered, 1973, was not necessarily his best. It was a season in which the Mets won their division title with only eighty-two victories, the lowest winning total in baseball history. McGraw and the Mets both struggled through the first four months of the season, but it was also the year in which they both learned that "Ya gotta believe."

"The first half of that season I just couldn't get anyone out," McGraw says. "I felt great, but for some reason I just wasn't pitching well. One afternoon, I was having lunch at the house with my wife and a friend of ours who was one of those guys who believed in positive thinking and that sort of thing, and he kept saying, 'You're not going to get anybody out until you start believing you can when you go to the mound, and right now you don't; you don't have any confidence in yourself.' He kept talking that way, and Phyllis was agreeing with him. When I left for the ballpark, they said, 'Remember, Tug, you gotta believe in yourself.'

"Then, when I went out the door and got into the car, I waved back and I said, 'Okay, see you later. Ya gotta believe, right?' And all the way to the ballpark, I kept it going, like one of those religious cult guys, 'Ya gotta believe, ya gotta believe.' By the time I got to the clubhouse I was really pumped up. I was saying it in the clubhouse, all during batting practice, 'Ya gotta believe, ya gotta believe.'

"Just before the game, M. Donald Grant (the Mets' chairman of the board) called a meeting in the clubhouse, and he told us that the front office still had confidence in us, that we were like family to him and Mrs. Payson (the Mets' owner), and that they believed in us and we had to believe in ourselves. Now, I'm over at my locker and I'm just pumped, and I yell out, I scream, 'That's right, Mr. Grant, you gotta believe. You said it, babeeey.' That was right in the middle of his talk, and he didn't know that I came to the ballpark a maniac and that I was chanting 'Ya gotta believe' all day. So he cut his talk short and stormed out of the room thinking, 'Who is this fucking kid mimicking me in front of the team, making fun of my talk?'

"Of course I didn't intend it that way, and I didn't realize he was insulted. But Eddie Kranepool came up to me and said, 'Tugger, you better go talk to that man; you just screwed up.' I said, 'Screwed up? Man, I'm agreeing with the guy.' But he didn't know that, so I called on the phone and went up to his office and explained it. But it all worked out, because then I got on a roll, I got on a roll like I never was on before in my life."

McGraw's roll was contagious. It helped carry the Mets to within one game of another world championship, and "Ya gotta believe" became a part of the language. It also became the title of his television show twelve years later in Philadelphia. Twice, sometimes three times a week, "Tug's Ya Gotta

Believe" tops off the evening news with a story that depicts the "triumph of the human spirit."

"We come on at the end of the newscast," McGraw says. "After you've heard all about the terrorists, the car wrecks, the murders, the bank robberies, the Phillies just lost three in a row . . . 'But guess what, folks? Ya gotta believe, and here's Tug McGraw with a story about some special person.' "

A "special person" to McGraw is anyone who needs help or anyone who gives it. That philosophy is the foundation of Tug McGraw Resources and one McGraw believed in long before his own success. As early as 1965, after his first season with the Mets, he formed the Youth Encouragement Program in Vallejo. The program, run out of his own apartment, involved local businessmen in an effort to keep teenagers from dropping out of high school. Tug McGraw Resources is engaged in similar projects, with much of its work aimed at helping young people in the Philadelphia area.

"The agency was formed to put different types of projects together," he explains. "Some are profit oriented, and some are for charities and civic organizations that need exposure. We act as advisors or consultants and offer help with marketing or public relations. A lot of the work we do is motivational. I give talks and speeches about caring and sharing and about having a positive attitude. That's what Tug McGraw Resources is all about."

It also is much of what Tug McGraw is all about.

"I look at it this way," he says. "One of the wonderful things about being gifted with big-league ability is that you can reach out and touch people without even trying. You can make people happy just by walking into a room, and you haven't even done anything. It's just that you share all those memories, you have something in common. It's really a wonderful thing.

"You know, I figure I'm the product of all the people that helped me when I was a kid; all the sponsors, the Little

League coaches, my parents, my friends. . . . I'm little bits and pieces of all the things those people gave me. Now I have the opportunity to spread all those little bits and pieces around and help other people. It's a way of returning the help I was given, of paying some of it back.

"We once did a 'Ya Gotta Believe' show on a lady from North Philadelphia, which is a densely populated black neighborhood. She had fourteen children and raised them all, and none of them had ever been in trouble. We asked her how she had managed to do it, and she said, 'The only thing I ever tried to teach them is that if you manage to climb to the top, just before you get there, when you think you have it made, you have to reach back and pull someone up with you, because it can get awfully lonely up there by yourself.' "

It is the kind of story McGraw appreciates, for it reflects his own sense of social responsibility, a state of conscience he has dared to express even when it might cost him. He is reminded of an incident that took place during spring training in 1970. The Mets were world champions, and the City of St. Petersburg chose to honor them with a New York Mets Day.

"The city was named Metville for that day," McGraw recalls, "and we were given a dinner in celebration. It was a time when the Vietnam peace movement was very active, and hippies were being chastised for their long hair and treated like the enemy, and our audience was made up mostly of older people from the area. Also, it was an election year, and the dinner was being run by local politicians who were making political speeches condemning demonstrators and activists and holding us up as an example of clean-cut American youth.

"Now there were a lot of us who thought like the kids who were making the protests, who these guys were ridiculing. For me, it was an especially confusing time. I was still in the Marine Reserves, and I was being trained to control campus riots, but I had a brother in college who was a member of the Peace and Freedom Party at San Francisco State when they were having the riots there. I had another brother and some friends who these guys would have described as dirty hippies, but they weren't. They were intelligent and they had something to say. I resented being used as an example against people I sympathized with and respected, for the political profit of people I disagreed with. I thought the whole idea of the dinner was wrong.

"So when I was called up to accept my award, I made the peace sign in the face of the guy who was making all the speeches. It was considered a dirty sign then, and as it turned out it stirred a bit of a storm. The next day, at my locker, there were reporters from *The New York Times, Newsweek, Time* magazine, local newspapers, and I realized then for the first time in my life that when you're a world champion your life is changed forever."

McGraw was not yet thinking about being a world champion on May 4, 1969. Despite their heroics in Chicago, the Mets still stood no better than fourth in the standings, leading Montreal and just a hair's breadth ahead of the Cardinals. They trailed the Cubs by six games. But they clearly had inched a step closer to respectability. The doubleheader sweep of the Cubs signaled a liberation from an old and persistent pattern. A pair of losses that Sunday would have dropped them ten games from first place and within a sniff of the cellar. Instead they had curbed their losing streak, sustained their place in the standings, and, perhaps most important, delivered a message to the Cubs. Seaver had informed them that the Mets would not shy from playing fundamental hardball, and the team served notice that a new intensity would mark future engagements. It was a message whose meaning would be read more clearly as the season progressed.

CHAPTER

5

THE METS NOW HAD COM-
pleted the first part of their schedule. Playing home-and-away
series against the other five teams in their division, they had
won eleven games and lost fourteen. For the next six weeks,
through the middle of June, they were to play only teams
from the Western Division. It would prove to be an eventful
period. By the time it was over, the Mets would have touched
history in their own special way and put a new cast on the
balance of the season.

They opened this segment of their schedule with an eight-
game homestand against Cincinnati, Houston, and Atlanta,
and with Hodges still searching for run production from a
team that collectively was hitting .210. Part of the answer came
from Tidewater, where Art Shamsky had completed his term
on the disabled list and was now eligible to be recalled. Hodges
also turned to his bench, where he found the rookie utility
infielder Wayne Garrett awaiting deployment. Garrett became the Mets' fourth third baseman of the month-old season, replacing Kevin Collins, who had hit .150 during his one
week of regular play. It was a move that paid quick divi-
dends. Garrett, showing unexpected power, homered his first

day on the job and put in a serious claim to long-term residence at the position.

The Mets, however, found themselves unable to put two wins together. They split a pair with Cincinnati, then took two of three from the Astros, winning and losing alternate games. But there were encouraging signs as well. Tom Seaver won the opening game against Houston with a four-hitter. It was his third straight win and his fourth successive complete game. At bat, the Mets' Mobile connection—Agee and Jones—asserted itself throughout the series with an impressive display of power. Jones contributed a home run, a triple, a pair of singles, and four walks to lift his batting average to .411. In the Sunday doubleheader, Agee connected for three home runs, giving him six for the season, one more than his 1968 total.

Early in Sunday's second game, nature seemed to send a signal of its own. Having scored only once in the opener against Larry Dierker, the Mets erupted for six runs in the first inning of the second game. No sooner had the inning ended than the sky brightened on what had been a dark, misty day, and the graceful arc of a rainbow appeared beyond the center-field fence. The phenomenon was duly noted in the next day's papers, but if it was indeed an omen, the fortune it presaged was not yet at hand, for the Mets played poorly in losing two of their next three games to the surging Atlanta Braves.

The Braves came to town as leaders of the Western Division and winners of ten of their last twelve games. They had not done it with pitching. The Braves were a run-making machine as potent as any in baseball, and they displayed their power in the opening game, winning 4 to 3 on home runs by Hank Aaron, Orlando Cepeda, and Bob Tillman.

The next day, the Mets mustered some power of their own in a game whose format was as improbable as many another they would engage in during the course of the season. Phil Niekro, the Braves' knuckleball pitcher, retired the first thirteen Mets he faced. With one out in the fifth, he lost his perfect game when he walked Ed Kranepool. He lost his no-hitter and his shutout in the seventh when Ken Boswell tripled and scored on a groundout by Jones. He lost his 3 – 1 lead and the game in the eighth when the Mets exploded for eight runs in an inning that featured a two-run double by Agee and a bases-loaded home run by Jones.

In the third game of the series and the last of their homestand, the Mets waited for the eighth inning again, but this time it was too late. They scored four times on hits by Agee, Garrett, Boswell, and Shamsky, but that still left them a run short at 6 – 5. They tried to salvage the game in the ninth and came within inches of succeeding. With the bases filled and two out, Jones lined a drive that appeared headed for the gap in right-center, but Felix Millan, the Braves' second baseman, leaped high and speared the ball backhanded for the final out.

The Mets thus concluded their homestand by dividing eight games. In the process, they had slipped to seven and a half lengths behind Chicago, which had won six of nine. However, another minor drama had been unfolding, almost unnoticed. Since the end of April, the Mets had been doggedly, though unsuccessfully, stalking the .500 mark. Never in their history had they attained that level beyond the fourth game of a season. With their opening victory over the Reds, they had crept within two games of evening their season's record. But for the next week, they proceeded to alternate wins and losses, and when it was over they were still three games shy of dead even. Now, they were packing their bags for return visits to Cincinnati, Atlanta, and Houston. Before they left, there was some extracurricular business that needed tending.

Hodges had not been altogether pleased with the team's performance in the last eight games, and he called a clubhouse meeting to tell them about it. The manager was not a man given to theatrics, but when he was angry one knew it, and his very restraint was enough to fill a room with menace. Clubhouse meetings were held sparingly, but their rules were fixed. They were not held in the town-hall tradition. Public participation was neither encouraged nor indulged. There were no question-and-answer periods, no discussions or debates. The format was basic: Hodges spoke and everyone else listened. When he finished speaking, the meeting was over. On this occasion, he informed his team that he was not satisfied with their play in recent games. They had been performing indifferently, he believed, careless of fundamentals. By all reports it was not a loud meeting. Writers who covered the team stood outside and heard nothing, they said. But it was no casual lecture either. Though the players would not discuss the details, they agreed that Hodges was angry—as angry, some said, as they had ever seen him.

"He didn't get mad often," Wayne Garrett says, "but when he did he was really intimidating. Without saying anything, just looking at you, he was intimidating. I felt it the first time I shook hands with him. I mean, his hand was so big and strong I thought it would crush mine. Right then I knew that I never wanted to get on the wrong side of this man; I never wanted him getting mad at me."

Garrett remembers Hodges with unqualified praise and obvious affection.

"He was the best manager I ever played for," he says. "The thing about Gil was that he never got on you, he never humiliated you. If you did something wrong, he would take you aside and ask you a question. He would make *you* tell *yourself* what you did wrong. He'd even ask questions while you were sitting on the bench. He'd come up to you and say, 'How many outs are there? What's the count on the batter?' He kept you in the game that way, and you always wanted to have the answer. You were always a little scared that you might get him angry."

Garrett, who was a twenty-one-year-old rookie in 1969, stepped as lightly as he could that first season. The dimensions of his life had grown larger, and he understood the need to adjust. Playing in the big leagues was just part of it. Before coming north with the Mets, Garrett had never been to a city the size of New York, and he found it every bit as intimidating as his manager.

"Until I started playing professional baseball," he says, "I had spent my whole life in Sarasota, Florida. In the minors, I played in cities like Atlanta and Dallas, and I thought they were large. But when I got to New York I could hardly believe it. You could take all of Sarasota and put it in Shea Stadium and have seats left over. New York is a very intimidating city to come to from a small town, and it's not just the size of it. Everything is magnified there. I was really nervous at first, about a lot of things.

"One of the things I was worried about was the press. They're all over the place in New York. They go anywhere they want to go. It seems they're always with you in the clubhouse, they're on the field and in the dugout before the game. You know they're there, and you know that you have to deal with them. But it's not all bad. The press can make you bear down; they can make you a better ballplayer. And it's the same with the fans. The enthusiasm of the people there is incredible. Everywhere you go, people recognize you. I mean, I was a rookie, you're not supposed to recognize *me*. But they did. The fans there really follow the game; they know the game and they know the players, and you have to adjust to that environment. You just can't go in there and do things the way you want to. It all makes sense after a while, but you have to be ready to make the adjustment."

Garrett had less trouble than most. His disposition was in his favor. He was a freckle-faced kid then, with a shock of bright red hair and the open, playful manner of a youngster who is doing what he enjoys most. He would have been at home in a Mark Twain novel, a fishing pole over his shoulder, or running the rapids on a raft with Tom Sawyer and Huck Finn. There was that small-town, country freshness about him. There still is.

You can pick him out immediately when you step off the plane. Not quite forty, he looks as if he could still slip into his old uniform and give a fair enough accounting of himself at third base. But more than that, his manner is precisely as one would have expected, as gracious and friendly to a new visitor as a Welcome Wagon host.

It is a Saturday afternoon in early spring. I have another plane to catch in three hours, and Garrett has offered to meet my flight and do the interview over lunch in the coffee shop at Sarasota's airport. The interview, then, is conducted amidst the clatter of dishes and the public address announcements of flights arriving and departing. The time allowed is not excessive. The pace is casual in Sarasota, even at the airport. Our lunch order is inadvertently delivered to two elderly ladies at the adjoining table, who appear to enjoy it as much as if the selections had been their own.

"It's not like New York," Garrett says, grinning. "Things are more relaxed here. You know, when I go to New York people still recognize me. Down here, they don't know me from Adam. People don't care who you are. That's the way I grew up; I like it that way. Even after we won the World Series, no one made a big deal about it when I came home."

That unassuming attitude became a part of Garrett's own understated style. He still seems surprised that what happened to him happened as suddenly as it did. He had spent three and a half years in the Atlanta Braves' organization when the Mets purchased his contract at the end of the 1968 season.

"I knew they would have to give me a major league contract," he says, "because I had played in triple-A the year before, and they're required to draft you at least one level higher. But that didn't mean I would make the team. I had never been to a major league spring training camp before. I had never even seen a big-league game except on television. But I figured this might be my only chance. Buddy [Harrelson] had had knee surgery during the off-season, and they needed someone to fill in until he was 100 percent. I also played a little at third and at second. I had a good spring and Hodges liked me, so when the season opened I was still there."

Garrett, who now is a major investor in an overnight courier system and its site-plan coordinator, recalls his first big-league season with an enthusiasm that belies the passing of nearly two decades. He went on to play for ten years in the majors and ended his career with two seasons in Japan, but when the subject is 1969 he is a rookie again. His voice rises an octave or two as he describes his feelings of making the team, of being inserted in the starting lineup, of playing alongside Bud Harrelson.

"Buddy was a big help to me," Garrett says. "He was a steadying influence, and just playing next to him taught me a lot. Playing defense is a matter of communication and concentration. It's not just fielding the ball. You have to know what to do with it when you get it. What do you do if the runner goes? What do you do if the ball is hit in the gap? You have to pre-program yourself, not just with every batter but on every pitch. You have to adjust every time the count changes. And Buddy taught me a lot of that. He communicated so well. He kept you thinking and improved your concentration.

"I learned a lot from Ed Charles, too. We ended up platooning most of the year at third, but neither of us minded not playing every day. Ed knew his time was coming to an end and mine was beginning, so he didn't complain. And I wouldn't have complained about anything. I was just elated to be there, to be experiencing all of that. Just being in the big leagues made me ecstatic. And scared. I was nervous a good part of that first season."

If Garrett indeed was nervous, he managed to hide it well. Since being inserted in the starting lineup, he had been hitting with authority and fielding his position cleanly. He contributed three hits and raised his batting average to .333 as the Mets opened their road trip in Cincinnati with a 10– 9 win. The team, in the meantime, seemed to have discovered the fuse to a hidden explosiveness. They scored six times in the seventh inning, and the next day they built a 10–0 lead by the fifth on their way to a second straight victory over the Reds. Now, having won seventeen of their first thirty-five games, they were just one game short of the .500 mark.

Seaver started the final game of the series on Sunday, and Cincinnati scored three runs in as many innings while the Mets went hitless in their first four times at bat. Then, for the first critical time that season, fortune intervened. It rained. Time was called and the field was covered and as the teams waited in their dugouts the rain came harder. Finally, after a delay of more than an hour, the game was terminated one inning shy of the four and a half innings necessary to make it official. It was as if the teams had never taken the field.

Thus rescued, the Mets moved on to Atlanta. It was Wednesday, May 21, and Hodges chose to start Seaver again, with only two days' rest. He responded by pitching a three-hit shutout for his fifth straight win. Jones drove in two runs and boosted his league-leading average to .391. Agee, who also was over .300 now, hit in his eleventh consecutive game. And the Mets, at the latest point in their history, were a .500 ballclub, five and a half games out of first place and third in the standings behind Chicago and Pittsburgh.

It was an achievement given its due by the press. New York papers deemed it the stuff of which headlines are made. But among the players, the responses were mixed. Those with some attachment to the Mets of the past found cause for satisfaction. Ed Kranepool, the senior Met in point of service, was foremost among them. "After all those losing years, it's a good feeling," he told Leonard Koppett of the *Times*. "Now that we're at .500, we can start proving we're a good ballclub."

Seaver spoke for most of the team when he asked, "What's .500? Let us reach first place. That'll mean something. We're looking far beyond .500."

But Seaver and the others might have done well to savor the moment, for the Mets proceeded to lose their next five games. After the Braves drubbed them 15–3 on Thursday night, they went down to the Astrodome and dropped three straight to Houston. Returning home for another long homestand, they were beaten by San Diego, the Western Division expansion team.

By now, they resembled the old Mets again. In losing the five games, they had scored a total of only nine runs. They had slipped to fourth place and were just percentage points out of fifth. They trailed the Cubs by nine games. Their season's record, 18 and 23, was no better than at that point the previous year. Their brief period of prosperity appeared to be a mirage. It was Wednesday, May 28, and the Mets once again seemed headed for oblivion.

PART THREE

Learning to Win

6

BASEBALL HAS ALWAYS BEEN A
game of streaks. Without warning and for no apparent reason, a team that has been playing on the margin all season
will become unbeatable for a week or two, winning eight, ten,
twelve games in a row. Later in the season, that same team,
its personnel intact, might as easily lose the same number of
games without being able to win one. In one pennant-winning year, the Yankees won nineteen straight games and then
lost their next ten in succession. In 1987, the Milwaukee
Brewers opened the season with thirteen consecutive wins and
proceeded to lose their next twelve games. Such streaks cannot be anticipated or explained, and they are a phenomenon
unique to baseball. Good football and basketball teams often
go on long winning streaks, but seldom do they lose more
than two or three in a row. Form can be trusted to hold more
closely in those sports. But baseball defies easy forecast, for
the variables that determine the outcome of a game are less
subject to calculation. The abiding characteristics of size, speed,
and power do not count for so much in baseball as they do
in other sports. Nuance and chance are more likely to have
their say, and so the term "upset" is rarely applied to a single
baseball game. It is taken for granted that, during the course

of a season, the best team in the league will be beaten on occasion by the league's weakest team and might even lose the season series to that team.

Given the uncertain texture of any one game, it is next to impossible to account for the extended periods of success and failure through which a team may tumble as a season progresses. One might as soon try to explain a run of hot or cold dice at a craps table. Still, streaks are a fundamental part of the logic of baseball, and championships are often won or lost on the rush of such tides of fortune.

The Mets, of course, were no strangers to losing streaks. They had, in fact, just begun a homestand by losing their fifth straight, to San Diego. But the next night they reversed the trend against the Padres, although it took them eleven innings to do it. Koosman, his arm sound once again, pitched ten shutout innings, allowed only four hits, and set a team record with fifteen strikeouts. But ten innings were enough for a pitcher on the mend. McGraw started the eleventh and twice had to work his way out of trouble. He walked the first batter on four pitches but escaped when Grote converted an attempted sacrifice into a double play. Then McGraw walked the next batter before striking out Nate Colbert to end the inning. The Mets scored the only run of the game in the bottom of the eleventh when Harrelson singled home Jones with one out and the bases full.

There was no reason at the time to attach any particular importance to the victory. The Mets were still a fourth-place team, still nine games out of first place, still four games under .500. But the course of the season had taken a turn. Gradually but inexorably, over the next two weeks, a new perception would begin to take focus. Exactly when it became apparent would depend largely on the observer, but all would agree that it began to take shape with that 1 – 0 victory on the night of May 28.

The next day, Thursday, was an off-day. The Giants and the Dodgers—twelve years gone from New York but still loved and hated as carpetbaggers—were due in next. The Mets, who in their last five games had been held to seven runs by Houston and San Diego, would soon be taking their cuts against the likes of Juan Marichal and Gaylord Perry, Don Sutton and Claude Osteen. Understandably, Hodges felt the need for greater production. He sent Jones to first base and Gaspar to left field. Ed Charles, the veteran, was assigned to everyday duty at third. Garrett and Al Weis would platoon at second base in the absence of Ken Boswell, who was off for two weeks of military service.

The Giants and Dodgers invariably attracted the largest crowds of the season to Shea, the pull of the past heightened by the hope, however frail, of the present. This Memorial Day weekend was no exception. Greeted by 52,272 customers, the Giants began their first game of the season against the Mets in a fashion that had become customary. Willie McCovey reached Tom Seaver for a home run, and San Francisco surged to a three-run lead. The Mets, meanwhile, were held hitless by Mike McCormick until the seventh, when Swoboda drove a pitch into the left-field bullpen. An inning later, Gaspar homered to draw the Mets within one. Before the inning ended Swoboda tied it with a single, and Duffy Dyer's pinch hit, his first since opening day, put the Mets in front 4–3. Ron Taylor relieved Seaver in the ninth and saved the game by striking out the Willies Mays and McCovey in succession.

The following day, McCovey got the Giants off early again, homering with a man on base in the top of the fourth. But the Mets responded quickly. Ed Charles connected off Gaylord Perry with two men on in the bottom of the inning and drove in another run in the eighth to account for all the scoring in a 4–2 decision. The sweep was completed a day later when the Giants' Joe Gibbon, a left-handed pitcher of ten years' vintage, walked four Mets in the ninth to force in the winning run.

The Mets now had won four in a row. The Dodgers, who were second to the Braves by half a game in the West, would be the opponent for the next three days. It was Monday, June 2, and the erstwhile Bums of Brooklyn were about to help the Mets make history.

The series opened with a one-run victory that lifted the Mets back to the .500 mark. Al Weis doubled home the deciding run, and Koosman, pitching brilliantly for the second straight time, held off the Dodgers, 2 to 1. A day later, Seaver and McGraw combined on a three-hitter, Kranepool hit two home runs, and the Mets were a game better than even, a level they had never managed to reach beyond the fourth game of a season. They also moved past Pittsburgh into second place, and their six-game winning streak brought them within one of their all-time record, achieved in July of 1966. So the next day's game, the last on their homestand, could provide a watershed triumph for the Mets. They would be two games above .500 for the first time in their history; they would equal their longest winning streak; and, perhaps sweetest of all, they would have accomplished it all with back-to-back sweeps of the Giants and Dodgers.

This pivotal game, arguably the most important in the franchise's seven years, would be entrusted to a young left-hander just up from Tidewater by the name of Jack Di-Lauro. An acquisition from the Detroit farm system, DiLauro had been added to the Met roster when Nolan Ryan was disabled with a pulled groin muscle. He was principally a relief pitcher with a reputation for being especially tough on left-handed batters, but Hodges was strapped for starters, so he turned to the twenty-six-year-old rookie. For DiLauro, who had spent six seasons in the minors, it would be his first big-league start, and he felt the pressure long before game time.

"Gil told me I'd be starting two or three days in advance," DiLauro recalls, "but it felt more like a month. I was really nervous, and it took me a couple of innings to settle down. I gave up a double in the first and another in the second, and I came within a couple of inches of giving up more. Buddy Harrelson saved a run with a great play at short, and Cleon caught a drive at the wall that the wind held up. The wind was blowing hard from left to right, and that's what kept the ball from going out. When I saw that Cleon had it lined up, I took a deep breath; from that point on I was all right. I held them hitless for the next seven innings, and I retired the last sixteen batters in a row."

DiLauro's two-hit shutout over nine innings was not enough to earn him the win, however, for the Dodgers' Bill Singer was matching him pitch for pitch. Singer also allowed only two hits, while striking out ten, and the game was destined to go deep into extra innings before the Mets finally won it. But when DiLauro left the mound after retiring the Dodgers in the top of the ninth, the crowd showed its appreciation of his effort.

"There were about 35,000 people there that day," DiLauro says, "and when I went back to the dugout they gave me a standing ovation. I was due to bat second in our half of the ninth, so they knew I would be lifted for a pinch hitter, and they stood and cheered me all the way from the mound to the dugout. That was the biggest thrill of my career. I had been pitching in the minors for six years, trying to make it to the big club; and now, after my first start, to get an ovation like that from a New York crowd . . . it's a moment I'll never forget. Of course it would have been even better if I'd have gotten the win, but still. . . ."

As it turned out, there would not be many wins in Di-Lauro's career and few standing ovations. It was an abbreviated career that sparkled occasionally with brief moments of promise but never really took root. He had another quality start against the Dodgers in Los Angeles, but some loose play afield cost him the game. For the balance of the season, he worked mainly in relief, winning only one of five decisions despite a creditable earned run average of 2.40.

"I was a victim of the Mets' outstanding pitching staff," he says. "I had always been a starter, and I wanted to stay in the rotation, but with the kind of pitchers they had on that team there was no way I could break in."

DiLauro started only two more games in 1969, and at the end of the season he was dealt to Houston. He became the Astros' number-one left-handed reliever, appearing in more than one-fourth of the team's games. At one point in the season, he made seventeen consecutive appearances without allowing an earned run.

"For two months," DiLauro says, "I was the best reliever in the majors, but from August 28 until the end of the season I never threw a pitch."

DiLauro had a falling-out with Harry Walker, the Astros' manager, and he did not get on any better with the general manager, Spec Richardson. He failed to make the team in spring training the following season. His future in baseball consisted of two seasons in the minors—one with Hawaii and one in the Atlanta Braves' organization. At the end of the 1972 season, he took a job with a sporting goods company for the off-season, and it turned out to be the start of a new career. Since then, he has managed three of the company's stores and opened a new territory in his native Akron, Ohio, not far from his home in Malvern.

"It's a good position for an ex-athlete," he says. "I wear my World Series ring for business purposes, and it really helps. People ask about it, they ask to see it. They still remember.

Everyone remembers the '69 Mets. You know, you really had to play for another organization to appreciate what the attitude was like on that club. Everyone was always pulling for everyone else. It was a great blend of players. We had some low-key guys like Cardwell, Koonce, and J. C. Martin, and some vibrant types like Tug and Swoboda. But the guy who impressed me the most was Seaver. He was a year younger than I was, but he carried himself so well. He knew how to handle everyone—the press, the fans, the other players. And he really believed we could win. That was so important. It was the younger guys on that team who made believers of the players who'd been around for a while. I was a cheerleader on the bench, and we were always alive and rooting for the guys who were playing. That kind of spirit really helps a team. I remember how I felt when I returned to the dugout after that game against the Dodgers and the other guys all jumped up to greet me; it was such a great feeling. I just wish we could have scored and won the game in the bottom of the ninth."

The Mets did not score in the ninth or in any of the next five innings, and neither did the Dodgers. In the top of the fifteenth, the visitors threatened, putting runners on first and third with only one out, but Al Weis saved it. He made a difficult backhand stop of a ball hit off the pitcher's glove, then wheeled and threw home, where Grote blocked off the plate and made the tag. Ron Taylor, pitching his second inning in relief of McGraw, got the third out and would soon own the win. In the bottom of the inning, with Agee on first and one out, Garrett lined a single to center. The usually sure-handed Willie Davis charged the ball with an eye toward holding Agee at second, but the ball skipped between his legs and rolled to the wall while Agee sprinted around the bases with the only run of the game.

So the Mets ended their first homestand against the West

with a seven-game winning streak and a season's record that was two games better than .500. They were a second-place ballclub now, and if it was still premature to think seriously in terms of a pennant, it was clear that the team's fortunes would have to be considered in a new context. For the first time in their quixotic history, the Mets were now in a position where failure could be looked upon as a disappointment. They had just swept six straight games from the Giants and the Dodgers—and that was, in a sense, a declaration of independence. Some part of the root to the past had been severed. After twelve years of weaning, New York fans could now look upon the Giants and Dodgers as just a couple of teams from California. Tug McGraw understood what the double sweep meant to New York.

"When the Mets were born," he says, "management did a tremendous job of public relations in making the team popular. The theme was: 'To err is human, but to forgive is to be a Mets' fan.' From the fans' standpoint, the idea was to take this little baby of a team, and they were going to feed it and bathe it and stroke it and change its diapers and forgive it when it messed up. They were going to give it love and affection, and some day this little baby was going to grow up, and when those Dodger bullies and those Giant bullies came to town it was gonna kick their ass so high they'd have to shit through their ribs. Finally, in 1969, that little Met baby had grown up. He was young and innocent and naive, but he was also strong and powerful. Nobody knew yet what he was capable of, but when we beat the Dodgers and the Giants it was like saying, 'Okay, folks, no more kicking sand in our faces.' "

Having tamed the out-of-town bullies before the adoring New York throngs, the Mets flew west for return encounters with the same three teams against which they had built their winning streak. On Friday, June 6, they opened a three-game series in San Diego. The Padres had a six-game winning streak of their own, a fair piece of work for an expansion team. It was even more impressive when measured against the performance of their Eastern Division counterparts. The Montreal Expos, playing up the freeway in Los Angeles, had lost eighteen straight and were closing in on the 1961 Phillies' modern-day record of twenty-three consecutive losses.

Only one of the three streaks survived the weekend. The Expos finally won one after two more losses, while the Mets swept all three games from the Padres. San Diego contested each game closely, but Met pitching had begun to reach its form now, and the Padres' batters were simply overmatched. In the opening game, Gentry won his fifth in a row, at one point retiring fourteen straight batters, then getting help from Taylor for the last two outs. The next day Koosman struck out eleven while allowing only six hits, running the winning streak to nine. The tenth almost got away. Seaver had fourteen strikeouts after six innings, but the Mets again were having trouble with Al Santorini, a young rookie from Fairleigh Dickinson who had handed them their last defeat almost two weeks earlier. They trailed 2−1 when they came to bat in the eighth, and Seaver retired for a pinch hitter, but the timing was flawless. Ed Charles singled, Harrelson walked, and Tommie Agee lined a double good for two runs and a 3−2 lead. Taylor came on to pitch two shutout innings, salvaging Seaver's ninth victory of the season, and the Mets headed for San Francisco with a ten-game winning streak.

It was Tuesday, June 10, and in the wind tunnel known as Candlestick Park, the Mets made it eleven in a row with a convincing, well-balanced effort. Agee hit two home runs while going 4 for 5, and Jones also hit one. Don Cardwell, in the meantime, contributed both from the mound and at the plate, stroking three hits and a sacrifice fly while pitching a two-hitter over eight innings. Taylor again finished up, earning his third save in the last four games.

That, however, was as far as it went. The streak ended the next day when Gaylord Perry throttled the Mets on four hits. During the course of their run, the longest in the major leagues that season, the Mets had solidified their second-place position in the standings, but they had cut only two games from the Cubs' lead, which now stood at seven. The Cubs, for their part, were almost as hot as the Mets, having just swept four games from the Braves in Atlanta. With the season exactly one-third over, Chicago already was twenty games over .500, with a nearly invincible winning percentage of .685.

Still, the Mets had cause for satisfaction. They had opened a four-game lead on both Pittsburgh and St. Louis. They had begun to establish themselves as a winning ballclub. First place still seemed beyond their reach, but a third-place finish, a long-shot chance for second, now loomed as a realistic possibility, and that was all they had hoped for. They were not thinking in terms of a pennant; not yet.

CHAPTER

7

THE UNEXPECTED SUCCESS OF the Mets was judged by many to beg explanation. It was as if a law of nature had been violated: one was prepared to accept the consequences, but if balance and symmetry were to be restored, the cause had to be uncovered.

Of course there is never a shortage of explanations when it comes to sports. The discerning eye can be trusted to supply all the reasons once the result is known. The long shot looks like a sure-bet winner after the upset is in the books. Causes are determined by effects in sports, and now with the Mets clearly established as a team capable of winning its share of games, a multitude of arguments was being advanced to define their sudden emergence.

Analysts were quick to point out that the changes in rules and format introduced at the start of the '69 season were most likely to benefit a team like the Mets. The addition of two new teams, they contended, had spread the talent a bit thinner and allowed the Mets to get healthy at the expense of the needy. Almost one-third of their victories, after all, had come against the Expos and Padres. Did anyone believe that the Mets would be in second place if they were playing in the ten-team league of 1968?

Also, it was argued in curious fashion, the lower pitching mound and smaller strike zone, designed to improve the lot of batters, would be of most help to a team whose strength was pitching. The reasoning went this way: Marginal pitchers would have the most difficulty adjusting to the new rules, while quality pitchers with good control would be less-adversely affected. Conversely, a light-hitting team like the Mets would benefit from the constraints placed on opposing pitchers. Therefore, the Mets could be expected to be more productive at bat while their pitching continued to prosper.

The most convincing argument offered was that the Mets had been aided by the institution of the amateur draft in 1966. Previously, teams had bid for the most promising talent with bonuses that had pushed well into six figures. But the draft, fashioned along the lines of those employed in football and basketball, brought order to the selection process and fiscal restraint to negotiations. Players were obliged to sign with the teams that drafted them, and since choices were made in the reverse order of finish—with the team lowest in the standings given first pick—the Mets had been skimming the cream from the top.

Certainly, there was some merit to such reasoning. The intent of the draft was, of course, to assure more balance among the major league teams and to prevent those with the largest bankrolls from building dynasties that might endure for decades. But still, only a small handful of the players now helping the Mets make their run—most notably Garrett and Boswell—had been drafted by the club. Most of the others had already been maturing in their minor league system or had come to the team in trades.

While searching to explain the Mets' sudden rise, few of the pundits noted that just two years earlier the Boston Red Sox had leaped from ninth place to a pennant in one quick swoop, improving their record by twenty full games, without the benefit of an amateur draft or any changes in format or rules. They had done it with the addition of some key personnel and the careful grooming of their younger talent. And the Mets were doing it in much the same manner.

They had been put together, if not with brickwork precision, certainly with a clear eye to fitting the pieces together. Some teams are built around a core of one or two world-class players, with the rest of the squad acting as a supporting cast. For decades, the Yankees had structured their championship teams around a centerpiece: Ruth and Gehrig, DiMaggio then Mantle. The Mets, by contrast, were being molded as an integrated unit, with each player accorded a role that he was expected to fill; if it worked as intended, the parts would constitute an organism that was greater than their sum.

At the start of the season, there were three everyday positions—right field, first base, and third base—that beckoned to any candidate who might come calling. There also was a handful of young players, numbering among them Amos Otis, Rod Gaspar, and Wayne Garrett, whose roles were uncertain. Hodges spent a good part of the season's first two months mixing and matching, sifting the inventory of talent at his disposal, determining who fit best where and what parts might still be needed.

Gaspar, who had started the season in right field, was now consigned to a bit part. He was valued for his speed, his sure glove, his shotgun of an arm, his occasional dexterity with a bat. All would be put to good use as the season wore on. Otis, whose potential was esteemed far more than that of the other rookies, was judged to be not quite ready for the majors. He had played in more than half the team's games, in both the outfield and at third base, but was batting only .136 and had struck out nineteen times in sixty-six plate appearances. In a matter of days, Otis would be optioned to a minor league team.

Right field, then, would be entrusted for the balance of the season to the combined talents of Swoboda and Shamsky.

First base once again belonged to Kranepool, but the search was still on for a right-handed batter with whom he could alternate. That would establish three platoon positions, for it had been settled during the course of the Western road trip that third base would be shared by Garrett and Ed Charles.

Third base had been a chronic problem for the Mets. Dozens of candidates had been tried there since the Mets opened shop, four during the first few weeks of the 1969 season. But Garrett, after filling in at second and short, had secured part of the position when tried there in May, and Charles's steady glove and solid if unspectacular bat had earned him the right-handed platoon. It would prove to be a more-than-adequate combination, providing as it did a near-perfect blend of youth and experience. Garrett, the twenty-year-old rookie, would make an eager pupil for the thirty-six-year-old Charles, now in his eighteenth professional season. For Charles, the opportunity was something of a resurrection, cherished the more because it was unexpected.

"I wasn't even supposed to be a part of the '69 team," Charles says now. "They were grooming Amos Otis to play third base, and I was trying to help him along, but it didn't work out. Finally, I got a chance to play, and I got some key hits and I ended up sharing the position with Wayne Garrett. I don't think anyone was too surprised that I was able to contribute. I had a good year in 1968, but they were looking to the future with youngsters like Garrett and Otis."

Nineteen sixty-eight, Charles's first full season with the Mets, was one of his best in the majors. He batted .276 with fifteen home runs and fifty-three runs batted in, while playing in 117 games. He had come in a trade from Kansas City early in the previous season, and at the time he was not happy about it.

"I had no bad feelings about New York," he says, "but I had been in Kansas City since 1962, and I thought I would finish up there. I was thirty-four years old at the time, and I had talked with Mr. Finley (the owner of the Kansas City A's), and he said they were thinking of making me a coach, so I was a little discouraged when they traded me. Any trade hits you hard, especially when it comes near the end of your career."

Charles's major league career was nearing its end not very long after it had begun. He was already twenty-nine years old when Kansas City purchased his contract from the Milwaukee Braves' organization, where he had labored for ten seasons in the minor leagues. By the time he was traded to the Mets, he had been a professional baseball player for more than half his life and had little to show for it. He had been born in Daytona Beach and raised in Fort Lauderdale at a time when blacks cast their eyes toward the majors with fond aspirations but only the thinnest of hopes. So when the Braves—then still based in Boston—offered him a tryout, he was quick to accept.

"I was in my senior year at Gibbs High School," Charles recalls, "and I was given a tryout with their Class B team. They told me I wasn't good enough, but I was thrilled because I was the first black to be given an opportunity to try out with them. After that I was offered a contract by the Indianapolis Clowns of the Negro-American League to play for them after I got out of school, and I was contemplating that offer. But one night the local team was playing an exhibition game against the Syracuse Chiefs there in St. Petersburg, and I decided to go to the game. As I walked into the stadium, the gentleman who was president of the club at the time, Vern Eckert, saw me and he called me into his office and said, 'Where are you going to play this year?' I told him, 'I don't know; I might go off and play with the Indianapolis Clowns.' He said, 'Wait a minute, let me make a call.' He called the Braves' organization in Myrtle Beach, South Carolina, and said he was going to send me up there for a tryout.

This meant I had to leave high school before my class graduated. I got permission from the principal and took off for Myrtle Beach, and I was assigned to the Quebec Braves team in Class C, and that's how I got started."

That was in the spring of 1952, and Charles was still a long way from the majors. The journey from Class C to the big time, never an easy one, was all the more tortuous for a black ballplayer in the early fifties. Integration was still a new idea in organized baseball when Charles signed his first professional contract. It was only five years since Jackie Robinson had broken the color barrier. Blacks on major league rosters were few in number, and they were chosen with consummate care. In the main, they were established stars from the Negro leagues, players like Larry Doby and Monte Irvin who, in some instances, had their best years already behind them. Blacks were given the opportunity to succeed as best they might during those first years of integration, but they were not afforded the luxury of the chance to fail. And so Charles would be obliged to serve an apprenticeship that was far beyond what a candid appraisal might dictate. His route to the majors passed through Quebec, Fort Lauderdale, Corpus Christi, Wichita, Jacksonville, and Vancouver. Still, he was prepared to be patient, for the years had accustomed him to adversity.

It had never been easy for Ed Charles. He was born during the worst of times in among the worst of places, and it might have seemed to a young man as if all the accidents of circumstance had conspired against him. The Depression was as deep as it would get in 1933, and in the forlorn Negro sections of St. Petersburg, it was as much a state of being as a period in time. What little food there was in the Charles household was shared among nine children, and there were no immediate signs of relief. But Charles soon discovered that he possessed a gift with market value. He was graced with the quick ease of motion, the sure hands, and the good eye that enabled him to perform those basic acts that were fundamental to baseball: he could catch the ball when it was hit, and he could hit it when it was pitched. Baseball was the way out for Charles, and he sensed it perhaps as early as 1946, when Jackie Robinson came to town.

"Jackie signed with the Montreal Royals for the 1946 season," Charles says. "Montreal was the triple-A farm team of the Brooklyn Dodgers, and the Dodgers trained in Daytona Beach, so I got to see him come down. That was a big happening for us. It was ushering in a whole new era when blacks and whites would be competing on the same field. No one down there had ever seen anything like that before, and it brought hope to the other kids and myself. I never dreamt at the time that I would be a major league ballplayer, but Jackie was my hero. I idolized him and I was happy to see him out there with the other players. He performed real well, and he was an intelligent person. He handled himself so well on and off the field, and it was great having him to look up to.

"I'll never forget one time, after my family moved to St. Petersburg, when Jackie came to town. The Dodgers were breaking camp in Daytona Beach and moving north, and they stopped in St. Pete for a game with the Yankees. After the game, a bunch of us kids followed the Dodgers' bus to the train station and stood on the platform until we located Jackie. We saw him through the window, sitting there, playing cards with some of the other guys; we waved to him, and he waved back. It was a big thing . . . it was a big thing to us kids seeing Jackie through the window and him waving back to us. Then, as the train started moving out of the station, we chased after it, all the time waving to Jackie. It was a big thing, it was an inspiration to us. We had some local figureheads on the scene that we could look up to but not a national hero like Jackie."

Even before Robinson's arrival, spring training was a special time for Charles and the other youngsters in the area.

"We used to go down to Al Lang Field in St. Petersburg and chase foul balls that were hit over the fence," Charles recalls. "That's how we made our spending money. We would wait outside the park for balls to be hit over the fence, then we would chase them down and try to sell the ball to the tourists. If you got a player to sign the ball, especially some-one like DiMaggio or Willliams or Musial, you could get as much as five dollars for it. For other players, you might get two or three dollars, but it added up.

"I remember one time," he says chuckling, "I was wait-ing over by the left-field area, across the street in back of the park, when I saw a ball headed my way. It was right at the edge of the water there, but I had my eye on the ball and I said, 'I got this one all the way,' and I kept backing up and finally backed right into the water, and I said, 'the heck with it, I'm not even going to look for it,' and I just let it lay there."

Charles laughs heartily as he recalls the incident. Youth has its nostalgic attraction even when its bounties have been meager.

It is a bright but chilly afternoon in late April. Charles lives in a small, old-style apartment building—the kind with fire escapes fronting the brick facade—in the Washington Heights section of Upper Manhattan. It is a friendly-looking neighborhood lined with trees and shrubs, and mothers with small children are in the streets tasting the first pale sun of springtime.

His visitor is a tad early, and Charles does not answer until the third ring of the doorbell. His mouth is foamy with toothpaste. He apologizes for not being quite ready, but by the time the tape recorder is set and notes are in order, Charles strides into the living room wearing sweat pants and a pull-over shirt. His hair is flecked with more than a touch of gray and his hard, square body is padded about the middle now, but he still moves with an athlete's grace.

He is being interviewed, as it happens, on his fifty-third

birthday, but nothing is planned by way of celebration. He has spent the day working on his autobiography, a somewhat ambitious extension of a taste for writing he has nurtured for more than twenty-five years. A deeply religious man, Charles began writing inspirational poetry when he was in San Juan, Puerto Rico, in 1961.

"I wanted to see if I could say what was on my mind and express it with clarity in a poetic way," he says. "I started writing some rough, crude stuff, but I was encouraged by some people that I respected, so I kept at it and finally put together some things that were pretty good."

Some of his poems have appeared in newspapers and as part of a collection of sports poems written by athletes. Now he is seeking a wider focus, attempting to draw together the bits and pieces of his life and orchestrate them into a harmony that is somehow comprehensible. It is not an easy task. He is living alone now, divorced from his wife of eighteen years, who still resides in Kansas City with their two sons. He has been unemployed since the end of the 1985 baseball season, when the Mets discharged him after twelve years of working for the organization as a scout and minor league coach. Except for the three years immediately following his playing career, Charles had earned his living in baseball since he was nineteen years old.

"I retired as a player after the 1969 season," Charles says. "I could have played a couple more years, but no one was keeping old players around in those days except for a few superstars. The Mets offered me a job in promotion, but I didn't take it. Instead, I did promotion for a record company in Kansas City for three years, and then the Mets signed me on as a scout. I covered Missouri, Iowa, Kansas, Nebraska, Colorado, Oklahoma, and sometimes Texas. I did that for nine years. After that, they wanted me to coach in their minor league system, and that's what I did for the next three years, until last October."

Charles is reflective but not bitter when he speaks of the deprivations of his younger years, but there is a deep resentment in his voice when he addresses his dismissal by the Mets. He is reluctant to discuss the details. He leans back in the corner of the sofa and puffs on long, thin, brown-colored cigarettes. He shakes his head ruefully and speaks instead of the prospects that might lie ahead.

"I'm trying to get started again," he says, "to resolve things with respect and with dignity. I've been trying to find employment, but so far I haven't been successful. I contacted a lot of teams, but most of them said they were set for this season. They said I should contact them later, but they didn't have anything for me now. I completed a correspondence course in hotel and motel management and I tried to get into that around the city. I had some interviews, but I haven't got anything yet. It's kind of tough. Of course I'd really like to get back into baseball. All my life has been baseball; that's where my expertise is, but right now I'd just like to find something to do."

Emblems of his attachment to baseball, his years with the Mets, are still plainly visible. In the corners of the living room are stashed blue-and-orange tote bags bearing the logo of the Mets. They sit there compressed in small spaces, reminders of better times. They have been there, one suspects, since the previous fall, the tangible evidence of a past that contains perhaps some promise for the future.

The season of 1969 was, of course, the best of times for Ed Charles. A career that had foundered on the twists of chance and the hard edge of bigotry was resurrected and carried to a peak that only the most dauntless romantic might have imagined. Charles was a welcome addition to the Mets' roster when he arrived and an essential ingredient in their championship formula. The Mets were a team that was being refashioned in the image of youth, and Charles brought with him an easy-going maturity that stabilized and brightened the mood of the clubhouse. The younger players called him "Pops" and referred to him at times as "the old man"; he took their jibes and responded with equally good nature. On the field, he was known as the Glider, a nickname given to him by Jerry Koosman for the fluid manner in which he moved to field ground balls. He played in only sixty-one games during the 1969 season, but perhaps it is no coincidence that his emergence as a role player began simultaneously with the start of the Mets' eleven-game winning streak.

Now the winning streak had ended, and the Mets were ready to conclude their western swing with a trip down the coast from San Francisco to Los Angeles. The last time the Mets played the Dodgers, just nine days earlier at Shea, they had extended their winning streak to seven when Willie Davis's error allowed the game's only run to score. Now it was the Dodgers' turn. They won the opener of the series by the same 1 – 0 score when Shamsky bobbled a single to right and Jim Lefebvre followed with the game-winning hit. Shamsky made amends the following night with a home run and a single, and Seaver drove in two runs to help himself to his tenth victory.

The last day of the Mets' road trip was a memorable one. Some writers who covered the team would later contend that this was the day that the Mets won the pennant. It was Sunday, June 15, and the record shows that Don Drysdale, the Dodgers' Hall of Fame – bound pitcher, came off the disabled list that day and beat the Mets 3 to 2. It also shows that just hours before the major league trading deadline, the Mets shipped four minor league players—infielder Kevin Collins and pitchers Steve Renko, Dave Colon, and Jay Carden—to the Montreal Expos for Donn Clendenon, a first baseman with home run power who was nearing his thirty-fourth birthday. Platooning with Kranepool, Clendenon would give the Mets the right-handed, long-ball potential they had been seeking since spring training. He also provided the youthful Mets with another veteran presence, a stabilizing influence whose cool demeanor had been forged in the pressure of pennant competition when he played for the Pittsburgh Pirates.

After eight seasons with Pittsburgh, Clendenon had gone to Montreal in the 1969 expansion draft. He was yet to be fitted for his new Expos' uniform when Montreal traded him and outfielder Jesus Alou to the Houston Astros in exchange for Rusty Staub. Clendenon was reluctant to make the move, perhaps because of differences that had surfaced between him and Astros' manager Harry Walker when both were with the Pirates. More than a month after the trade was made, on the eve of the opening of spring training camps, he announced his retirement from baseball.

It was not an idle maneuver, and the principals in the controversy knew it, for Clendenon was a man with diverse interests and a few options of his own. A resident of Atlanta, he had set roots in the business life of the community that were expanding in more than one direction. He recently had been named vice-president of the Scripto Pen Company, was in the process of opening a new restaurant, and was on his way to earning a law degree from Morehouse University. He said he planned to use his resources to help black ballplayers obtain jobs when their baseball careers were over.

According to baseball's regulations, Clendenon's retirement nullified the trade, and the other players involved were to report back to their original teams. But that created new complications. Rusty Staub, it seemed, had welcomed the move to Montreal and had quickly developed strong ties in the city that would soon affectionately christen him *La Grande Orange*. Now Staub said he would quit rather than return to Houston.

With spring training nearly over, Commissioner Bowie Kuhn and his assistant, former Giants' outfielder Monte Irvin, intervened. The Astros were persuaded to accept two young pitchers—Jack Billingham and Skip Guinn—and a cash payment of $100,000 in lieu of Clendenon, who then was coaxed out of retirement with the added incentive of a raise in salary. The deal was cemented on opening day, and thus the pieces were put in place for the trade that, two months later, would provide the Mets with the missing link in their quest for the pennant.

Precisely what Clendenon meant to the team cannot be measured in terms of his on-field production alone. He was a unifying element, a clubhouse presence that eased the tension and lightened the mood on a team that was unaccustomed to the pressures of contending.

"He was the catalyst on the team," Art Shamsky recalls. "You can talk about our pitching, which was great, and whatever else, but until June we were just a potentially good team. When Clendenon joined us, he gave us the right-handed power we needed, some more experience, and we became a really good team from that point on."

"He was a take-the-pressure-off kind of guy," says Tug McGraw. "He'd been through it all before, he was a very intelligent man, and he loved to talk. He was our pressure exorcist. He scared the demons right out of the clubhouse. He and Charles were a good combination that way. Charles had this kind of silent wisdom. He was real cool. When things would get a little tight, you would look over at him and say, 'Hey, the Glider doesn't look worried; I guess we're all right.' They complemented one another. Clendenon was more vocal, a fun kind of guy to have around."

Wayne Garrett agrees. "Clendenon was probably the key to our whole season," he says, "because when he came over we really came alive. We needed run production, and he gave us the potential to score four, five, six runs a game. He also helped some of the younger players, like myself. He kept us going when we got down on ourselves. It took him a while to get started with us, but he slowly came into the picture, and when he did we really took off. He was just the ingredient we needed, the last piece of the puzzle."

Clendenon joined the Mets in Philadelphia, where they were scheduled for a four-game series before returning home. They opened by splitting a twi-night doubleheader, with Gary Gentry winning the first game in the most impressive performance of his young career. He retired the first fifteen Phillie batters on his way to a two-hit shutout, jealously guarding the run he had been given on a seventh-inning single by J. C. Martin. He also collected nine strikeouts, the last of them against the formidable Richie Allen for the final out of the game.

Allen, who already had hit seventeen home runs in the first ten weeks of the season, faced an unusual defense when he came to bat in the ninth. Looking to deprive him of an extra-base hit, Hodges aligned four outfielders against him. Al Weis, the second baseman, was sent to the left-field corner, with the remaining three fielders spaced between left-center and right. This novel deployment was rendered academic when Gentry struck Allen out for the third time in the game, and it was rendered useless in the second game when Allen hit a 460-foot home run over the left field roof to help salvage a split of the doubleheader.

The Mets won the next day behind a Koosman shutout and closed out the series with a free-swinging 6–5 victory in which Shamsky hit two home runs and Boswell delivered the tying and winning runs with a two-out single in the ninth.

So the Mets concluded their two-week road trip with eight wins in twelve games. They now were six games over the .500 mark, but that once-elusive goal was no longer invested with magic. More significant was the fact that the Cubs had lost their last five in a row, cutting their first-place lead to five and a half games.

It was Friday, June 20. The Mets had won fifteen of

their last nineteen games. If they were to make a move for the top, now was the time. They would be playing their Eastern Division rivals, including the Cubs six times, right up through the All-Star break on July 23. The month's work would begin with a nine-game homestand. When they returned to Shea, the largest National League gathering of the season, 54,083, turned out to welcome them back. It was a crowd whose tone was a shade different from that of crowds of the past.

PART FOUR

Racing with the Moon

CHAPTER

8

THERE IS A SPECIAL ALLURE AT-
tached to rooting for a loser. It is a no-risk proposition that
offers immunity from the despair of defeat while extending
the promise of unexpected triumph. For the underdog, every
victory has a spiritual message; it speaks of the conquest of
forces larger than itself. Winners, and those who back them,
carry with them always the relentless burden of their own
success.

The 1962 Mets, who forever will remain the prototype
of the losing cause, could not have come upon the scene at a
better time. The early sixties was a fairly blissful period in
America's history. The serene but monotonous years of the
fifties had given way to breezier days. Camelot had opened
its gates to a new generation. A sense of subtlety, of irony
and wit, was more the fashion than the ponderous sincerity,
the unwinking commitment to purpose that had given the
Silent Generation its name.

In New York, sports championships had become as routine as the turning of the seasons. In 1962, the Yankees were
on their way to their third straight pennant, and two more
would follow. The football Giants were winning division titles
with almost equal regularity. So when the Mets came to town,

it meant more than the return of National League baseball. Here, at last, was a team one could root for and remain free of the anxiety of defeat. If fans drew sustenance from a winner, there were nonetheless few who could easily identify with one. The Yankees and the Giants might reflect our fondest hopes and aspirations, but the Mets—ah, the Mets!—embodied the harsh reality of our workaday lives.

In 1963, a survey was conducted that sketched a profile of the typical Met fan. The result was summarized by Robert Lipsyte in *The New York Times*:

> The Metophile is a dreamer. He believes that one day he will punch out that arrogant foreman at the plant square on his fat nose; that he will get in the last word with his wife; that he will win the Irish Sweepstakes; that the Mets will start a winning streak. The odds on the final possibility are somewhat higher than those on the first three. That is the main reason he comes to the Polo Grounds.

The survey concluded: "The pure Metophile is likely to disappear in a few more years. Even now, more and more ordinary people go to the Polo Grounds to watch a baseball game. As the Mets progress from incompetency to mediocrity, their psychological pull will be gone."

Whether the last assessment was truly prophetic remains a matter of conjecture, but indications point in its favor. Attendance had slipped some by 1968; perhaps more significantly, a delicate shift could be discerned in the mood of the crowds. Some of the enthusiasm seemed to have drained from the surface. A touch of derision had muted its voice. Supporting a loser can be uplifting for a time, but it finally begs relief. In the long run, it is the memory of the experience one yearns for rather than the experience itself, the wish to know that one came from humble roots but rose above them.

If the Met mystique had begun to wear thin, the tenor

of the times had also changed vastly in the past seven years. The frolicsome spirit of the early sixties had turned surly in the second half of the decade. Those spirited gadflies with a healthy contempt for authority had recently developed a taste for its blood. Passive disobedience had mushroomed into open rebellion. The flower children had been replaced by urban guerrillas. It was no longer sufficient to avow one's alienation from the Establishment; the need now was to seize it by the throat.

The Mets of their infancy, therefore, no longer gave shape to the dreams of their fans. What was wanted now were real heroes, brash upstarts with a bit of swagger to their gait and a touch of arrogance to their manner. The day of benign defiance had passed; the time had come to storm the gates. Joe Namath had shown how it could be done earlier in the year. He guaranteed that his lightly regarded Jets would topple the Colts in Super Bowl III, and he had made good on his promise. Now here were the Mets, sticking it to the big boys just as Broadway Joe had done. So when they returned home, the Mets, on the very brink of contention, were greeted by a throng that had begun to learn to feel for the jugular.

The opposition was the Cardinals, who had faltered for much of the season but were still considered the chief threat to nudge the Cubs from their perch atop the Eastern Division. Despite their poor start and their fourth-place standing, the Cards were just one game under .500 and eight and a half games out of first. Nolan Ryan, making his first start since coming off the disabled list, was matched with Bob Gibson in the Friday night opener, and the Mets quickly demonstrated that they still had Gibson's number. They reached him for three runs in the first inning and another in the second, and four was precisely the number they needed. With the score 4 to 2, McGraw relieved Ryan in the seventh, gave up a leadoff home run to Gibson, then retired the next nine in a row, striking out the side in the ninth.

The Mets lost to Nelson Briles the next day, but on Sunday, before a crowd that exceeded Friday's record, they swept a doubleheader, 5 – 1 and 1 – 0, behind Gentry and Koosman. The Cards scored in the first inning of the opener but came up empty for the next seventeen innings. For Koosman, it was his third shutout of the season, and it extended his string of consecutive scoreless innings to twenty-three.

It was not, however, a very good day for Ron Swoboda, who was batting just a shade over .200. He left nine men on base in the first game while becoming only the thirteenth player in major league history to strike out five times in one game. During the course of the season, the fans had been developing a complex relationship with Swoboda, whom one cynic had described as a Marv Throneberry with talent. He was booed and cheered from day to day with equal vigor, and on this day he had it both ways. The crowd jeered after each of his first four strikeouts, but when he came to bat in the eighth he was accorded a standing ovation, the intensity of which increased with each strike until he had fanned for the fifth time. It was, all told, a good-natured display, and even if tainted with a touch of hostility, it was no doubt easier to accept with the Mets on their way to winning three of four from the National League champions.

The Phillies, who led only Montreal in the standings, were in next, and they proved to be no match for Met pitching in a Tuesday doubleheader. Seaver beat them 2 – 1 in the opener, and McAndrew was even tougher in the second game, retiring the first seventeen batters he faced on his way to his first win of the season, 1 – 0.

By the end of the day, the Mets had won twenty of their last twenty-five games; they were ten games over .500 and only four and a half games behind the Cubs. But the engine that had powered them for the past month was about to stall briefly. Ryan started the next day's game much as McAndrew had the previous one. He struck out eight of the first twelve batters and did not allow a runner until the sixth inning. Then it all began to unravel. The Phils scored a run in the sixth and three more in the seventh, and won the game in ten innings, 6 to 5. Grant Jackson shut the Mets out the next day, striking out ten batters, including Swoboda four more times. In the two games they lost to the Phillies, the Mets struck out twenty-four times, and they failed to score a run in their last fifteen times at bat.

The number of scoreless innings reached twenty-three the following day before the Mets broke through against Pittsburgh's Steve Blass in the ninth, but they lost that game and the next one too. Seaver halted the four-game skid on the last day of the homestand with his twelfth victory of the season, but it gave the Mets little cause for celebration. During their short stay at Shea, they had won six games while losing five and had slipped to eight games in back of the Cubs. One could not help notice, as well, that they owed their winning record to a facility for beating teams in the Western Division. Against Eastern Division clubs, they had done no better than an even split of forty games. During the next three weeks, between the end of June and the All-Star break, they would try to tilt the balance in their favor, beginning with visits to St. Louis and Pittsburgh.

McAndrew got the Mets off well, pitching a three-hitter in a lopsided win, to close out the most successful month of play in the team's history. Their 19–9 record in June marked only the third time that the Mets had played a winning month of baseball. However, they opened July by dropping a doubleheader, which gave them six losses in their last eight games. It could not really be called a losing streak nor a slump of any dimension, but it was fuel for those who suspected that as the season progressed the Mets might begin to stumble. As it turned out, more than a week would pass before they lost another game.

The Mets rebounded with the kind of victory that lifts a

team and silences its skeptics. Koosman, who had the lowest earned run average in the National League, appeared on his way to another shutout. He was protecting a four-run lead with two out in the eighth when he seemed to lose sight of home plate. He walked the next three batters and was relieved by Ron Taylor, a right-handed pitcher. Red Schoendienst, the Cardinal manager, countered by sending up Vic Davalillo, a left-handed batter, to hit for Julian Javier; Davalillo proceeded to tie the game with one of only two home runs he would hit all season. McGraw came on in the ninth and loaded the bases with none out, but he managed to escape without allowing a run to score. For the next five innings, McGraw pitched his way in and out of trouble, stranding eleven runners in six innings of relief, before the Mets pushed across the two winning runs in the fourteenth. It was a difficult, exasperating game that appeared to be won early, then lost on several occasions, and finally won in what seemed to be a contest of will and endurance. But that is the kind of inelegant game that quality teams seem to win so often, and for the Mets it marked the start of a winning streak that would establish them as serious contenders.

They ended their stay in St. Louis with Gary Gentry throwing a five-hitter for his eighth win of the season, then moved on to Pittsburgh where Seaver won his thirteenth— and seventh in a row—to open a sweep of a July Fourth doubleheader. After a rainout, they made it three straight against the Pirates, coming back from an early five-run deficit. Ed Charles hit a solo home run, and Clendenon hit his first as a Met with two men on as the Mets scored seven times in the middle three innings on their way to an 8–7 victory.

That gave the Mets a five-game winning streak and a 6-and-2 performance on their brief road trip. Just three games short of the season's midpoint, they were eleven games over .500 and, more importantly, back to within five games of first place. Now, for the first time in seven years, a Met team was preparing to play a critical series of games. It was Tuesday, July 8, and the Chicago Cubs were in town.

The Cubs arrived at Shea having lost their last three games. Still there was little evidence to support the notion that they viewed the Mets with alarm. Ernie Banks, the future Hall of Fame—first baseman with the disposition of spring sunshine, was customarily chipper before the start of the first game; Ron Santo, the third baseman and team captain, who was never known to be reticent when it came to discussing the opposition, was said to have scoffed at the lack of power in the Met lineup. The Cubs had, after all, won five of the first eight games between the teams, and they still viewed the Cardinals, rather than the upstart Mets, as the chief threat to their chance for a title.

The Cards had dominated the Cubs for decades, and the resentment cut deep, for the two teams felt that they were competing for the rooting heart of middle America. Chicagoans tended to look upon St. Louis as a small town with pretensions to the status of a metropolis. Those in St. Louis were similarly contemptuous of Chicago. They viewed it as possessing all the size and arrogance of a big city but none of the sophistication and class. But even as the Cubs were looking over their shoulders in the direction of St. Louis, the Cards seemed to be slipping out of contention. They were in fifth place now, fourteen and a half games behind the Cubs when the Mets finished with them. All the Cubs had to do to secure their place at the top was to polish off the New Yorkers.

The three-game series at Shea would be followed by another three games in Chicago a week later, and Gil Hodges did not underestimate the importance of the confrontation. "We need to take two out of three each time," he said. "If we don't win against the Cubs, they'll open up a lead in double figures." It was clear now that the Met manager was taking dead aim on first place. "Who thought the Red Sox could win in '67?" he asked. "We're a little like them—young."

Of course Hodges had planned ahead. He had structured his pitching rotation so that Koosman, Seaver, and Gentry, in that order, would be ready. Durocher, apparently, had prepared his staff in like manner, for he had Ferguson Jenkins, Ken Holtzman, and Bill Hands ready to go against the Mets. Jenkins, who had won twenty games in each of the two previous seasons, was on his way to another such year, with an 11−5 record. Koosman, though only 5−5 at that point, had been nearly unhittable when he was in his rhythm.

Both pitchers were at their meticulous best at the start of the game, but Jenkins blinked first. He yielded a home run to Ed Kranepool in the fifth inning for the first run of the game and the Mets' first hit. But Ernie Banks got it back in the sixth with a drive over the left-field fence, and the Cubs kept the pressure on Koosman. They went ahead in the seventh when Jenkins walked, advanced to second on a sacrifice, and scored on Glenn Beckert's single to left. In the eighth, they made it 3−1 when Jim Hickman, an original Met, homered with two out.

The Mets, meanwhile, went to the ninth with Kranepool's home run still the only hit off Jenkins. Ken Boswell, who was replaced at second base that day by Bobby Pfeil, pinch hit for Koosman to open the inning and lifted a soft fly to short center. Don Young, the Cubs' rookie center fielder, had trouble locating the ball, then charged hard, but it was too late. The ball fell for a double, and the crowd of more than fifty-five thousand roused to the possibilities. Agee fouled out to Banks, but Clendenon, batting for Pfeil, raised the fever of the crowd still higher. He drove a Jenkins pitch to deep left-center that sent Young racing to the fence. This time the youngster got a quick start. He made a backhand catch of the ball just as he hit the wall with his right shoulder, and the impact jarred the ball loose. Boswell, who was forced to await the outcome, got no further than third, while Clendenon slid into second with what could be the tying run.

That brought Cleon Jones to the plate and Durocher to the mound. The Cub manager was wary of Jones, who was leading the league in hitting, but he did not wish to put the winning run on base. "Battle him," he told Jenkins. Jones won. He slashed a drive down the left-field line for the third double of the inning, and now the game was tied. Shamsky was walked intentionally to set up a double play that would end the inning, and Garrett almost obliged. He hit a slow grounder to second base—too softly for a play to be made anywhere but at first. So the runners moved up a base each, and it came to a showdown between Jenkins and Kranepool. With first base open, Jenkins pitched carefully to the Mets' first baseman. He nipped at the corners for a 1-and-2 count, then he teased him with a slow curveball, low and just off the outside of the plate. Kranepool was ready for it. In a sense, he had been getting himself ready for that pitch for the last seven years, since he had joined the Mets as a teenager in 1962; now he reached out and nudged the ball over shortstop, a soft wisp of a hit, neither a pop-up nor a line drive, that landed lightly in left-center field while Jones was being mobbed at home by his teammates.

"In a way, that might have been the turning point of the season," Kranepool says now. "From then on, we kept applying the pressure and the Cubs knew they were in a pennant race. Every time we played a big series, we won it. We beat the Cubs head to head in every series after that. We got some breaks—but look, a winning team makes its breaks.

"We had a good ballclub. We had outstanding pitching, and we had young kids coming up who were used to winning. That was a big thing. It doesn't matter at what level you're playing—high school, college, or the minors—if you're used to winning, you expect to win wherever you are. Those kids began to change the attitude on the club. Then, in June, Clendenon came over in a trade, and that helped us. He and

I platooned at first base, and between the two of us we hit over twenty homers and drove in a hundred runs."

Kranepool conjures his memories of that season in a matter-of-fact, almost businesslike manner, as if taking stock of the inventory in the plant he owns and operates in the Jamaica section of Queens, New York. A manufacturer of marketing displays for stores and exhibit booths, Kranepool is attentive to his day's work even as the interview proceeds. It is a Tuesday morning and the plant is in full swing as we chat in his paneled office under the steady gaze of an elk's head, a trophy from a hunting trip he made with Jerry Koosman. The door to his office swings open periodically; the plant foreman offers a bit of information or asks a question, and Kranepool responds while still leafing through the papers and cards that cover his desk. He makes an occasional note, shifts it from one stack to another, and continues to answer the questions put to him even as the interviewer suspects he has lost his attention. Only now and then does a particular reply seem to warrant the interruption of his paperwork. He is a cordial and hospitable subject, but he gives the impression that business comes first and that he is clearly capable of attending to disparate chores without losing concentration. But then Kranepool always had more than one side to him, even when he was playing with the Mets.

As early as 1963, when he was a nineteen-year-old, second-year player, he worked as a stockbroker and was more than mildly successful at it. He had his own desk at the Wall Street firm of Brand, Grumet & Siegel, and the Lincoln Continental he drove was not purchased solely with the money he earned playing baseball.

"I had always worked in the wintertime," Kranepool says. "Most of the players did. In those years, we didn't have the luxury of long-term contracts, and no one was making $2 million a year. If you took the winter off, you suffered for it financially."

Kranepool became acquainted with the financial exigencies of life at an early age. His father had been killed in the Battle of the Bulge before Ed was born, and he was raised by his mother in modest circumstances. He grew up in the Castle Hill section of the Bronx, where he was a regular at the neighborhood playground.

"My whole life was sports then," he recalls. "The playground was right next to my house, and we played whatever sport was in season. We spent all our spare time playing ball. That's how it was then. You'd go to the playground right after school and spend all day there on weekends. At lunchtime you'd run home for a sandwich and then go right back to the playground."

But it was his exploits at James Monroe High School, not far from his home, that attracted the notice of big-time scouts. At six feet three and 205 pounds, Kranepool was a good enough basketball player to be offered scholarships at several universities. Baseball, however, was his sport. Steve Ray, the athletic director at Monroe, was touting the youngster as a big-league prospect right from the start, and with good cause. Ed had a level swing that rippled with power, and by the time he was seventeen years old he had eclipsed all of the school's home-run records—which until then were owned by another muscular first baseman, Hank Greenberg, a Hall of Famer, who once hit fifty-eight home runs in a season.

A number of teams expressed interest in Kranepool, but the Mets were the most eager. They already were off to a horrendous start in their inaugural season, and it certainly could not hurt to have a local kid with home-run power on the roster, especially one who had not yet turned eighteen. They wasted no time in making an offer. The day after graduation, Johnny Murphy, the general manager, and Bubba Jonnard, a scout, appeared at the Kranepool home, and when they left they had a signed one-year contract for $85,000.

Kranepool, however, was not quite ready for the big leagues, not even with the Mets. In late June, shortly after signing, he accompanied the team on a western trip, strictly as an observer, then was farmed out to Syracuse. After fourteen games, he was shipped down a notch to Knoxville, and after only seven games there, to Auburn in Class D. At Auburn he batted .351, with eighteen RBIs in twenty games. When the Mets recalled him at the end of the season, he appeared in three games, getting one hit (a double) in six times at bat. He made the team a year later, and by 1964 he was a fixture at first base. He was still only nineteen years old, the same age at which Mickey Mantle broke in with the Yankees, but the experience was not quite so glamorous for Kranepool.

"It wasn't that easy making the adjustment," he recalls now. "I was still just a teenager, and I was in awe of some of the older players. I had been a Yankee fan until the day I signed with the Mets, and Casey Stengel was an idol of mine. Now I was just out of high school, and he was my manager. At that age, you might look the part of a big-league player physically, but mentally you're not prepared to cope with certain situations. The toughest part was that it was hard for me to relate to the other players on the team because of the age difference. My first roommate was Frank Thomas, and he was a man thirty-five years old. He did everything he could to help me, but he was old enough to be my father and we had different interests. The following year, Larry Bearnarth joined the ballclub out of St. John's, and he was three years older than I was, but he was the first guy I could relate to and we palled-out together. Then, guys like Swoboda and McGraw started coming up, who were more my own age, and it got to be fun."

What never got to be fun for Kranepool, however, was the losing, and the Mets did little else during the first five years he spent with the club.

"It was frustrating," he says. "As a ballplayer, all you

have is your professionalism, and you set goals for yourself, and by the time of the All-Star break, all your goals are destroyed. Anyone who's ever played for a losing team will tell you that as you continue to lose the season gets longer. It's not a good place to be. Young players shouldn't spend too much time on losing teams, because winning is contagious and so is losing, and after a while you form a negative attitude, and playing baseball stops being fun.

"It got to the point where I would have welcomed a change. Did I ever want to be traded? Yeah, I wanted to win. Growing up as a high-school player, I was always involved with championship teams and with winning. So during those first years it was frustrating. Whatever you did, it wasn't enough. All you ever kept reading about was the circus atmosphere, the clown atmosphere, and after a while you just can't read the papers anymore because no matter who they're writing about, it's not just one guy, you're a part of that act, and you get tired of being written about as a joke all the time. On a winning team, when someone makes a bad play, someone else compensates for it. On a losing club everything is magnified. You make an error and the next batter hits a home run and your error stands out."

During those losing seasons, it helped somewhat to be playing for Casey Stengel.

"Casey took a lot of pressure off the players," says Kranepool. "When the writers were around and the cameras were on him, he put on an act for them. He would joke a lot and double-talk, and he would talk baseball with them into the wee hours of the morning. He was entertaining them, giving them something to write about to divert their attention and camouflage the result of the game. But in the clubhouse he was right to the point. He was very witty, very sharp—exceedingly sharp for a man seventy-five years of age—and you knew exactly what he was saying if you were willing to think about it.

"For instance, one year at the All-Star break he told us that with our record we ought to be working out those three days instead of going home. 'But,' he said, 'take the three days off and go home . . . but take your records with you.' Now, if you analyze it, he was saying we were horseshit, and we should take our records with us and reflect on what we did wrong in the first half of the season, because working out wouldn't make any difference anyway. That's the way Casey was. He had a dual personality—one for the public and another for the team.

"Gil, on the other hand, was altogether different. He was set in his views of how the game should be played, and you did things his way. He was very straightforward and a strong disciplinarian. From spring training on, he molded the ballclub the way he wanted it. He never played favorites. He had one set of rules, and either you lived by it or you died by it. Everyone knew his position on that team. 'These are the guidelines,' Gil would say, 'this is the way you win.' And the guys stuck to it. Of course winning helped. You could see it coming together that first year, 1968. A lot of young players were coming up, and for the first time since I was there, I thought we had some potential. Then, as the 1969 season wore on, you could see the players had the ability and were beginning to believe in themselves. After all those years, playing on a winning team was like a dream come true.

"But being a part of that team was special in a lot of ways. People will never forget the '69 Mets. We caught New York by surprise, we caught the world by surprise. No matter where you go, people still want to talk about '69. Nothing ever replaced it. We won the pennant in '73, but people don't even mention it. They just want to talk about the '69 Mets.

"Just before the start of spring training in 1986, a hospital foundation in Phoenix got us all together out there to play an old timers' game against the '69 Cubs. Ron Swoboda helped to coordinate it for the benefit of the hospital, and we played the Cubs and beat them again. One of the situations we recreated was the hit I got that beat Ferguson Jenkins in the ninth inning of that game in July. We walked out to left field and marked the spot where the ball fell. That was a turning point not only for us but for the Cubs too. After that game, the Cubs seemed to slip a little, they began to feel the pressure."

Indeed, the Cubs gave every evidence of feeling the pressure after that game, and by all accounts they did not react to it with the composure of a championship team. Don Young, the rookie center fielder who had lost two fly balls that he might have caught, was berated by both the manager and the captain of the ballclub in front of a group of reporters in the Cub lockerroom after the game.

"Two little fly balls," Durocher is reported to have said. "He just stands there watching one and he gives up on the other. It's a disgrace."

"The only reason he's in the lineup is for his glove," Santo is said to have shouted loud enough for all parties to hear. "It's ridiculous," he added. "There's no way the Mets can beat us."

To his credit, Santo apologized to Young the next day and then apologized in public through the press. "It wasn't like me at all," he said.

But it was perhaps the first sign that cracks had begun to appear in the foundation. The Cubs might have reacted differently had it been a team like the Cardinals who had beaten them. The Cardinals, after all, were champions; they were supposed to beat teams like the Cubs with late-inning heroics. But the Mets were another matter entirely. They represented a threat to the very core of a rival's image of itself, for if you lost to a team that you felt could not beat you, you might be obliged to contemplate the character of your competitive instinct. It was not your ability that would be called into question so much as the quality of your nerves.

Santo had expressed it himself: "There's no way the Mets can beat us," he said, which means: "We're a better team than the Mets; even if they beat us we're better than they are." Thus the question of supremacy has already been decided, and the result becomes a matter of incidental concern. It is a sentiment often expressed by a contestant who is fearful of losing and who needs the assurance that the outcome is less than vital. It prepares one for the possibility of defeat, and if the Cubs were getting themselves ready to lose, it was not for nothing, for the Mets would beat them again the next day.

CHAPTER

9

IT IS A COMMONPLACE OF SPORTS that games are won with defense. Football teams that have yielded the fewest points invariably are those that contend for the championship. Even in basketball, a game preeminently devoted to offense, it is the teams most adept at containing the opposition that finish at the top. But the ultimate sport of defense is baseball. It is the only game, after all, in which the team playing defense is given control of the ball.

Through the decades, it has been estimated that pitching represents at least 75 percent of a team's chances of winning. The batter becomes almost an incidental figure, as one succeeds another, in orderly procession, to take his turn against the same pitcher. The best hitters in a team's lineup are likely to be successful in no more than three out of every ten turns at bat. By contrast, a good quarterback is expected to complete more than 50 percent of his passes, a basketball player to score on at least half of his shots.

Though defense is usually the decisive factor in other sports, it is the offense that creates the plays most appealing to the eye. The highlight films are mainly devoted to the long run or pass play, or the fast break that ends in a spectacular shot. But the esthetics of baseball are fashioned around the concept of prevention. What image of a run-scoring hit could live in memory with the clarity of Willie Mays's catch in the 1954 World Series? The pictures of baseball that remain engraved in memory are most often those of defense: Brooks Robinson diving to his right, spearing a ball backhanded, then throwing to first while still on his knees; Billy Martin charging in from second base to make a shoestring catch with the bases loaded; and those wondrous outfield plays that would turn the 1969 World Series in the Mets' favor.

Yes, baseball is a game whose geometry and rhythm were designed to favor the defensive team. The very soul of the sport is not action but anticipation, the possibility of an event that has not yet taken place but might at any moment. It is not surprising then that the most thrilling spectacle in baseball is a game in which nothing at all happens on offense— no runs, no hits, no walks, not a single baserunner. Such an occurrence is called a perfect game. It is an event that is somehow typical of baseball, for it develops gradually, at a leisurely pace, and its possibility is often unnoticed until the game is more than half over. Then, once one is aware of it, the tension winds pitch by pitch, inning by inning, like a vise tightening down on the nerves. It takes a full nine innings to materialize, but it can end abruptly, on any one of more than a hundred pitches. For sustained drama, there is no event in any sport that is quite its equal.

From the turn of the century until the dawning of the 1969 season, through more than eighty-five thousand baseball games, only eight perfect games had been pitched. There had never been one in the National League until 1964, and that one took place at Shea Stadium on Father's Day when the Phillies' Jim Bunning retired twenty-seven Mets in a row. A year later, Sandy Koufax, who had pitched no-hitters in each of the three previous seasons, was perfect in his fourth one against the Cubs. Now, on the night of Wednesday, July 9, Tom Seaver was looking to add his own name to the list.

Seaver looked strong right from the start. He struck out two of the first three batters in the first inning and all three in the second. For added impetus, he went to the mound to start the third inning already holding a three-run lead. The Mets had gotten to Ken Holtzman early. Agee drove the Cub left-hander's first pitch into the right-field corner for a triple, and Bobby Pfeil followed with a double to left. In the second, successive errors by Santo at third and Kessinger at short led to two more runs when Seaver singled and Agee lined a double to right.

So now it was Seaver, with three runs in the bank, winding it down tighter and tighter. His command of the game was complete. The three key elements in pitching, Seaver would explain some years later, were velocity, movement, and location, and he had them all that night. His fastball was as trigger-quick as he could have it, and it was rising suddenly as it approached the batter. His breaking pitches, darting sharply, were shaving slivers off the edges of the plate. He was working as if the man with the bat cocked was no more than a prop on a stage set, a statuary adornment whose only function was to lend symmetry to the scene. If the pitches were perfect, it would matter little who tried to hit them. Seaver pitched that way inning after inning, as if each were a discrete composition of its own, with a beginning, a middle, and an end: prelude, refrain, coda.

By the fifth inning, the spectators had begun to stir to the possibilities. It was a large crowd, more than fifty-nine thousand, for the third time that season a new Met record, and if you listened attentively, you could follow the progress of the game without even watching. On an occasion such as this one, it is not so much the crowd noise as its absence that signals the event—the length and depth of the hush as the next batter approaches the plate, like that moment of high drama in a theater when no one surrenders to the need to clear his throat. It built that way through the middle innings of the game, the periods of silence growing deeper and the quick, almost polite rush of applause when the batter was retired just a bit louder each time but of no longer duration; then the tension would take its grip again, tighter this time, each time tighter, and the silence deeper and more expectant.

The applause was no more than courteous when Cleon Jones hit a home run in the bottom of the seventh to make the score 4 to 0. When a no-hitter is in progress and the outcome of the game looks secure, the leading team's turn at bat seems superfluous. One would be willing, even eager, to forgo it and get on with the business at hand. Just let the Cubs keep coming to bat, let Seaver keep the clock ticking to his own rhythm.

When he came out to start the eighth, it appeared that everyone in the ballpark was standing, reacting to every pitch. It is the normal cycle of response as a no-hitter nears completion for the pauses to grow shorter and the cries of encouragement more frenzied, and so it was when Seaver recorded his tenth and eleventh strikeouts and walked to the dugout with twenty-four consecutive outs notched in his belt.

Randy Hundley, looking to break the spell, opened the ninth inning with a bunt, but the ball rolled in the direction of the mound and Seaver was quick to field it, and he threw out the runner easily. The next batter was Jimmy Qualls, a twenty-two-year-old rookie who was playing in only his eighteenth major league game and coming to bat for the forty-eighth time. He was a center fielder and was playing in place of Don Young (who had had his troubles the previous day) because he batted left-handed and Seaver was right-handed. When he came to bat, Qualls had a batting average of .243, but he had hit the ball hard off Seaver in the third and sixth innings, pulling the ball each time. Now, Seaver tried to keep the ball on the outside of the plate, but Qualls reached out and drove it sharply to left-center, where it fell in almost the identical spot that Kranepool had dropped his game-winning hit the day before. The crowd, which included Seaver's father, booed Qualls briefly and then rewarded Seaver with a lasting wave of appreciation. Grote came out to the mound to congratulate his pitcher and give him time to allow the excitement, and the disappointment, to settle. Seaver got the next two outs quickly, completing what through the years would be known as his "imperfect" game.

"That was the best game I ever pitched," Seaver says now. "It was better than my [1978] no-hitter with Cincinnati. I had great stuff that night, superb control, and a mastery of all my pitches. It was obvious even before the game. I felt it when I was warming up in the bullpen. Sometimes you get that feeling, but it doesn't work out that way during the game. Other times, you feel that you don't have much when you're warming up, and you turn out to be very good. You can't always trust what you have in the bullpen. But that night I really felt that I had it. Rube Walker [the Mets' pitching coach] saw it too. He told Hodges at the start of the game that I might throw a no-hitter that night."

It perhaps seemed ironic that in a lineup packed with hitters of consistency and power, it was Jimmy Qualls, who got only twenty-nine other hits that season and only one more after 1969, who would thwart Seaver's bid for perfection. But it does not seem so unlikely to Seaver.

"I had never faced Qualls before," he says. "That was the first time he played against us, so I wasn't sure just how to pitch to him. I knew he had hit me hard his first two times up. He drove one deep to right and then he hit a hard shot to first base. So I pitched him outside, it was a fastball, and he reached out and got it. But that was still the best game of my career. It was not only the best pitched, it was also the circumstances in which it was played. It came right in the middle of the pennant race, and it helped turn things around against the team we were chasing."

When Seaver cites his "imperfect" game as the best he ever pitched, it is a selection made from among more than three hundred victories that include a no-hitter, a handful of one-hitters, and a game in which he struck out nineteen batters including the first ten in a row. It is a career that numbers three Cy Young Awards and that is certain to land him in the Hall of Fame precisely five years after his retirement.

But most of that is behind him now. As we speak, he is wearing the uniform of the Chicago White Sox and contemplating the end of his days as a player. It is not the happiest of times for Seaver. He is in his third season with the White Sox and is eager for a trade that would bring him closer to his home in Greenwich, Connecticut.

"I'm tired of traveling," he says. "Playing in Chicago, I'm always on the road. I've only seen my family four days since the season started, and it's too much for me. I've been away too much already. I don't know how many more years I'll pitch, but if I'm not traded to New York or Boston, '86 will be my last season."

It is a Tuesday afternoon in late June, and we are sitting in the White Sox dugout in Comiskey Park about four hours before a game with the Minnesota Twins. There is an early-summer chill in the air, and Seaver is wearing a blue warmup jacket over his home uniform. His cheek is puffed with a wad of Red Man chewing tobacco. Periodically, he turns his head and squirts a sepia-colored stream onto the rickety wooden floorboards of the dugout. Even to an observer who has never met him before, it is clear that he is somewhat distracted. It had been a difficult spring.

His mother had died early in the season, and during her illness Tom had flown to her home in California and returned to the team in time to make his next start. Then, for weeks, there had been reports of attempts to trade him to either the Yankees or the Red Sox, but the June 15 trading deadline passed without a deal having been made. But even as we speak, his days with the White Sox are numbered. Four days later, he would be sold to the Boston Red Sox, a team that was on its way to the American League pennant. The Red Sox would mark Seaver's fourth change of big-league uniform, counting his second brief tenure with the Mets. But a change of teams was something that Seaver had grown accustomed to even before he played a professional game. He had, in a sense, already been affiliated with two franchises by the time the Mets signed him to his first official contract.

Seaver was in his junior year at the University of Southern California when he was chosen by the Los Angeles Dodgers in the first amateur draft. The Dodgers backed off when they heard his asking price, and the Atlanta Braves drafted him the following year. He came to terms with the Braves quickly and signed a contact to take effect at the end of his senior year, in June. The college baseball season had already started, however, and major league rules stipulated that a player cannot be signed to a contract once the collegiate season is underway. At the same time, the National Collegiate Athletic Association declared Seaver ineligible and lifted his athletic scholarship on the grounds that he had forfeited his amateur standing by signing a professional contract. So the twenty-one-year-old Seaver found himself caught in the crosscurrents of two seas of bureaucracy; he was neither amateur nor pro.

Seeking to clarify his position, he called the office of the commissioner of baseball, General William Eckert, and was referred to Eckert's assistant, Lee MacPhail. MacPhail ruled that Seaver's contract with Atlanta was void and that he would be permitted to sign with any club except the Braves that was willing to meet the original bonus price of $50,000. Three teams—Cleveland, Philadelphia, and the Mets—expressed interest, and a lottery was scheduled for April 1. The commissioner called Seaver's home; with Tom on one phone and his father listening on the extension, MacPhail narrated the drawing.

"It was like the Academy Awards ceremony," Seaver says. "Lee MacPhail described how the commissioner was reaching into the hat; then he said, 'The team is . . . the New York Mets.' And that was fine with me. The team I didn't want to go to was Cleveland, because they had a pretty stable pitching staff with guys like Sam McDowell and Sonny Siebert. It would have been hard breaking into that rotation. I figured my best opportunity would be with the Mets. It was a young franchise, and I thought I might not have to wait too long to make it with them."

He didn't. Seaver spent the 1966 season with Jacksonville, the Mets' triple-A affiliate, and he made the Met staff the following spring. His quality was immediately apparent. He won sixteen games and was named National League Rookie of the Year with a team that finished last, forty games under .500 and forty and a half games out of first place. The Mets had their first player who was truly of star magnitude, and he joined the growing nucleus of youngsters who did not appreciate the charms of losing.

"There was never really a losers' perspective that I could see," Seaver says. "It might have been that way in the fans' eyes, and the media built the Mets up as the lovable clowns, but the players didn't buy that. I never saw it. I spent most of my first year getting my feet on the ground, but we had the beginnings of what was going to be a good, well-rounded team. Then, in '68, Koosman came up and won nineteen games, and the big thing that happened that year was that Gil Hodges came over and brought a different attitude towards the game. Gil was very serious and professional in his approach, and he demanded that from his players, young and old alike. The following spring, in '69, we knew that we had a good ballclub. We had good pitching and an outstanding defensive catcher, shortstop, and center fielder. So we were strong up the middle and had some other good young players, but mostly the difference was Hodges.

"He was a pillar of strength. He was big and strong physically, but he was also mentally tough. He never rattled; he was always in control, and he was always there for you. Every player felt that he had his complete support. You felt that *he* always knew what he was going to do and *you* knew what he was going to do, and that nothing would deter him. Hodges was a great man and an outstanding manager. The only thing he lacked was overt compassion. As time went by, you discovered that he was compassionate, but it was not something he expressed openly. He didn't show his emotions. But there is no doubt that Gil was the leader of the club, not any of the players. He was a father image, someone the players could always count on.

"Our winning the pennant and the Series was not as complicated as people sometimes make it out to be. We were the best team in baseball that year, and that's why we won. If people took it to be a symbolic victory for the underdog, all well and good, but it was the fans and the press that related to it that way, not the players. We just happened to win during a particularly difficult period in this country, and people took from it whatever they could. The Vietnam War was at its peak then. It was a political war that went on too long and was terribly divisive to the country, and if the Mets helped to salve those wounds, good; but we certainly weren't conscious of it."

Now the interview proceeds with the sounds of batting practice in the background. Some early arrivals drift through the dugout and out onto the field. Harold Baines steps into the batting cage, and the late afternoon air trills with the ring of bat against ball. Seaver is a studied subject. He responds to each question thoughtfully, without enthusiasm but apparently with total candor. If he does not choose to address a subject, he says so without camouflaging his response.

"How did you feel when the Mets traded you to Cincinnati?"

"Actually, I welcomed it. I didn't like the guy I was working for."

"I assume you mean M. Donald Grant. What were your differences with him?"

"I'd rather not get into that."

If the question is not one that he can answer with conviction, he lets it pass.

"In the spring of 1969, was there a feeling among the players that they might contend that season?"

"I really don't remember," he says.

A New York newspaper recently had carried a headline announcing that Seaver planned to run for the U.S. Senate.

"That's nonsense," he says. "I have no political ambitions. I don't know what my plans for the future are. When I retire, I'm going to take one year off and do nothing except the things I like to do. I want to be with my family, take them to Paris for a vacation; play some tennis; and just spend the first year relaxing and catching up and deciding what I want to do with the rest of my life."

The field is studded with players now, each performing those rituals that prepare him for the playing of a game, each moving to his own practiced pace. Seaver is relaxed and patient. His hands are thrust in the pockets of his warmup jacket. From time to time, he removes them to replenish his chew of tobacco. He turns to his left and sprays the dugout floor, then turns back to await the next question. I am aware of his personal difficulties during the early part of the season and impressed that despite them he remains gracious and accommodating. I know, too, that his mood cannot be helped by the fact that neither he nor the White Sox have gotten off to a very good start in 1986.

Now forty-one years old and in his twenty-second year

as a professional pitcher, he can no longer trust the turning of a game to his fastball. Some of the speed and pop have been lost to the years, and he must rely more on finesse and the encyclopedic knowledge of pitching and hitting that he has acquired since he began playing the game. In a curious sense, he was counting now on a manner of pitching he had developed as a teenager.

"I was not very big as a youngster," he says. "I was not the kind of pitcher who could go out and throw the ball by people. So I began to learn the mechanics and techniques of pitching. I learned that location and change of speed are as important as velocity, and that you have to use your pitches to set up a batter. You have to set up the batter for a particular pitch, not only in each at-bat but early in the game for late in the game, and even early in the season for late in the season. You don't just see these guys one time around. You know you're going to come up against them again and again. What you show them one time dictates what you might get them out with later in the year."

Seaver, therefore, was not entirely shocked that it was a hitter like Jimmy Qualls, whom he had never seen before, who cost him his perfect game. The following day, Qualls again was trouble for the Mets, sparking a rally that salvaged the final game of the series for the Cubs. With the Mets leading 2 – 1 in the fifth and threatening to sweep the three games, Qualls lined a double to right field. Bill Hands tried to bunt him over to third; when the throw got to the base ahead of the runner, Qualls kicked it out of Weis's glove, and the Cubs were on their way back. Kessinger singled in the tying run, Gentry bobbled Beckert's bunt to load the bases, and Billy Williams put the Cubs ahead with a sacrifice fly. Another run scored on a throwing error by Grote, the Mets' third error of the inning, and Santo put the game away with a two-run homer.

After the game, a reporter asked Durocher, "Were those the real Cubs today?"

"No," Durocher replied, "those were the real Mets today."

Whichever the case, the Cub series marked the halfway point of the season for both teams. The Mets had won forty-seven of their first eighty-two games, four fewer than the Cubs. The two teams were preparing to meet again, in Chicago, four days later. It was Friday, July 11, and no one doubted that the Mets were in a real pennant race now. The local papers were beginning to carry the results of Chicago's games in separate stories, under their own headlines, rather than as part of out-of-town roundups. Those reports announced that the Cubs went on to spend a fruitful weekend in Philadelphia, winning three out of four against the Phillies. The Mets, meanwhile, lost the opener of their series at Shea to the Expos and then, after a rainout, scored comeback victories in both games of a Sunday doubleheader.

Kranepool carried them in the first game, tying the score with a sacrifice fly in the sixth inning, then winning it in the eighth with a run-scoring double after twice failing to lay down a bunt. In the second game, the Mets had to come from behind twice before salvaging the game with the help of one of the ironic twists of circumstance that had begun to mark their season.

Cleon Jones had been ejected from the game in the third inning after protesting too strenuously when he was called out at second base on an attempt to steal. At the end of the inning, Ron Swoboda, who was hitting .224, was booed roundly as he went out to left field to replace Jones, who was hitting .350. But Swoboda's recent troubles at the plate were forgotten when he pumped a single into right field for the winning run in the seventh.

On Sunday evening, when they left for Chicago, the Mets had won nine of their last eleven games. More than two months had passed since their last visit to Wrigley Field. At that time, their quest had been for respectability. Now they had the opportunity to make a further statement. Hodges had said that they needed to win at least two games at home and two in Chicago. If they did, the Cubs might find themselves watching the scoreboard for the rest of the summer.

CHAPTER

10

THE LAST TIME TOM SEAVER
pitched against the Cubs, five days earlier, he had retired the
first twenty-five batters he faced. Memories of that game were
no doubt roused in the Chicago dugout as Seaver proceeded
to set down ten in a row before being touched for a hit in
the fourth inning. Two innings later, the Cubs finally broke
through for a run when Kessinger bunted his way on, moved
to second on a groundout, and scored on a single by Billy
Williams. In the meantime, Bill Hands held the Mets in check.
He choked off a threat in the seventh and escaped again in
the eighth. In the ninth, with the tying run on base and two
out, Durocher called for Phil Regan when the count went to
2 and 0 on Donn Clendenon. Regan, who was nicknamed the
Vulture, was making his forty-first appearance in the Cubs'
ninety-first game. He worked the count full before Clendenon hit a broken-bat liner to short right field that Beckert
gloved with one hand, over his shoulder, to end the game.

Now the Mets had to win the next two games to avoid
losing ground in the standings, and they got help from a
most improbable source. Al Weis, the utility infielder who
had come from the White Sox in the Tommie Agee trade,
had been starting at shortstop while Harrelson served a two-

week tour with the Army Reserves. Harrelson returned to the Mets over the weekend, but Hodges had chosen to stay with Weis until his regular shortstop worked his way into playing shape. And it was Weis who led the Met offensive. In the third inning, he singled and scored the first run of the game on an Agee triple. But it was in the fourth, after the Cubs had tied the score, that he really flexed his muscles. With Shamsky and Kranepool on base, Weis drove a Dick Selma pitch over the ivy-colored wall, beyond the bleachers and the screen that topped them and onto Waveland Avenue, where the ball bounced once and landed on the porch of a house across the street. It was Weis's first home run of the season, his fifth in eight years in the majors.

An inning later, Boswell hit his third homer of the season for what turned out to be the game's deciding run. When the Cubs rallied against Gary Gentry in the eighth, with Santo and Williams hitting home runs, Ron Taylor emerged from the bullpen to get the last four outs and preserve the Mets' 5 – 4 victory.

Wednesday's game, though not a tidy affair, was over early. The Mets pounced on Ferguson Jenkins at the opening bell. Agee hit his first pitch for a double, Boswell and Jones singled, Garrett walked, Kranepool and Martin singled, and the Mets had four runs before the Cubs came to bat. They padded their lead in the second with two more runs including a home run by Agee. The Cubs responded with four runs of their own in the bottom of the second and another in the third to draw within one run of the Mets, but that was as close as they got. Cal Koonce established order with five shutout innings in relief of Cardwell and Mc-Andrew, while the Mets continued their assault on Cub pitching. Weis equalled his season high for home runs when he hit another one in the fifth, and Shamsky delivered one with a man on in the eighth to bring the final score to 9 – 5.

When the Mets had finished their work in Chicago, they

were three and a half games behind the Cubs but only one back in the "loss" column. Their record stood at 51–37 to the Cubs' 57–36. In the seven weeks since they had embarked upon their eleven-game winning streak, they had won thirty-four of forty-eight games, a winning percentage of better than .700. Perhaps more importantly, they had proved they could beat the Cubs. They had won six of the last eight meetings between the teams, four out of five at Wrigley Field. Now, as they left Chicago and headed for Montreal, there were some among them who dared to dream of a championship. One of those was Ken Boswell, the young second baseman whose home run had provided the margin of victory in the second game.

"I think that series in Chicago was the turning point of the season for us," Boswell says in his Texas drawl. "We beat 'em pretty good, and we came out of there thinking that maybe we could win it. We were young and confident and we started to feel the momentum building up. It was really a great bunch of guys on that team. We all pulled for each other, and everyone played his part, and Hodges kept everyone alert and in the game. He had such a high level of concentration; he was thinking about the game all the time, and he tried to get the players to think that way.

"It didn't always work, though. I remember one night in L.A., one of our guys flied out to end the game, and Hodges tells 'Peepee' Gaspar to go out to left field. Well, Peepee (I don't know where he got that name, but that's what everyone called him), old Peepee grabs his glove and starts out to the outfield. He didn't realize the game was over. Gil let him hear about that, but he never held a grudge. If you did something wrong, he told you about it and that was the end of it.

"He got the most out of everyone on the team. He was a master at juggling the lineup. He used all twenty-five players, and that kept everyone fresh and well rested. When it came to a game situation, a guy came off the bench and he was ready to play. He knew what a curveball looked like, what a slider looked like. He hadn't just been sitting on the bench all season. Everyone knew that he might be called on at any time. Gil changed the whole attitude on the club. He was a real disciplinarian, too.

"One of his rules was that we had to wear a coat and a tie when we were on the road. I remember one night in Houston, me and Sham were sittin' in our room around one, two o'clock in the morning, and Sham says, 'Man, I'm hungry.' I was hungry too, and room service was closed, so Sham says, 'I'll go down and get us some cheeseburgers from the White Tower across the street.' So Sham goes down and he walks right into Hodges in the lobby. What does Gil do? He fines Sham a hundred dollars for being out after curfew and another fifty for not having a coat and tie on."

Boswell enjoys the story even as he tells it. He is clearly a fun-loving type who seems to cherish the humor and good feelings of that season as much as the drama of winning. We had met on a steamy Texas evening in the bar of Austin's largest hotel. I had driven up from San Antonio, where I met with Jerry Grote earlier in the day, and on the way there I realized that we had not discussed how we would recognize one another. My only recollection of him was from photos of his playing days, more than ten years earlier.

So I got to the bar early, took a place as close to the front door as possible, and carefully scrutinized each new arrival. But when Boswell walked in, there could be no mistaking him. He looked as if he had come from a Texas roundup rather than from his job as sales manager of a local auto dealer, complete with pale red cowboy boots and a ten-gallon hat. He apparently picked me out with equal ease, perhaps because I was the only one in the bar dressed according to Gil Hodges's rules of the road.

"Hi, I'm Kenny," he says.

Over drinks and dinner in the hotel restaurant, we talk about people and places, about changing times and lifestyles. How, I wonder, did a twenty-one-year-old youngster, who even now would appear to be more at home on a ranch than in the concrete canyons of the Big City, adjust to life in New York?

"I had no problem there," Boswell says. "I got to like it right away. I lived right in midtown Manhattan—at the Shelton Towers on Lexington Avenue—and I loved walking the streets, riding the subway. It was great. Of course being an athlete opens a lot of doors, and I think New York has a specially warm place for people from Texas. I was well taken care of.

"The first time I'd been in New York was in 1966. I was playing for Williamsport in the Eastern League. We had a rainout followed by an off-day and three of us jumped on an airplane—Piedmont Airlines—I'll never forget that. We flew up to New York, and I just couldn't believe it. I had seen Houston and Dallas, but I just couldn't believe New York. I liked the bright lights and these were some of the brightest lights I'd ever seen."

Williamsport, a double-A team, was not Boswell's first stop as a professional ballplayer. He had spent the previous season at Auburn, New York, after being chosen by the Mets in the first amateur draft in June of 1965. Boswell was pleased to be going to the Mets, but he believes that he could have gotten a lot more money had he signed for a bonus before the draft rule was instituted.

"I had talked to seven or eight teams while I was in high school and playing American Legion ball," he says, "and I think I could have gotten twenty or thirty thousand dollars. Ray Culp, the pitcher, was the first big 'bonus baby' out of the Austin area, and he had gotten a hundred thousand. I probably could have signed with the Yankees right out of high school, but my folks wanted me to go to college. So I went to Sam Houston State on a baseball scholarship, but I realized right away that it was a mistake. I was tired of school, and I wasn't your best student in the world anyway. I wanted to play baseball. I always knew I wanted to be a baseball player. It was just a matter if I was gonna grow enough. I was awful small when I graduated from high school—five feet seven and 130 pounds—and I had to grow some to do that.

"So I knew I wanted to play ball, but now I had a problem. The rule was that once you started school, you couldn't sign a professional contract until your class graduated. The only exception was if you flunked out, and that's what I did. I pretty much stopped going to classes and I didn't take my finals, and I just flunked myself out intentionally.

"Red Murff, the Mets' scout, was the only one who did his homework on this thing; he told me he thought I was eligible to sign and that I should call Philip Piton, the president of the minor leagues, to make sure. So I called Piton, and he said I was eligible, and the Mets drafted me either number three or four, I don't remember. Anyway, I know I was taken ahead of Nolan Ryan. I signed for $8,000, which was a lot less than I would have gotten before the draft, but I guess it was more than my dad ever made. Actually, I was awfully lucky to be drafted by the Mets, because they needed ballplayers and I didn't have to wait very long before being called up."

Boswell began his professional career auspiciously. He broke in with Auburn by hitting safely in his first nineteen games and was named Rookie of the Year. After hitting over 300 for Williamsport the following season, he was invited to spring training with the Mets in 1967 along with two other youngsters—Tom Seaver and Bud Harrelson. But Boswell spent the spring and the first half of the regular season in the army, so it was not until the tail end of the season that he got to play in a major league game.

"I played my first game in Shea," he says, "but I remember ending up that first year in L.A. We had a lot of old heads on the ballclub who I guess were just looking to draw a paycheck and finish out the season. We were in an extra-inning game and I made an error. This big guy, Len Gabrielson—remember him? a left-hand hitter, a great big son-of-a-bitch—he hit a ball right through my legs. I mean it had error written all over it, and the winning run came in. Over in the clubhouse I was a big hero. It was the last game of the season, and a lot of the guys had plane reservations. They were going to Hawaii, Reno, Vegas, and they didn't want to play any more extra innings. They wanted to catch their planes and get out of there. That's how it was over there in '67.

"I didn't have too many at-bats that season, but I remember that same series I got my first home run off Don Drysdale. I was the only Met to hit a home run in Dodger Stadium that year. As a matter of fact I got three hits off Drysdale that night. Then, my next time up, he got me out on three spitters—three straight wet ones. After I hit that home run, someone got the ball back for me, and I asked Drysdale to sign it. He signed it, but he was pretty nasty about the whole thing. He was a tough one, Drysdale. There were a lot of tough ones around then.

"That guy in St. Louis, number forty-five, he was as tough as they come; I mean he was nasty. I'll tell you how bad Bob Gibson was. I used to hit him real well. (Now don't put that in your book or he'll come around after me.) I got three hits off him in St. Louis one night. Then, when the Cardinals came to New York, Gibson's pitching and I'm coming up to bat, and Tim McCarver, the catcher, says to me, 'Kenny, don't dig in, don't get too set in there.' I said, 'Oh, man. . . .' And he threw one and I mean, I think the ball went through me. I think it went right through me. I don't know how I ever got out of the way. I don't think I ever got another hit off Gibson. Yeah, there were a lot of tough ones around then.

"But I think I hit the good pitchers better than the guys

who were 2 and 11 or something. I didn't concentrate as much against them. I think I always hit better when it meant something. I'll bet I never got a hit with two out and nobody on. I just couldn't concentrate in those situations. I liked to hit when there were men on base and it meant something."

The record seemed to confirm Boswell's taste for the clutch situation. He would deliver a number of key hits as the season progressed, but perhaps none was more significant than the home run that helped the Mets capture their second straight series from the Cubs.

Right after the third game in Chicago, the Mets took off for a weekend series in Montreal. A day later, three U.S. astronauts took off on a three-day trip to the moon. The Mets had more trouble in Montreal. They managed to gain a split of their four games with the Expos, but it was not without difficulty and not without cost. Koosman won the first game with the help of home runs by Grote and Shamsky, but Jones was ejected for the second time in a week. Against the Expos at Shea, he had been fined $150 for remarks he made to umpire Frank Dezelan after being called out at second base. Now, five days later, he was tossed out again when he came up throwing punches at catcher Ron Brand after being called out at home.

The events of the following day were even more alarming. Seaver, who had won eight in a row and thirteen of his last fourteen decisions before losing to the Cubs earlier in the week, now lost for the second straight time. He gave up four runs and seven hits before he could get anyone out in the third inning, and he left the game complaining of a sore right shoulder.

The Mets' problems continued during the next day's doubleheader. They lost the opener 3–2 when Gentry was hit for home runs by Mack Jones, Bob Bailey, and Bobby Wine in the fourth inning. Some late-inning heroics salvaged the second game for the Mets, but not before they blew two leads and watched, stunned, as Tommie Agee knocked himself nearly senseless crashing into the centerfield fence. Agee lay on the ground, virtually motionless, for ten minutes before being helped to his feet and hobbling off the field with an assortment of bruises. His game effort, however, did not prevent the tying run from scoring in the bottom of the eighth, and the Mets had to rally twice more to win the game. They manufactured a run without benefit of a hit in the top of the ninth, but Coco Laboy tied it with a home run off Taylor. Finally, they won it in the tenth: Swoboda doubled with two out and dashed home as Bobby Pfeil's bunt was allowed to roll down the line until it nudged the third-base bag. Jack DiLauro pitched the tenth and was credited with his first win even though Taylor was technically the pitcher of record.

That Sunday, July 20, while the Mets were struggling north of the border, the Yankees were playing at home in the Bronx. At precisely 4:18 that afternoon, their game was temporarily halted and the crowd stood and cheered. The spontaneous swell of applause had nothing to do with what was taking place on the field. Two hundred forty thousand miles from both New York and Montreal, Apollo 11 had just touched down on the moon. More than six hours later, Neil Armstrong climbed out of the lunar module, descended a short ladder, and planted his foot firmly on the moon's surface. His gingerly walk and his brief, muffled message were transmitted back to Earth via satellite; hundreds of millions watched and marveled at the technological triumph that had transported men on a three-day space journey of nearly a quarter of a million miles.

The Mets, meanwhile, found themselves unable to negotiate the routine flight from Montreal to New York. They watched the moonwalk on a small television screen in a deserted passenger terminal in Montreal's airport. Their chartered 727 had been grounded because of a defect in its oil system. So while the rest of the nation celebrated the "giant leap for mankind," the New York Mets waited for more than five hours before they could begin the ninety-minute trip home.

Still, it was not an altogether unhappy band that prepared now for the three-day All-Star break. It was, after all, a second-place pennant-contender that finally arrived at Kennedy Airport at 2:45 A.M. They had come to the midsummer break four and a half games behind the Cubs and six and a half games ahead of the Cardinals. Seaver, Koosman, and Jones had been named to the National League team that was scheduled to play the American League All-Stars on July 22 in Washington, D.C. While it was true that they had lost their race with the astronauts—men had indeed walked on the moon before the Mets ever set foot in first place—it was not the race but the quest that teased the imagination. And the quest was just now beginning in earnest. Besides, the "moonmen" had set a tone for that summer of '69. From that point on, even the most distant possibility would be measured against the wonder of their odyssey.

"If men can walk on the moon. . . ."

1969 New York Mets team photo

Gil Hodges relaxes at his Brooklyn home the day after his team won the National League Eastern Division title at Shea Stadium, September 25, 1969.

New York Mayor John V. Lindsay is doused with champagne by Jerry Grote, left, and Rod Gaspar after the Mets clinched the National League pennant with a 7-4 win over the Atlanta Braves.

Tom Seaver winds up for a pitch in the opening inning of Game 1 of the 1969 World Series.

"Sign Man" Karl Erhardt holds up a "Met Power" sign after Ed Kranepool hits a home run in the eighth inning of the third game of the 1969 World Series.

Tommie Agee connects for a first inning home run off of Baltimore Orioles pitcher Jim Palmer in Game 3 of the 1969 World Series at Shea Stadium.

Centerfielder Tommie Agee chases Paul Blair's drive in the seventh inning of Game 3 of the 1969 World Series.

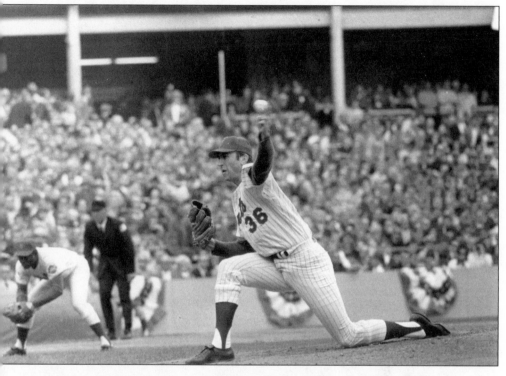

Jerry Koosman throws a pitch during the decisive Game 5 of the 1969 World Series.

Jerry Grote, Jerry Koosman, and Ed Charles celebrate on the mound after after the final out of the 1969 World Series.

Mets fans swarm the field at Shea Stadium in celebration of the team's first World Series championship, October 16, 1969.

PART FIVE

Relapse

CHAPTER

11

IT IS THE BURDEN OF THE HA-
bitual loser that his taste for winning is too easily satisfied.
One grows accustomed to defeat after a while. It becomes a
condition that is tolerated like many another of life's persistent woes. The relief that occasional victory brings is welcome, but it is embraced as an unexpected bounty that one
has fallen upon by chance. Success makes the loser uneasy.
He treats triumph as an alien, a beautiful stranger who has
happened upon his doorstep in search of another destination
and is certain to depart.

The Mets had stumbled into the All-Star break after a
shaky four-game series in Montreal. Prior to that, they had
won twelve of their last fifteen games. They had beaten the
Cubs at home and on the road. They had cut three games
from Chicago's lead. They were in second place. Though the
season was barely half over, these Mets had already earned
the distinction of being the best team the franchise had ever
fielded. They had set a new team mark for consecutive victories; they were certain to establish a new standard for winning percentage; deep into the heart of summer, they were
still a second-place contender. If they won no more than half
their remaining games, they would still finish well over .500

fifteen games better than they had the previous season. Wasn't it Gil Hodges who had set the goal at twelve? If the season ended now, who among the Mets or their followers would not deem it a success?

Indeed, shortly after the All-Star recess, the Mets would begin to play as if their season were already behind them. Of the seventy games remaining on their schedule, the first forty were to be against Western Division clubs, which were no easy pickings. Four teams in the West—the Braves, Reds, Giants, and Dodgers—were engaged in a dogfight for first place, and even the Astros were not far behind.

The Mets no doubt welcomed the opportunity to begin this segment of their schedule with ten games at Shea Stadium. They were not, after all, in the best physical shape. Agee, still sore from his collision with the wall in Montreal, would be available for pinch-hitting duty, but he was not yet ready to start. Seaver's condition was a matter of greater concern. His right shoulder was still giving him trouble, and he was kept out of the All-Star game while being treated with Butazolidin, a drug that relieves inflammation. He would be given a few days' more rest before testing his arm for the first time since being battered in Montreal.

The first team in was Cincinnati, which had six regulars hitting over .300 and more than enough home-run power from players like Lee May, Tony Perez, and a youngster named Johnny Bench. Met pitchers seemed able to deal with everyone except Perez, who hit three home runs while the teams divided four games. Each of the first three was decided by one run. Perez won the opener with a twelfth-inning homer off Tug McGraw, but the Mets rebounded the next day, scoring three times with two out in the eighth, the last two on a home run by J. C. Martin.

The third game was designated as the one in which Seaver would determine how much good a week's rest had done him.

The results were encouraging though not conclusive. He earned his fifteenth victory of the season, 3 to 2, but it was not a typical Seaver performance. He gave up eight hits, was in frequent trouble, and needed help more than once from his fielders. In the second inning, with men on second and third and one out, Cleon Jones threw a runner out at the plate to complete a double play. In the sixth, Seaver came to his own rescue. With a run in, men on first and third, and none out, he struck out Perez and May and picked Chico Ruiz off second. Two innings later, a double play staved off another Cincinnati rally, and in the ninth Seaver was bailed out again by his outfield. With one out and the tying run on first, Rod Gaspar charged in from his position in right field, speared a sinking line drive at his knees, and fired the ball to first base, where he doubled off Bobby Tolan to end the game.

Gaspar, who had watched the first eight innings from the bench, had been sent to the outfield at the start of the ninth in the expectation of just such an occasion. He had, in recent months, become a role player in Hodges's scenario, used now and then as a pinch hitter but mainly held in reserve for situations where his considerable speed and powerful throwing arm would be of greatest value. And those strategies had worked for Hodges more often than percentages would seem to allow. Gaspar already had seven assists; by the end of the season he would have an even dozen while leading the league in double plays started by an outfielder, an exceptional feat for a part-time player. He had started the season in right field, but his inconsistent bat and the return to form of Art Shamsky had left him with only a cameo part. The twenty-three-year-old Californian did not mind at all. He was happy just to be there.

"I knew I wasn't supposed to make the ballclub that spring," Gaspar says from his home in Mission Viejo, California, "*I* thought I would, but no one else expected me to make it. I was just up from Memphis, which was double-A ball, and they didn't even know who I was. Hodges didn't know who I was, the coaches didn't know . . . no one did. But Shamsky had a bad back, and Gil started me in the outfield, and I went on a hitting streak. I think I hit in thirteen or fourteen straight games, and they ended up keeping me. They had no choice, right? They had to keep me with Shamsky out and with the kind of spring I had. So I got a chance to play regularly when the season opened, but after about a week I had a couple of 0-for-4 games and I was benched for a while. Then Shamsky came back from Tidewater, and I was on and off the bench for the rest of the year. But I have no complaints, none at all. I played in about a hundred and twenty games, and it was a great year."

It was, in fact, the only good year Gaspar enjoyed in the major leagues. He spent most of 1970 in the minors, playing in only eleven games for the Mets, and at the end of the season he was traded to San Diego. For the next four years, he was mostly a minor league player. He appeared in only forty-nine games for the Padres during those four years, then spent two full seasons with Hawaii's triple-A team. When he failed to be chosen in the American League's expansion draft at the end of the 1976 season, Gaspar retired from baseball at the age of thirty. It was an abbreviated career that had begun with much promise, and Gaspar attributes his stunted success to his own disposition.

"I had a terrible attitude in those years," Gaspar says now. "When I was sent down by the Mets in 1970, I thought they were being unfair. But it wasn't them; it was me. I was spoiled rotten. I felt everyone owed me something. How can they send Rodney Gaspar to the minor leagues? That was my attitude. But I brought it on myself. For the first time in my life, I didn't work out after the 1969 season. Gil wanted me to play in Venezuela. I said, 'Heck, what do I have to go down there for?' So I didn't play any ball over the winter, and I reported to spring training out of shape. I was out of shape at the age of twenty-four. If I hadn't been sent down to the minors, there would have been something wrong with *them*. I *should* have been sent down."

Gaspar believes that the attitude that plagued him is common to many major league players.

"Do you know a lot of ballplayers?" he asks. "Have you been around them a lot? Because if you have, you'll know what I mean. A lot of players, they think the world owes them something. They're used to having everything done for them, to people taking care of them. They think that's the way it's supposed to be. Ballplayers much better than I was had their careers ruined by that attitude. That's why so many of them have a hard time with life. If you don't know how to work when you get out of baseball, then you're in trouble."

Retired from baseball and seeking a new life at the age of thirty, Gaspar soon learned how to work. He moved to Southern California and began selling life insurance, with more success than he had anticipated. He also discovered religion. The insurance office he worked in offered Bible studies classes, and Gaspar embraced Christianity. It had a dramatic effect on his life, he says. He continues to be active in the church and to prosper, to a reasonable degree, in the insurance business. He also coaches Little League baseball.

"I enjoy coaching the kids," says Gaspar, who has five of his own. "If anything, I'm more competitive now than I was when I was playing ball. My aim is to take a team to Williamsport, where the Little League championship is played. I played on a championship team, and now I'd like to manage one."

Gaspar recalls the championship team he played on with an obvious sense of awe and wonder.

"Looking back on it now, seventeen years later, it seems

like a dream," he says, "like it never really happened. That year was so incredible, it went so fast, I have a hard time remembering it. It was like Fantasyland."

Now, as July neared its end, the aura of fantasy that had surrounded the Mets for much of the season had begun to dissipate. They lost the fourth and final game of their series with the Reds, 6–3, and they did it in a fashion reminiscent of past Met teams. In the first inning, loose play afield put two runners on base and Tony Perez delivered them both, as well as himself, with his twenty-fifth home run of the season and his third of the series. The Reds scored twice more in the fourth without any muscle from their batters. They parlayed one well-timed hit with three Met errors—two of them by Al Weis at shortstop—to put the game out of reach.

The next day, Monday, was an off-day. On Tuesday it rained hard in New York, hard enough to postpone the opening of a three-game series with the Astros, hard enough to turn the outfield into something of a swamp for the next day's doubleheader. It was Wednesday, July 30, and the Mets were about to suffer through a day of humiliation that would revive memories of their forlorn past. They already trailed Houston 5–3 when the Astros came to bat in the ninth inning of the first game. When the inning was over, fourteen batters had come to the plate and eleven of them had scored. Eight of the runs were produced by a pair of grand-slam homers, one by Denis Menke off Cal Koonce and the other by Jim Wynn off Ron Taylor. It was the first time in the history of the National League that a team hit two bases-loaded home runs in the same inning.

Matters did not improve much in the second game, and in one critical sense they even deteriorated. After catching their breath for the first two innings, the Astros exploded for ten runs in the third, all of them scoring after two were out. The inning included a two-run homer by the pitcher, Larry

Dierker, but in Met lore it will always be remembered for a defensive change made by Hodges. In the midst of the third-inning mayhem, Houston catcher Johnny Edwards drove a routine double down the left-field line. Cleon Jones chased it down gingerly, then lofted a soft, almost casual, throw back to the infield. That brought Hodges out of the dugout. His hands thrust in his hip pockets, the Met manager ambled deliberately across the diamond, past the pitcher's mound, past the skin of the infield, and onto the sodden outfield grass. Bubbles of moisture oozed from the ground with each step he took, and he didn't stop walking until he arrived at the spot where his left fielder was standing. Hodges began to talk and Jones listened, each with his hands on his hips, and then Hodges turned and headed back to the dugout, walking with no greater urgency than had moved him on his departure. Trailing behind him was Jones, his glove dangling from his hand, his steps as measured and no more rapid than those of his manager. After the game, Hodges told the press that Jones had been removed because he was suffering from a pulled hamstring muscle.

"I saw him favor his leg that inning," he told the *Times*'s George Vecsey. "I didn't think he should play if he was hurting."

Jones was unavailable for comment. He was given the rest of the day off and he left the ballpark immediately. But many years later, his recollection of the incident is still fresh.

"When I saw him come out of the dugout, I had no idea he was coming out to see me," Jones says. "I thought he was going to talk to the pitcher. When he passed the mound, I thought he was going to say something to the shortstop. Then he passed the shortstop, and the only thing I could think was that he was going out to the bullpen. Then he comes right up to me and he says, 'What's wrong with you?'

"I said, 'What do you mean?'

"He says, 'I don't like the way you went after that last ball.'

"I said, 'The ball was hit down the line. There was no way I was going to keep him from getting a double. You know I've got a bad leg. I don't know why you walked out here.'

" 'If you have a bad leg,' he says, 'then I think you better come out of the game.'

"Then he turns around and starts walking back to the dugout, and I followed him off the field. It must have been a pretty weird sight," Jones says, amused now by the recollection. "The field was soaked and we're standing out there talking, with both our feet under water. It might have looked like he was trying to embarrass me, but he wasn't. Gil was just trying to make a point. We were getting our ass kicked and something had to be done, and that was his way of showing us that he wasn't satisfied with the way we were playing. We got the message too. It turned the team around. Not long after that, we got back on track and started playing good ball again."

Jones, after a brief spell on the bench, continued to pace the Mets at bat for the balance of the summer. He led the league in hitting during most of the season, but a cracked rib slowed his bat, and his .340 batting average placed him third in the race for the title, eight points behind Pete Rose and five in back of Roberto Clemente. But that didn't bother Jones very much.

"I wasn't thinking about the batting title," he says. "It really never entered my mind. I was just thinking about winning. Any personal goals I had were way in the back of my mind. When we beat the Cubs in Chicago that summer, I thought we had a good chance of winning it. The whole team seemed to feel that way. Hodges had instilled that winning attitude in us. When we left Chicago, our feeling was, 'We're gonna beat you guys. You're just a bunch of old men.' We felt we were as good as anyone then."

For Jones, the expectation of winning was particularly sweet. He had been with the Mets longer than anyone but Kranepool, and he had carried his potential through the lean years, finally blossoming in 1968 and then putting together his career season a year later. It must have seemed a long time coming.

Jones had begun playing baseball and football on the sandlots of a segregated neighborhood in Mobile, Alabama. His father had been a professional baseball player, pitching and playing the infield for teams in the Negro leagues. But Cleon, a talented all-around athlete with the foot speed of a sprinter, appeared to be most gifted at football. Playing halfback on the same team with Tommie Agee, he set a state high-school football record by scoring twenty-six touchdowns in one nine-game season. In college he ran for seventeen touchdowns, including consecutive kick returns of 107 and ninety-seven yards, in his one season at Alabama A & M after transferring from Grambling. At the time, Grambling had sent more players to the National Football League than any college but Notre Dame. The school's publicity director for athletics, Collie Nicholson, said of Jones: "[He] was a fantastic baseball player, but he would have been the greatest football player in Grambling's history."

But Jones preferred baseball. He was slight of build then and did not relish the pounding that a running back was obliged to absorb. And of course his baseball skills were considerable. A natural left-hander, he had learned to bat right-handed as a youngster because his early batting heroes were Joe DiMaggio, Willie Mays, and Roy Campanella. He hit the ball hard and with occasional power, and he soon caught the eye of a number of major league scouts. It was Clyde Grey, team captain of the Mobile Bears and an older friend of

Cleon's, who first brought him to the attention of the Mets. Jones worked out for the team for four or five days in Salisbury, North Carolina, and the Mets' scout in that area, Julian Morgan, was impressed. In July 1962, one month after Kranepool joined the organization, Jones signed a contract and became the second enlistee in the Mets' Youth of America program.

It did not take him long to prove he could hit. He batted .360 at Auburn and .305 at Raleigh in 1963, then was brought up by the Mets in time to play six games at the Polo Grounds before the venerable old park was razed in favor of a housing project. The following season, promoted to the triple-A team at Buffalo, Jones batted .278, with sixteen home runs and seventy RBIs. He played his first full season with the Mets in 1966, but it would be another few years before he showed signs of fulfilling his promise. His first big year was 1968, when his .297 batting average was the sixth best in the National League. Perhaps not coincidentally, that was Agee's first year with the Mets. Jones was a shy, rather soft-spoken youngster, and the companionship of his more effusive childhood buddy (whom Jones admiringly referred to as "Number One") could not help but aid his performance.

Ironically, Agee himself suffered through the worst season of his career in 1968. But a year later, the two graduates of Mobile's sandlots combined to lead the Met offensive. Between them they accounted for thirty-eight home runs and 151 runs batted in—seventy-six for Agee and seventy-five for Jones. One or the other led the Mets in every offensive department.

Jones and Agee, once described as the Damon and Pythias of the Mets, remained close friends. For a while, they were co-owners of a restaurant, called The Outfield, near Shea Stadium. In recent years, Jones has been in the roofing business while Agee has been working in youth programs for the New York City Police Department. But the two continue to see one another regularly. When Jones was interviewed, he was at the Agee home on a visit to New York, where they were exploring the possibility of new business ventures.

Only in the sweetest of reveries might they hope for a partnership as productive as the one they shared in 1969.

"It was an incredible year," Jones says. "Nothing will ever duplicate '69. If the Mets win this year [1986] it will be great, but it will never be like the first one. Kids remember me who never saw me play. The '69 Mets are like a part of history. It was a family thing then and everyone, even the fans, was a part of the family. It was not just winning, it was the way it happened. It didn't belong just to the ballplayers; it belonged to all New Yorkers."

Jones was part of the Mets' pennant-winning team in 1973, but it did not mean nearly as much to him.

"There was no comparison," he says. "We won, but to this day I don't know how we did it. We never did manage to put it all together that year. Someone always seemed to be injured. Grote was out a lot, and I was hurt a good part of the year."

Jones had only a moderately good season in 1973, and he never came close to equaling his 1969 performance.

"Pitchers started pitching around me," he explains, "especially left-handed pitchers, and I became a little impatient. I guess I lost my cool, so to speak. Also, my legs were hurting. I had bad knees, and they gave me more trouble as the years passed."

So perhaps there was some basis for Hodges's contention that it was an ailing leg that caused him to remove Jones from left field that soggy afternoon in Shea Stadium. But no one really believed him—not Jones, not the other players, not the press. Hodges, as Jones said, was delivering a message, and to reinforce it he kept Jones on the bench the next day when the Mets were beaten again by the Astros, 2 to 0.

It was their fourth loss in a row and their fifth in seven games since the All-Star break; they now found themselves six full games in back of the Cubs. If those who followed the fortunes of the Mets closely were beginning to suspect the worst, and many of them were, Hodges nonetheless managed to keep his composure.

The team was experiencing "a little dry spell," he told the press. "They'll be all right tomorrow."

CHAPTER
12

JULY WAS OVER NOW. THOUGH
it had ended in an atmosphere of disarray, it had been a
winning month for the Mets, their second in a row. They had
won fifteen games and lost eleven, paring the Cubs' lead from
seven and a half to six games. August initiated the portion of
the baseball season called the stretch drive. It is a term derived from the race track. A horse, or a team, that trails the
leader must make its move somewhere at the head of the
stretch if it hopes to catch the front-runner. If pennants traditionally are won in the crisp, autumn-gathering days of
September, they are often lost in the snare of August's heated
grip.

Hodges had called the Mets' collapse during the Houston series "a little dry spell. They'll be all right tomorrow,"
he had said. He proved to be at least half correct. The Mets
were all right the next day. They squeezed by Atlanta 5–4,
defeating Phil Niekro, whose fifteen victories at that point in
the season included nary a one against the Mets. And they
were all right again the following day, when McAndrew and
McGraw combined to blank the division-leading Braves 1–0.
The only run of the game was delivered by Cleon Jones, who
came off the bench to drive home Swoboda in the seventh

inning. Jones, who was leading the National League in hitting, at .346, was still officially sidelined with a "pulled hamstring." He was on the bench again on Sunday when the Mets made it three straight over the Braves with another one-run decision. This time they came from behind, erasing a five-run deficit, and again Jones made a contribution in his new, though temporary, role as a pinch hitter. Trailing 5 to 0, the Mets got even in one gulp in the bottom of the sixth, with pinch-hit singles by Jones, Clendenon, and Shamsky. The game was not decided until the eleventh when Grote, who had a triple and a home run in the first game against Atlanta, drove one over the left-field fence to give the Mets a sweep of the series. Grote remembers it as one of the high points of his season.

"I only hit six home runs that year," he says, "but I think three or four of them won ballgames. That one came at a good time, because we were struggling a little then, and it gave us a win when we needed it. There were so many highlights that season. I still get goosebumps when I think of the one-hitter Seaver threw against the Cubs. Of course I didn't have a whole helluva lot to do with it except that I caught it. Seaver pretty much threw his own game.

"By 1969, he and I had gotten so well geared to one another that he hardly ever shook me off. I didn't take it too well when most pitchers shook me off, but with Tom I didn't object. If he didn't go for the first sign I gave him, I knew he had something special in mind. What never ceased to amaze me about Tom was that he always seemed to be one step ahead of the hitters. If he got someone out this year pitching him a certain way, next year he's going to go somewhere else with him. Tom was the only guy I've ever seen who could get away with ten, fifteen mistakes in a ballgame. The hitters were never expecting him to make a bad pitch and they'd be frozen at the plate. In Atlanta one night, you could have run a

Little League team out there and if they didn't know it was
Tom Seaver pitching they would have beat his butt something fierce. And yet it was no contest. He didn't throw hard
enough to break an egg that night, but every time a hitter
got a good pitch to hit he was just paralyzed up there.

"With Gary Gentry, it was just the opposite. He was very
deliberate on the mound. He'd make one mistake and it would
cost him the ballgame. Now Nolan Ryan, he threw even harder
than Tom did, about four or five miles an hour faster, and
that makes a big difference at that speed. But Nolan didn't
go after a guy the way Tom did. He'd get two strikes on a
batter and then waste a couple of pitches. That's the way
American League pitchers pitch. In the American League,
the count goes to 0 and 2, you can almost automatically take
the next two pitches. You *know* they're not going to throw a
strike. That's one thing I never believed in. When I got a guy
0 and 2, one more pitch, baby, and you're gone. That's the
way Tom pitched. He went right after him."

Grote, who is animated and unhesitating in ordinary
conversation, becomes positively effusive when he discusses
pitching. While we are talking, in his real estate office on the
outskirts of San Antonio, he regularly bounces up from behind his desk to demonstrate a proper or flawed pitching
motion—the knees bending, the back coming down as part
of the follow-through, the precise point at which the hand
releases the ball. More than a student of the art, he is a ver-
itable scholar, and he has been thinking about pitching and
dissecting its every nuance since he was in high school, where
he started out as a pitcher.

"I had excellent form as a pitcher in high school," Grote
recalls, "and I always had a strong arm and good control. But
I tried to figure out what I could do to throw the ball harder,
and I began analyzing various aspects of my motion and release. I switched to catching because I wanted to play every
day, but I learned to throw every pitch, I learned the me-

chanics of every pitch a pitcher could throw so that I'd be able to help a guy when he was off.

"For instance, Seaver had a habit of sometimes throwing his slider so that it would come up there like a football and then back up instead of breaking down and away from a right-hand batter. But when he did that, I could spot the spin on the ball immediately, as soon as he released it. I'd catch the ball and show it to him and give him this. [Grote shapes his hand as if gripping a baseball and flicks his wrist with an overhand, downward motion.] Tom would see that and he would nod; he knew what I meant. I didn't have to go out there and tell him. The next slider he threw would break down hard, and it would be all right after that. You could sometimes prevent a big inning by spotting something like that and correcting it right away.

"A catcher should be a second pitching coach. I literally ran with the pitchers, ate with the pitchers, lived with the pitchers. I warmed them up on the days they threw between starts. If they were working on something new, I wanted to be there. I wanted to know what's going on, what their problems were. I wanted to know what to tell them if they were doing something that wasn't just right."

Given the quality, the depth, and the youth of the Met pitching staff, the arrival of Grote in 1966 was a piece of good fortune that could hardly have been calculated at the time. He was not considered an especially valuable property when the Houston Astros traded him to the Mets in October of 1965 for a six-foot, seven-inch pitcher named Tom Parsons, who had compiled a record of 2–12 in two seasons with New York and never earned another big-league decision. But then Grote's record with the Astros was not particularly encouraging either. He batted only .181 in 1964 and spent the entire 1965 season with Houston's farm team in Oklahoma City.

"The Houston club had given up on me," Grote says now. "After the 1964 season, I played with Venezuela in the winter league. Spring training opened two days after we finished our season there, and I told Houston's management that it would take me a couple of days to get my family together and get to camp. They said it would be no problem, but when I got there, there were problems. I felt I was in shape to play when I arrived, and I didn't work as hard as they expected me to. I didn't need to; I had been playing ball all winter and I was ready then. But when the season started, they assigned me to Oklahoma City. I wasn't worried, though. I always felt I could play in the majors. I had signed with Houston right out of high school and played my first season in double-A ball right here in San Antonio. I could have signed with the Dodgers, and the Yankees were interested in me, but I chose Houston because I would be able to get to the big leagues quicker. And after one year in the minors, I made the Houston club."

Red Murff, the scout who had signed Grote to an Astro contract, had since become a scout for the Mets. Shortly after the 1965 season, he phoned Grote and told him of the trade.

"I was enthusiastic about coming to the Mets," Grote says. "I knew that they needed a catcher and that I might be able to get a starting job right away."

He did, but those first two seasons with the Mets were not always easy. Grote was a competitive, exceptionally aggressive type of player, and he did not get on well with the manager, Wes Westrum, a former catcher of much milder disposition. Westrum thought Grote to be a bit ill-tempered, too outspoken with umpires, and far too tough on his own pitchers. When a pitcher's concentration seemed to flag, Grote was not timid about firing the ball back at a velocity that most Met pitchers would have paid a price to muster from their own arms. He was considered, in short, tough to handle, but he nonetheless played in 120 games in each of his first two seasons with the Mets. In 1968 Gil Hodges arrived, ringing in a new era for both Jerry Grote and the Mets.

"Gil instilled some respect in the team," Grote says. "Respect had been lost during all the years of losing, and Westrum just couldn't handle some of the players over there. Gil turned everything around. He was as knowledgeable a baseball man as I've ever seen. You can't compare anyone with Hodges, except maybe Walter Alston. There are a few guys who come close—Chuck Tanner and Gene Mauch, but Mauch overmanages a little. I would have loved to have played for Tanner, to get into his mind a little and learn more about baseball. I'll tell you a story about Tanner.

"One day during spring training we were fixing to play Pittsburgh, and I got to talking to Tanner. He asked me, 'Did you ever pitch out three times in a row?' I hadn't. He says, 'Would you do it?' I said, 'Try me.' Now, he's got a speedster on first base and he hollers out to me, 'You gonna pitch out?' I said, 'Send him and find out.' I knew he wouldn't go, so I get a strike on the first pitch. He says, 'You better get ready.' I pitched out, but I knew he wasn't going. I knew what was coming. I said to myself, 'I'm going to do it three times and the third time I'm gonna nail his ass.' And that's what happened. Tanner says, 'Well I'll be a son of a bitch. I don't believe you did it.'

"To me, that's what spring training was all about. It was a mind game. That's when I played with the hitters. I pitched to their strengths, not to their weaknesses. The idea in spring training is not to get guys out with pitches you know you can get them out with. Let 'em think they can hit you. In spring training, the pitchers aren't ready yet. They can't throw at full speed. They might not be able to get in a guy's kitchen then, but two weeks into the season they might. Pitching is a mind game.

"Gil was always thinking four, five innings ahead, and

he taught me to be that way. By the fifth or sixth inning, I knew who I wanted coming up there in the ninth. Sometimes I'd ease up on a batter—let him hit the ball and if he gets on, okay, because I was setting up the order. I didn't want numbers one, two, and three walking up there in the ninth, so I played with the batting order a little. The ideal thing is to have the number-five hitter leading off. How many fifth hitters in the league can run? If he gets on, let him block up the bases, set up the double play with the bottom of the order coming up.

"Let me throw something at you and see what you think. There are seventh- and eighth-place hitters in the league who bat around .230 and don't drive in many runs—glove men. Now, would you rather have a hitter like that up in the eighth or ninth inning with an 0 for 3 on the day or a 1 for 3? That type of hitter only expects to get one hit a game. He comes up hitless and he'll battle you like hell not to take an oh-fer. But if he already has his hit, he'll ease up a little. Now, I'd get a guy like that up early in the game with two out and no one on and I'd give him a chance to get his hit. I didn't want him looking for it late in the game."

If there is any truth to the maxim that each man, no matter how broad his range or varied his interests, has only one true subject, Grote's clearly is pitching. For him to be traded to the Mets in 1966 was a little like dispatching a gold-seeker to Sutter's Mill in 1849. McGraw was beginning his first full season, and Ryan made his appearance late in the year. Seaver came up in '67, Koosman and McAndrew in '68, and finally Gentry in '69. A treasure-trove of young talent was being gathered in increments, assembled around a veteran catcher whose passion it was to discern nuance in the finest detail and share his insights with strong-armed pitchers eager to learn. Grote says he could see the team taking shape right from the start.

"They were grooming good young pitchers in their minor league system and bringing them up one at a time," he says. "By 1968, you could tell we were building a contender. It was such a young team. In 1969, I was about the eighth-oldest player on the team, and I didn't turn twenty-seven until the day we won the National League title. Gil kept just enough veterans around to mold those kids, and in spring training that year I felt we had a good shot to win the pennant. You can ask Jack Lang, the sports writer who covered us for a Long Island paper. I told him I thought we could win it in '69, and he wrote it. Jack said I was crazy, but at the end of the season I reminded him of it. He forgot he wrote it, but I told him to look it up in his own column."

Grote helped mold the young staff and watched it grow into maturity during his eleven-year tenure with the Mets. In 1977 he was traded to the Dodgers, another team with a bountiful group of pitchers and one that was on its way to the first of two consecutive pennants.

"It was great to be with a winner and play in the World Series again," Grote says, "and playing in Los Angeles was phenomenal, but it was nothing like playing in New York. New York was amazing in 1969. We actually had New Yorkers talking to one another. People in New York won't even meet your eye when you pass them on the street, but in 1969 strangers were talking to one another. The people there have such an intense love of the game. Players on other teams hated to come to New York. I didn't realize how bad it was until I got with the Dodgers. We had to go to New York to play the Yankees in the World Series, and the players would have been willing to forfeit those games rather than go there and play. They especially hated to go to Yankee Stadium. They were afraid of being in that area of the Bronx, but mostly it was the fans. They just feared the intensity of the New York fans. The Los Angeles fans are great; they know their baseball, they appreciate their baseball, they know their players, but they're quiet, they're not like New York fans. Where would I rather play? Are you kidding? In New York. I want those fans on my side.'"

One aspect of playing in New York that did not appeal to Grote was dealing with the swarm of writers that covered the team.

"I didn't get along with the writers," Grote says, "and I made no pretense about it. They'd ask questions that all they had to do was look in the press guide to find the answers, and sometimes they'd ask questions that were just plain stupid. One time after I was totally misquoted, Hodges called a clubhouse meeting and I got my ass chewed. It was about two months before the end of the '69 season, and I told the press they could all go fuck themselves. 'You'll never misquote me again,' I said. 'You can't hurt me worse than you already have, so the hell with you.'"

Art Shamsky believes that Grote's poor relationship with the press cost him the recognition he deserved.

"Jerry Grote was the best catcher I've ever seen," Shamsky says. "I played a little with Johnny Bench, and he wasn't too far behind, but Grote was the best. He did things so naturally. He was the quickest catcher behind the plate, and he had an outstanding arm. If you ask guys like Lou Brock and Maury Wills—base stealers—which catcher they feared most, I'd venture to say that Grote would be at the top of the list. And he was also a great handler of pitchers. He did wonders with a lot of the young pitchers we had on that team. But he was vastly underrated because he didn't get along with the press. My locker was right next to Jerry's, so I know that he didn't like the writers and they didn't like him."

Grote acknowledges some exceptions, however.

"Joe Durso, who covered the team for *The New York Times*, was as fine a man and as good a reporter as there is," Grote says. "He was one of the few I talked to. But near the end of the season there were a hundred or more reporters there every night. You couldn't get into the clubhouse to take a shower. Some of the guys on the team used to ride me about not talking to the press, but then some of them finally did the same thing. Hey, this old country boy learned in a hurry, and I put a stop to it right away. I had enough to deal with in August and September without worrying about being misquoted in the press."

If the Mets had to contend with more pressure than they were accustomed to as the season entered its late stages, Grote believes it had little effect on the team's performance.

"We were the kind of guys who didn't know when we were beat," he says. "We didn't know we were supposed to be horseshit. We just went out there and we never quit. We never felt we were out of a game; we never felt we were out of anything."

But to the outside observer, the Mets appeared to be slipping as the season moved into August. Even after sweeping Atlanta, they were still six games behind the Cubs as they prepared to make return visits to Cincinnati, Atlanta, and Houston. It was only a ten-day road trip, but by the time it was over the Mets would be perilously close to falling out of the race.

The first stop on the trip was Cincinnati, where the Mets dropped three out of four. The Reds had just inched past Atlanta in the Western Division race, and now they seemed to welcome the opportunity to solidify their lead. Cleon Jones, restored to the starting lineup, went hitless in the opening game, but so did most of his teammates as Jim Maloney pitched a two-hitter to beat Koosman 1−0. The Mets managed to split a doubleheader the next day, but Nolan Ryan's well-pitched victory was overshadowed by a recurrence of Seaver's arm problems. His aching right shoulder caused him to leave after the third inning, having already given up four runs and five hits. Over the past month, his record now stood at two victories and four defeats. Seaver was concerned, but he tried to keep things in perspective.

"When you've been pitching since you were nine years old and never had a sore arm until now, it's impossible not to worry," he said. "But I'm intelligent enough to know my trouble is a strained muscle, not a torn muscle and not a joint." Still, as Seaver admitted, it was impossible not to worry.

While the Mets were losing their third game to Cincinnati, the Cubs were completing a sweep of Houston in the Astrodome. It was their seventh straight win, and it enlarged their first-place margin to a relatively comfortable eight and a half games. The Mets, staggering a bit now, conceivably welcomed their visit to Atlanta. The Braves' power-heavy lineup appeared to hold little menace for Met pitchers, and indeed they allowed only four runs in as many games while winning three of them. For added encouragement, Seaver pitched seven and a third innings with only minor discomfort, earning his sixteenth victory of the season. Ever the student of pitching mechanics, Seaver said he had kept his motion as compact as possible to reduce the strain on his shoulder. The decision gave him a lifetime record of 10–2 against Atlanta, and the Mets concluded the regular season's business between the teams with eight wins in their twelve meetings.

If the Mets had developed the habit of breathing new life when they played the Braves, the Astros were the team that choked it out of them. Since the two teams joined the league together in 1962, Houston had beaten the Mets eighty-five times and lost only forty-nine. So far in 1969, the Mets had dropped seven of nine games between the teams, including the last six in a row. In the past three seasons, they had won only five times in the Astrodome. Now, with the promise of their first season as a contender beginning to show signs of wear, they were on their way to Houston for three games of indoor baseball in what had been termed, perhaps cynically, "the Eighth Wonder of the World."

What followed might have been the final act of a season-long script. The Astros outpitched the Mets in the first game, outhit them in the second, and embarrassed them in the third. Tom Griffin, the twenty-one-year-old rookie pitcher who had held the Mets scoreless in two previous starts, made it three in a row. He shut them out for eight innings, allowing only four hits and recording nine strikeouts. In three appearances against the Mets, Griffin had pitched twenty-five innings, struck out twenty-eight batters, and failed to yield a run. (The three victories accounted for more than twenty-five percent of his total for the year.) After the game, Jim McAndrew, whose misfortune it was to draw Griffin as an opponent, reflected on the Mets' inability to deal with the Astros. A former psychology student at the University of Iowa, McAndrew looked to his academic background for an explanation.

"In life, as in baseball," he said, "patterns are often hard to fathom. If you admit there is a pattern, sometimes you're trapped by your own premise."

Whatever it was that entrapped the Mets tightened its grip the next day. This time they jumped ahead 5−1 when Kranepool hit a three-run home run in the fourth, but two innings later Curt Blefary hit one with two men on for Houston, and the Astros later increased their lead before hanging on to win 8−7. The final game was never a contest. Houston opened up on Gary Gentry for three runs in the first and added five more in the third while Larry Dierker was holding the Mets to five hits, collecting his fourteenth victory on his way to a twenty-win season.

So now the Mets had lost nine straight to the Astros, six of six in the Dome, and ten of twelve on the season. But that was not nearly the worst of their woes. Their record since the All-Star break was 9 and 12. In those three weeks, they had fallen five more games in back of the Cubs and now trailed Chicago by nine and a half, the farthest behind they had been all season. The Cardinals, resurgent now, had passed them in the standings, and they led Pittsburgh by only three and a half. Their eleven-game winning streak, their heroics against the Cubs, their ascent to within reaching distance of first place on the day of the moon landing—all seemed to be part of another season now. To all appearances, the Mets had made their run but finally were overtaken by reality. They had stirred the sauce of new possibilities and raised the lid a crack on what the future might hold. Now they could read-just their sights and focus on what their goal had been at the start of the season: a realistic chance for third place, a long-shot's hope for second.

It was Friday, August 15, when the Mets returned home from Houston. There were only forty-nine games left to play in the '69 season.

PART SIX

'Look Who's No. 1'

CHAPTER

13

BASEBALL HAS LONG BEEN CEL-
ebrated for its independence from time. It is a sport in which
the clock has no dominion. Each game theoretically has eter-
nity at its command. No matter how great the deficit or how
late the inning, the possibilities linger. Its relation to time is
what lends baseball part of its mythological dimension. It
confirms the injunction that it's never too late.

That, of course, is true of a single baseball game. It is
not true of a season. If baseball is free of the clock, it is nonetheless a prisoner of the calendar. The inexorable passing of
the days narrows the limits of a team's chances. It can run
out of season in the same way that a fast-closing racehorse
runs out of track. As the days fall away and the season ebbs,
each team's hopes will finally be governed by the bane or
benediction of time.

In 1951, the New York Giants trailed the Brooklyn
Dodgers by thirteen games on August 12, yet closed to finish
the regular season in a tie. Their comeback, climaxed by a
dramatic three-game playoff, was christened the Miracle of
Coogan's Bluff. Now, eighteen years later, the mountain that
the Mets had to climb was very nearly as steep. They would

have to make up only nine and a half games, but they would have almost a week less in which to do it.

The chase was to begin with a ten-game homestand against the three teams from California, and the Mets could not but appreciate that the first visit would be paid by San Diego. It was, after all, against the Padres that they had started their eleven-game winning streak; they had won four of the first five meetings between the clubs; and while the Mets had been struggling of late, San Diego came limping into Shea with a six-game losing streak and the poorest won-lost record in baseball.

The four-game series was to consist of single games on Friday and Saturday and a doubleheader on Sunday. Hodges had planned to open with Seaver, but when Friday came up cloudy and wet he named Gentry as his starter. It was a strategy that suited the turn of the weather. The start of the game was delayed thirty minutes; then, after only four batters had come to the plate, the rain came harder and more persistently. After a second delay of almost an hour, the game was called and rescheduled as part of a Saturday doubleheader. Hodges still had a fresh Seaver to open with.

The pain in his shoulder gone, Seaver, who had won sixteen games in each of his first two seasons, proceeded to win his seventeenth of 1969 with a 2–0 shutout. In the second game, the Mets again were able to score only twice, but that was once more than the Padres could manage. Jim McAndrew, also physically sound now, earned his fourth victory of the year with the aid of two innings of relief from Tug McGraw and a neat piece of managing by Hodges. With the score tied at one in the seventh, San Diego pitcher Gary Ross fielded a routine grounder by Swoboda and threw the ball down the right-field line, putting Swoboda on third with nobody out. Hodges then sent up a succession of left-handed pinch hitters in an effort to get the run home. The first two,

Wayne Garrett and Ed Kranepool, failed to deliver; and the third, Bud Harrelson, drew a walk. Then, with Shamsky in the on-deck circle to bat for McAndrew, Padres' manager Preston Gomez pulled Ross in favor of a left-hander, Dave Roberts. Hodges countered by sending up Grote to hit for Shamsky, and the inning's fifth straight pinch hitter lined Roberts's second pitch to right field for the winning run.

The next day, Sunday, was Banner Day at Shea. It was an old tradition that annually filled the stadium and sent hundreds of fans parading across the field carrying banners of various motifs. On this day, the winning entry bore the legend: "One small step for Hodges, one giant leap for Met-kind." The Mets, whose "giant leap" appeared earlier in the week to have fallen short, responded appropriately. They whipped the Padres twice more, by identical scores of 3 to 2, scoring all their runs in a single inning of each game.

In the opener, Koosman, who had won only once in his previous six starts, was trailing 2–0 in the fifth when Clendenon and Harrelson singled and Duffy Dyer, the third-string catcher, homered to give Koosman his tenth victory of the season. For Dyer, who had spent a good part of the year at Tidewater, it was the kind of hit that can pry loose an opening on a big-league roster.

"I had just been recalled by the Mets that weekend to take Nolan Ryan's place when he left for military duty," Dyer recalls. "About three weeks earlier, Gil had called me into his office and said he wanted me to go down to Tidewater for a while so I could get myself into playing shape. I hadn't had much chance to play, and Grote was struggling a little, and Gil said he wanted me ready for the last part of the season. I wasn't too happy about it at the time. A lot of players are told that and they never make it back up. But Gil was as good as his word, and three weeks later I was back. Then, right after being called up, I hit the home run against San Diego. It was a great feeling, but nothing like the one I hit on opening day.

"That was also a three-run homer, and I can remember it as clearly as if it happened yesterday. It was my first game in New York. I had played one game at the end of the 1968 season, but that was on the road. I was down in the bullpen and I wasn't expecting to be called. There were two out in the ninth. Then the phone rang and Gil said, 'Get down to the dugout. If Jerry [Grote] gets on, you're going to hit.' I jogged down through the tunnel, and all the way to the dugout I could feel my heart beating. When I got there I put my batting helmet on, and then Jerry singled and I started to go up to hit. I was numb. I remember distinctly that my knees were shaking while I was at bat. As soon as I hit the ball I knew it was a home run but I started sprinting to first and I was still sprinting halfway to second. Then I realized the ball was gone and I slowed down, and when I touched second base I remember saying to myself, 'My God, I hit a home run in the major leagues.' "

Now, almost two decades later, Dyer describes that home run in its finest detail. He summons it with a clarity reserved for those rare moments in a man's life that live always in the present. But then he is quick to leaven it, to lend it proportion.

"Of course, when you hit thirty home runs in your whole career it's not hard to remember them; they're all special." Dyer chuckles with the good humor that befits a man who all his life has answered to the name of a radio-comedy character.

"The name 'Duffy' comes from *Duffy's Tavern*," he says. "That was my mother's favorite radio program, and she was listening to it when she went into labor. When I was born, the first thing she said was 'How's Duffy?'—and that's what I've been called all my life. My real name is Don Robert, but few people even know that. I've always used the name Duffy."

So it was as Duffy Dyer that the young catcher signed with the Mets after graduating from Arizona State in 1966. He spent the second half of that season and all of the next with Williamsport in the Eastern League, then moved up to Jacksonville in 1968. A year later, he was a rookie third-string catcher with the Mets. There is perhaps no more precarious position in all of baseball, but it has its advantages.

"I learned while playing, but I also learned a lot just sitting on the bench," Dyer says. "Grote and J. C. Martin were both veteran catchers, and they knew a lot about setting up hitters. I used to call my own game, pitch for pitch, from the bench and compare it with the way they called the game. As the season progressed, the pitches we called differed less and less."

His role as third-string catcher and his occasional sojourns to the minors afforded Dyer a perspective somewhat detached from the day-to-day run of events. He is one of the few members of the team who does not object to its being called the Miracle Mets.

"Not at all," he says when asked about it. "I know we earned it, but it still seemed to me that we were a team of destiny. On opening day, not many of us thought we would be contenders. We felt sure that we would be better than in '68, there was no doubt about that, but most of us were just hoping to play better than .500 ball.

"It really began to change after that series with Chicago, when Young dropped the fly ball and Seaver pitched the one-hitter. You could see a difference in the Cubs after that, the way they reacted, like 'Oh, my God, we're choking.' It affected the whole ballclub. I just don't think they were the same after that series. And then we started getting some breaks, and it seemed that every day it was someone else making the key play, getting the big hit, and we really started to believe that we could win it. We had such a good blend of players—a lot of young guys and some veterans like Charles,

Cardwell, and Koonce. Some of the players were quiet and stabilizing while others, like Tug and Koosman, kept everybody loose. I was really surprised and upset that we didn't win much after that year."

Dyer enjoyed another pennant with the Mets in 1973 before being traded to Pittsburgh two years later. After brief stays with Montreal and Detroit, he wound up his playing career in 1981, spent one season out of baseball, and then embarked on a new career as a coach and manager.

"I always thought I would remain in the game," Dyer says, "but after all those years I was tired of the traveling, and I enjoyed spending a year at home. I got a real estate license and I practiced right near my home in Phoenix. I was making a good living at it, and I was happy, but in 1983 I got a call from Lee Elia, the manager of the Cubs, offering me a job as bullpen coach, and I took it. I really enjoyed that season, but I wanted to try my hand at managing, and the following year I got the chance with the Twins' organization. I managed the Kenosha [Wisconsin] team in the Midwest League, which was Class A ball, and in my second season we won the league championship. In 1986, I accepted an offer to manage in double-A with El Paso, a Texas League affiliate in the Milwaukee system, and we won the whole thing there."

Dyer's early success bodes well for an opportunity to manage in the major leagues. He would like the chance to recapture some of the glow of the world championship he knew as a twenty-four-year-old rookie in 1969.

Although he played in only twenty-nine games for the Mets that season, Dyer was an integral part of the team. His nineteen hits seemed, very often, to come at critical times, not only of a game but of the season as well. After his opening-day home run, he did not get another hit for almost two months. But the next one, a pinch hit on May 30, gave the Mets their third straight win in their streak of eleven. Then, just up from another stay at Tidewater, his home run against

San Diego provided the winning margin in what again was a third straight victory for the Mets. This time, it prolonged a run that would revive the team's hopes as a contender. Within a week, the Mets would be right back on the heels of the Cubs.

In the second game of Sunday's doubleheader, the Mets earned a sweep with a three-run surge in the seventh inning. It was their fourth win in the past thirty hours and their eighth straight over the Padres. With the Giants and Dodgers coming in next, the Mets' latest revival stirred a sense of *déjà vu*. It was against the same three teams that they roused themselves in late May, climbed past the .500 mark, and embarked on a journey from fifth to second place. Now, almost three months later, they seemed poised to use the same three teams as a springboard back into contention. It was Tuesday, August 19, and if the Mets indeed had begun to make their stretch move, they would have to proceed next against two of the league's premier pitchers—Juan Marichal and Gaylord Perry.

Marichal, on his way to another twenty-win season, met all expectations. He held the Mets to two hits across the regulation nine innings, but that was not enough to win. Gary Gentry, though not quite as stingy, managed to keep the Giants from the plate, and the game moved into extra innings.

The Mets almost won it in the twelfth. Cleon Jones, who already had two hits off Marichal, beat out an infield single to open the inning. Then Tug McGraw, who had relieved Gentry in the eleventh and was batting fourth as part of a two-man switch, bunted towards the mound. Marichal fielded the ball and threw to first. Ron Hunt, covering from his second-base position, arrived at the same time as the runner, and McGraw jarred the ball loose as he crossed first base. The ball rolled thirty-five feet down the right-field line, with Hunt in pursuit and Jones circling the bases and heading for home. Hunt retrieved the ball and made a perfect throw to the plate, where Jack Hiatt tagged the runner in another collision that sent both men sprawling.

In the thirteenth, it was the Giants' turn to come within inches of winning the game, and once again it was Jones who figured in the critical play. With two out and no one on base, Willie McCovey came to bat. McCovey was the most productive hitter in the league that season. He already had thirty-six home runs and nearly a hundred RBIs on his way to leading the league in both departments. Hodges, accordingly, decided it was time to deploy his four-man outfield alignment. Bobby Pfeil, who was playing third, moved into the left-field corner, Jones and Agee occupied the power alleys, and Gaspar guarded the right-field line. McCovey came close to making the strategy academic. He lined McGraw's first pitch deep to left-center; but Jones, ideally positioned to make the play, raced to the wall, made a leaping, backhanded catch, bounced off the fence, and tumbled onto the warning track. Finally he arose with his hand held high and the ball still clutched in his glove.

In the bottom of the fourteenth, Marichal, who had already made 150 pitches, threw one too many. Tommie Agee, who had struck out three times earlier in the game, hit Marichal's second pitch of the inning hard and deep to left. Marichal did not turn to watch it clear the visiting bullpen. He simply lowered his head and walked off the mound as Agee rounded the bases.

It was the kind of game that often suggests the changing tone of a season for a team, a signal perhaps that luck is prepared to cooperate. Just a year ago to the day, the Mets had lost a similar game—1 to 0, in seventeen innings—to these same Giants. Now it appeared that fortune had begun to turn in the Mets' favor.

Luck, however, played no part in the following night's game. Art Shamsky led a six-run assault against Gaylord Perry, and Jim McAndrew pitched a two-hit shutout, his second impressive start within four days. Met pitching now had kept the muscular Giant lineup scoreless for twenty-three straight innings. But that was as far as it went. The next day, the Giants took dead aim at Tom Seaver. Bobby Bonds, the young outfielder who was being heralded as the second coming of Willie Mays, hit two home runs, one with a pair of runners on base, and the Giants snapped the Mets' winning streak at six. Still, the Mets did not go easily. They rallied from four runs behind and tied the game with two out in the ninth, but finally succumbed in the eleventh when Agee lost Ken Henderson's fly ball in the sun.

It was, nonetheless, a good week's baseball for the Mets. They had won six of seven games and sliced three games from the Cubs' lead. There also were other, more subtle, indications of the Mets' revival. Help was coming from new, sometimes unexpected, sources, and it seemed as though each day spawned its own hero. McAndrew, who had only three victories through the middle of August, added two more in the past week. Cal Koonce, who had been hit hard early in the year, had now won five in a row coming out of the bullpen. Art Shamsky had been hitless in his last eighteen appearances before unloading a three-run homer and a double in the second game against the Giants. And Ron Swoboda, who had struggled at bat for most of the season, was in so smooth a hitting groove that Hodges was playing him against both right- and left-handed pitchers.

It was Swoboda who would now lead the Met offense in a three-game sweep of the Dodgers. He hit a two-run homer— his first in almost three months—in the opening game and was virtually a one-man attack in the third, driving in four runs, scoring twice, and throwing out a runner at third.

In the middle game of the series, Shamsky hit his eleventh home run of the year, but the Mets needed help from the Dodgers to win it. Don Cardwell, who had pitched well but without luck for most of the season, had a three-hit shut-out and a two-run lead going into the eighth, but neither survived the inning. The Dodgers tied it on a single, a triple, and a throwing error. The score stood at two runs apiece when Clendenon walked with one out in the ninth. Jim Brewer, throwing his knuckleball in relief, then got the next two batters to hit soft infield pop-ups—and lost the game in the process. The first was hit by Rod Gaspar and caught by Wes Parker at first base. The second was lofted high in back of second base by Jerry Grote and was caught by no one, although three Dodger fielders could have handled it. Willie Davis trotted in from center field; Maury Wills, the short-stop, and Ted Sizemore, the second baseman, each drifted back on the outfield grass; and all three looked first at the ball and then at one another as the ball fell untouched among them. Clendenon, meanwhile, was looking at neither the ball nor the fielders. With two out and a 3-and-2 count on the batter, he was off with the pitch, and he scored the winning run unchallenged.

The three wins gave the Mets a six-game sweep of the Dodgers at Shea. It was the first time they had ever swept a team at home over the course of a season. More significantly, it marked the end of a homestand in which they won nine of ten games. They had survived a time of crisis, emerging with their confidence intact and their hopes alive. Now, with just over five weeks remaining in the season, they were back in the race, and the belief was growing among them that they would finally overtake the Cubs.

"It was after that homestand that I really thought we could make it," says Cal Koonce. "When we came back from Houston, we were about nine, ten games behind, and then the Giants, the Dodgers, and San Diego came in, and I think we pretty-near swept them. We began closing the gap on a day-to-day basis, and we had a sense that however far behind we were and no matter what happened during the game, we'd figure out a way to win it. We had extreme confidence in Hodges, and he seemed to be on a roll too. All the moves he was making—the pitching changes, the pinch hitters, the platooning of players—all seemed to be working. Everything was falling into place, and we figured that someway, somehow, we were going to get it done."

Koonce, of course, was one of the role-players who gave Hodges the flexibility to make those changes. He had lost three straight decisions early in the season, and the burden of right-handed relief was carried, almost exclusively for a while, by Ron Taylor. Taylor had appeared in more than one-third of the team's games by the middle of August; but Hodges came back to Koonce as the weather and the pennant race heated up, and the right-hander from Hope Mills, North Carolina, began to deliver. From around midseason on, he never lost another game. He won six straight times in relief and earned seven saves on a pitching staff that required less help than most.

"It took me a while to get in a groove," Koonce says. "I didn't pitch that often early in the season, and then when the weather warmed up, that helped too."

Koonce is discussing the 1969 season in an atmosphere conducive to such recollections. We are in Shea Stadium, seated in front of his temporary locker in the clubhouse of the 1986 Mets. It is a Saturday afternoon in the middle of July, and the Mets are celebrating their twenty-fifth anniversary with an Old Timers' Day. Dozens of former Mets, including most of the 1969 team, are milling about the clubhouse, renewing acquaintances, squeezing into uniforms with their old numbers on the back. Some are chatting about the current edition of the Mets, which is far ahead in the Eastern Division.

Outside, the field is covered with a tarpaulin. It is raining hard, and the old-time Mets will not get to play their three-inning game. Instead, they will each be given a brief introduction over the public-address system, step out of the dugout, and wave to the crowd. There is some disappointment at losing the opportunity to trot onto the playing field once again, to see how much snap is still left in the arm and how much greater the distance has grown between the batter's box and the outfield fence. But spirits are nonetheless high. Memory, jostled and revived by the familiarity of place, leaps the gap in time and the past edges that much closer to the present.

Koonce recalls that his was one of four lockers on one side of the clubhouse. The others belonged to Don Cardwell, J. C. Martin, and Ron Taylor.

"Three of us were southerners," Koonce points out. "Cardwell and I were both from North Carolina, and J. C. was from down in Virginia. Ron, of course, came from Toronto. One day, Nick Torman, our clubhouse man, hung a sign over that side of the room that said, 'Y'all's-Row.' Someone asked Taylor what he was doing there, and he said, 'I'm from South Canada.' "

Koonce relives the camaraderie, with obvious delight. "We were a loose group," he says, "but we were very close. There were no real cliques. When we were on the road, you might go to dinner with three or four guys one night, and the next night you would go with three or four others. Probably the best way to describe that '69 team is that we were like a big group of kids having a good time, playing loose and pulling for one another. We each accepted the roles we were given early in the year, and we went about our work."

Koonce's role was quite clear. He would be the right-handed relief pitcher working behind Ron Taylor, a role similar to the one he had filled during more than five seasons with the Cubs. He had been signed by the Cubs as a bonus player in 1962 and sold for cash to the Mets near the end of the 1967 season. The change of uniform had a rejuvenating effect on Koonce. He had never had a winning record in Chicago, but he was 6 – 4 with the Mets in '68 and 6 – 3 during the 1969 season. The difference, he says, was the Met coaching staff, which included three former catchers, and the manner in which Hodges (who also had done some catching) handled his pitchers.

"With the Cubs," he says, "Leo [Durocher] would use the same reliever game after game until he ran out of gas. If you were on a hot streak, you knew you'd be the first one to be called every day until your streak ended. During one period, I warmed up in the bullpen fourteen days in a row, and that takes something out of you. That was Leo's style of managing. He did the same thing in 1969, not only with his pitchers but with his infielders too. He played them every day, and by September they were pretty well burned out. With the Mets it was different; we took turns. If you were brought in one day, you knew you would have a day or two to get ready before you were called on again. That's why we were fresh at the end of the season."

Koonce's presence on the staff and his effectiveness late in the season allowed Taylor the rest he needed for the drive down the stretch. It also added the stabilizing influence of another veteran player to the young Met team. Koonce, in his eighth big-league season, would play only two more years, and he was already looking ahead to the end of his career. During the off-seasons, he worked as a stockbroker and developed his own practice. But not long after his retirement, he gave it up in favor of a life closer to baseball.

"I went back home to Hope Mills as a teacher and coach at Southview High School," he says, "and then I moved on to become the baseball coach at Campbell University."

Seven years later, in 1987, he was embarking on an entirely new career. He had just been named general manager of the Class A Fayetteville (N.C.) franchise in the South At-

lantic League. The team, part of the Detroit Tigers' organization, was the first professional team in Fayetteville in more
than thirty years.

"I was looking for an opportunity to get back into
professional baseball," Koonce says, "and I wanted to see how
things looked from the other side, the administrative view.
But I suspect that winning feels as good no matter what your
role is. When a team wins a championship, everyone connected with it feels involved—the front office, the traveling
secretary, the ground crew—everyone's a part of it, and I
think the feeling would be very much the same as winning it
on the field. There's really no feeling like it.

"I can honestly say that the World Series money was nice,
but when people see that ring on my finger, that says it all.
They may not know me from Adam's cat, but when they see
that ring . . . Well, there's only one like it in Fayetteville,
and when I show it to someone they never ask me how much
money I got for winning it."

There was a double irony in Koonce's winning a championship with the Mets. Not only was he an emigre from the
team they chased all summer, but in coming to the Mets, he
arrived in the city that he "hated more than any other in the
big leagues."

"I had always told my wife, Peggy, that if I ever got traded
or sold, New York was the one place that I did not want to
go to live. Of course, when we visited New York we were
always downtown. I never got to see the residential areas, but
once we moved there and settled down, I fell in love with it.
We lived in Roslyn Heights, out on Long Island, and out
there it was just like it was back home."

But the most satisfying part of it was beating the Cubs.

"When we were out in Chicago that summer, the Cubs'
wives had already spent their World Series checks," Koonce
recalls. "The guys were very cordial to me, but they thought
they had it in the bag. I kept reading in the papers that Mrs.

So-and-so was going to buy this and Mrs. So-and-so was going to do that, and I looked around and said, 'I think these guys might just be jumping the gun a little.' "

With the season entering the last week of August, the Cubs might have begun to sense by just how much they had jumped the gun. While the Mets were winning nine of ten on their homestand, the Cubs were splitting a pair of four-game series with the Giants and the Astros and losing two of three to the Braves. The nine-and-a-half-game lead that the Cubs held on August 15 had been cut to five; and on Monday, August 25, while the Mets were flying to San Diego for ten games on the Coast, the Cubs were losing to Cincinnati. By the time the Mets landed in California, they trailed Chicago by only four and a half games, and going to San Diego was like going home.

CHAPTER

14

SAN DIEGO WAS THE ONLY
Western Division team not contending for the title. If the
intent of divisional play was to enliven interest with tighter
races, the plan was succeeding beyond all measure in the National League West. A recent winning streak had carried the
Giants into first place. They led Atlanta by half a game, Cincinnati and the Dodgers by one, and Houston by two and a
half. Each day's games produced a new alignment of the teams,
with only the hapless Padres secure in their position. They
remained outside the swirl of excitement, their chief purpose
seemingly to provide the Mets with a ballast to counter the
Houston Astros. For while the Mets had lost their last nine
games to the Astros, they had won their last eight against the
Padres, and in no time at all they made it eleven straight.

On Tuesday, they won a doubleheader, Seaver earning
his eighteenth win with his first complete game in a month
and McAndrew pitching his second straight shutout. On
Wednesday, Koosman won for the sixth time in a row, allowing two hits in the first inning and none for the next eight.
The Met pitching staff was reaching its peak at the season's
most critical point. For added encouragement, the telling hits
continued to be distributed among a wide variety of batters.

In the first game of the doubleheader, Clendenon and Swoboda hit home runs. In the second game, the winning runs were driven home by Weis and Shamsky. The following day, it was Jones and Shamsky who led the attack.

When the Mets completed their business in San Diego, they had seventy-four victories for the season, one more than their record number in 1968. They had won their last six games and twelve of their last thirteen. The Cubs, meanwhile, were losing twice more to Cincinnati and now had lost eight times in their last ten games. Their lead, all in the win column, was down to two. Seven and a half games had been pared from their cushion in less than two weeks, and the Mets were closer than they had been at any time since April.

With thirty-six games left to play over the last five weeks, the National League office made a request of the Mets that could hardly have been contemplated at the start of the season. They were asked to print tickets for the league's first playoff. Of course the same request was made of Chicago, St. Louis, Pittsburgh, Los Angeles, San Francisco, Atlanta, Cincinnati, and Houston, but nonetheless it was an acknowledgment of no small substance. It was official now: the Mets were involved in a pennant race.

On Wednesday, August 27, while the Mets were flying north to San Francisco for the second stop on their road trip, Ferguson Jenkins was halting the Cubs' four-game slide with a five-hitter against the Reds. But even this return to form did not serve to conceal the unrest that was brewing in the Cubs' lair. Durocher was adhering relentlessly to his four-man pitching rotation—using Jenkins, Ken Holtzman, Bill Hands, and Dick Selma on three days' rest—and the pitchers were beginning to show signs of wear. Jenkins had asked for a day off and was denied it. Phil Regan was being given little assistance in the bullpen. He already had appeared in almost half the Cubs' games. Catcher Randy Hundley and the infield of Ernie Banks, Glenn Beckert, Don Kessinger, and Ron

Santo were playing every game, and the rigors of an unre-
lieved daily schedule were magnified in Wrigley Field. Since
the park had no lights, all of the Cubs' home games were
played in the midday heat of a Chicago summer. Hodges, on
the other hand, was using all twenty-five men on his roster,
juggling his lineup, resting his pitchers in a five-man rotation, employing three catchers, and dividing the bullpen chores
among McGraw, Taylor, and occasionally Koonce. Before the
season was over, attrition would prove to be an ally of the
Mets.

In San Francisco, the Mets found that they had other
allies. Some local storeowners—perhaps displaced New
Yorkers or possibly Californians responding to the link, mainly
in the person of Willie Mays, that connected the Giants to
the New York of Polo Grounds vintage—displayed signs in
their windows declaring, "Let's go, Mets." They doubtless
harbored visions of a Mets-Giants pennant playoff, and at
the time it looked to be a reasonable enough parlay. The
Giants had an eight-game winning streak and the Mets had
won their last six, but the Mets' run was halted abruptly.

Juan Marichal shut them out on four hits, and this time
nine innings was all he needed. When Bobby Bonds tagged
Gentry for a three-run homer in the first inning, the game
was effectively over. In his last two appearances against the
Mets, Marichal had allowed just one run in twenty-three innings, and he extended his career record against the New
Yorkers to 22 and 3.

The Mets evened the score the next day in one of those
games of bizarre turnings that had long been their trade-
mark. With the score tied at 2–2, the Giants put a total of
five runners on base in the eighth and ninth innings only to
see two of them thrown out at the plate and another at third
base. In the bottom of the eighth, with the bases loaded and
one out, Jim Davenport hoisted a pop fly near the foul line
in short right field. Boswell drifted back from his second-

base position and caught the ball with his back to the plate, then wheeled and threw home. Ken Henderson, who had no thoughts of trying to tag up and score on the short fly, had gone back to third. But Boswell's throw plunked Wes Westrum, the Giants' first-base coach, in the back and rolled onto the skin of the infield. Now Henderson broke for home. Clendenon chased down the loose ball and whipped it to the plate, where Grote made the tag, absorbed the force of the collision, and held on for the third out of the inning. For Clendenon and Grote, it was a warmup for an even more unorthodox series of events that took place an inning later.

With one out in the bottom of the ninth and the game still tied, Bob Burda singled. McCovey then sliced a drive down the left-field line, an area left unprotected by the Mets' defensive shift. Gaspar, who had been sent into the game for defensive purposes in the eighth inning, retrieved the ball, and Burda chose to test his arm. Gaspar made the throw on a dead line to the plate, and the wily Grote decoyed the runner. He stood idly at the plate as if no play were imminent, until the ball was nearly upon him. Then he snatched Gaspar's throw on the fly and made a lunging tag on Burda for the second out. But then came the strangest turn of all.

Thinking the inning was over, Grote casually rolled the ball back in the direction of the mound. McCovey, who had not attempted to advance on the throw to the plate, lit out for third, and Clendenon found himself in pursuit of a loose ball for the second time in as many innings. He scooped it up in front of the mound and fired to Bobby Pfeil at third in time to get the sliding runner. For Grote, it was an uncharacteristic and momentary lapse.

"The ball had just left my hand," says Grote, "it hadn't hit the ground yet, and I knew there were only two out. I went right out after it, but Clendenon called me off; he was moving in the direction of third, so I stopped and he cut in front of me and made the play. I don't think I ever did anything like that in all the years I played baseball. But Gaspar's throw stunned me. The fact that a person could throw the ball from the left-field corner to home plate in Candlestick Park, at night, with that wind blowing, and *whooosh,* a perfect strike, shocked me so much that I totally forgot there were only two outs."

Gaspar, who picked up his tenth assist of the season on the play, also remembers it clearly.

"McCovey didn't hit the ball hard," he says. "It was kind of a dying quail and I knew it wouldn't roll to the wall. It was cold that night in San Francisco, the grass was wet, and the ball just stuck there. I picked it up bare-handed and said to myself, 'Just get it and throw.' I knew Burda was the winning run, so it was a do-or-die situation, and I just happened to throw a strike."

After Gaspar's strike closed out the ninth with the kind of doubleplay one is not likely to see twice in a lifetime, the Mets promptly won it in the tenth. Clendenon, perhaps weary of chasing stray baseballs around the infield, took matters in hand with two out and drove a Gaylord Perry pitch far over the left-field wall for the winning run.

The next day, a Sunday and the last day of August, the two teams divided a doubleheader. The split of the four-game series did neither of them any good. The Giants, who had won ten of their last twelve games, slipped out of first place behind Cincinnati, and the Mets lost ground to the Cubs, who had rebounded with four straight wins. So when the Mets arrived in Los Angeles on Labor Day, they were four games out of first place; when they left, having lost twice in three days, they trailed by the same five-game margin with which they had started their road trip.

The series with the Dodgers was a particularly trying one for the Mets. It began with a strafing of Koosman, who gave up five runs in the first inning before he could get two men out. The next night, Gentry took a 5−1 lead into the

ninth, but the Dodgers pieced together three runs off him
and Ron Taylor; they had runners on first and third when
McGraw came in to strike out Willie Davis and preserve the
win. Davis got even in the third game, driving a two-out double for the winning run in the ninth. It was a painful loss for
the Mets. They had tied the game at 4–4 in the eighth on
two-run homers by Agee and Clendenon only to see it slip
away an inning later, and they used four pitchers in the process.

Now they were heading home to begin the last segment
of their schedule: twenty-nine games, all against teams in the
Eastern Division. It did not promise to be easy. Early-season
cancellations were being made up in September, and the Mets
were slated to play twenty-five games in twenty consecutive
days. Not for nothing had Hodges spared his pitchers during
the months of summer. But the schedule also conferred its
benedictions. While the Mets opened with four games against
the fifth-place Phillies, the Cubs would be obliged to play their
first three with Pittsburgh, a team on the move with an eye
on third place. So if the Mets could gain some ground over
the weekend, Shea Stadium would crackle with the sounds of
Armageddon on Monday night. For the Cubs were due in
next.

It was Friday, September 5, and before the Mets took
the field for their twi-night doubleheader, the scoreboard told
them that they had already inched a step closer. At Wrigley
Field that afternoon, the Pirates had beaten the Cubs, 9 to 2.
Seaver advanced the Mets another quick step before darkness set in, pitching a tidy five-hitter to become the first Met
ever to win twenty games in a season. However, another fine
effort by McAndrew was wasted in the second game when a
throwing error allowed the Phillies to edge their way to a 4–
2 decision. Still, the Mets had picked up half a game, and the
best was yet to come.

On Saturday, Cardwell and McGraw teamed up for a

three-hit shutout while Pittsburgh was pounding Cub pitching for thirteen runs. The Cubs' lead was down to three and a half games.

On Sunday, the Mets broke open a close game with two runs in the seventh and four in the eighth. Meanwhile, the Cubs were staging a similar comeback in Chicago. They came from two runs behind to pull ahead 5–4 on a home run by Jim Hickman, the former Met, in the eighth. But they held the lead only briefly. Willie Stargell answered with a tying homer in the ninth, and the Pirates scored twice to win it in the eleventh. Now the lead was down to two and a half, and the Cubs were headed for New York.

The showdown between the teams would not, of course, be decisive. They would be playing only two games, and even if the Cubs won them both, there would be time enough for the Mets to make a stretch run. More than twenty games remained to be played, and the season was due to end with another series between the teams in Chicago. If the Mets won both games, the Cubs would still leave town with a tenuous hold on first place. But the tide seemed to be running against the Cubs now.

The Mets had won eighteen of their last twenty-four games. Their pitching staff was well rested, deep, and at the height of its form. Hodges had reached even further down the length of his bench, and everything appeared to be working. In addition to the platoons he had employed since early in the season, he was now splitting second base between Al Weis and Boswell. J. C. Martin often spelled Grote against right-handed pitchers. With Jones nursing a sore right hand, Gaspar had filled in for him during the series with the Phillies, and now Swoboda was to start against the Cubs, with Shamsky moving from right field to left.

The Cubs, by contrast, were a team with few alternatives. As the race tightened and the season shortened, Durocher's already overworked pitchers were working even harder, occasionally pitching on only two days' rest. By the end of the year, Jenkins, Holtzman, and Hands would have started among them the incredible total of 122 games. And the infielders knew they would get no respite. Coming into Shea, the Cubs had lost their last four games and were no doubt eyeing the Mets with the trepidation of the front-runner whose margin is shrinking and who suspects that his legs will no longer carry the load. The burden of their pace now was upon them.

The Cubs had led their division every day since the first week of the season. They had outrun the Cardinals, whose closing rush they had awaited with dread all season long but which now, even if it came, would clearly be too late. Just three weeks earlier, the Cubs owned a lead—almost ten games—that should have been conclusive. Now the lead was nearly gone, and they were being pursued, harried, by a team they had not taken seriously, that they had felt could be intimidated, and that they had been certain would fold. There is nothing more unnerving in sports than the conviction that one is superior to an opponent but is somehow unable to seal his defeat.

For the Mets, no matter what the outcome, the rest of the season would be gravy. They had already gone further than anyone had anticipated. They had won more games than any of their predecessors. They were certain to finish well above the .500 mark that had been their preseason goal. They had managed to hold tight long after the race appeared to be over. No matter what happened now, no one would ever accuse them of folding, of failing to play up to their promise. And there is no more dangerous adversary than one who takes the field with the assurance that he has nothing to lose.

It was Monday, September 8, and in came the Cubs.

CHAPTER

15

IT WAS NO NIGHT FOR BASE-
ball. It was cold for early September, and a fine, wet mist was
in the air. A dense haze gathered around the floodlights,
providing effective cover for the snap of Jerry Koosman's
fastball. Wasting little time between pitches, Koosman got Don
Kessinger to open the game with a weak fly ball and then
struck out Glenn Beckert and Billy Williams.

Bill Hands approached things differently in the bottom
half of the inning. He fired his first pitch directly at the head
of Tommie Agee, who went sprawling backwards and barely
escaped being hit. Two pitches later, just to be certain the
message was received, Hands knocked Agee down again before inducing him to ground out. Then he quickly dispatched Garrett and Clendenon.

Ron Santo, the Cubs' vocal captain and the principal tar-
get in a beanball duel earlier in the season, led off the second, and Koosman's first pitch hit him just below the right
elbow. Santo picked himself up and went to first base. He
said nothing to Koosman. No one made a move from either
dugout. The umpire issued no warnings. Those were somewhat grittier times in baseball, and the players were given
room to settle things among themselves.

In the third inning, Agee responded to Hands's message. With Harrelson on first, he hit a 1-and-0 pitch over the left-center-field wall for his twenty-sixth home run of the season and a 2–0 Mets' lead. The Cubs tied the game in the sixth on successive singles by Kessinger, Beckert, and Williams, and a sacrifice fly by Santo. But Agee took charge again in the home half of the inning. He lined a shot past Santo at third, and with the wet grass slowing the course of the ball, he stretched it into a double. When Garrett followed with a single to right, Agee scored on a rolling slide to the infield side of home, just eluding the tag of Randy Hundley. Koosman allowed nothing the rest of the way. He struck out the side in the ninth, giving him a total of thirteen for the game. The final score was 3 to 2.

Now the Mets trailed by only a game and a half, and what little life was left in the Cubs appeared ready to flee the body. In the Cubs' locker room before the next night's game, Santo, apparently immune to the lessons of the past, summed up his team's position: "Even if we lose tonight," he explained to the press, "we'll still be in first place, and how bad can you feel about that?" It was an observation that raised the image of the Roman emperor Caligula, near death, standing before his mirror and repeating, "I'm still alive, I'm still alive . . ."

Santo, of course, had few partisans among rival players. He had adopted the habit, early in the season, of marking each Cub victory by leaping in the air and clicking his heels together, a ritual that delighted the Bleacher Bums in Wrigley Field but filled opponents with a silent, simmering rage.

"He really pissed us off," says Jim McAndrew. "No one liked Santo. During the course of a season, it's hard to get yourself up for every game, but when it came to playing the Cubs it was easy because of just one man. He planted the adrenalin in us every time we played them. He was a great

competitor, but if I was his teammate I would have been tap-
ing his mouth shut."

On Tuesday night, with the game about to start, an unexpected but clearly visible omen appeared. With Don
Kessinger ready to lead off against Seaver, a black cat emerged
from under the stands. It sprinted to the batter's box, stopped
and stared at the Cubs' batter, then skittered past Glenn
Beckert in the on-deck circle and headed for the visitors'
dugout. There, it raised its furrowed tail, hissed at Durocher,
and then scurried back beneath the stands. The message was
clear.

But for those who might disdain such primitive signals,
the Cubs' manager was furnishing more tangible evidence of
his team's unraveling. Having lost the opener, he chose to go
with Jenkins on two days' rest. It was Holtzman's turn to pitch,
but Durocher was looking ahead to a weekend series with the
Cardinals. If Holtzman pitched against the Mets, his next turn
would come up on Saturday, which was the Jewish holy day
of Rosh Hashanah, and he would be unavailable to work. So
rather than entrust this game to one of his other starters,
Durocher tapped the already arm-weary Jenkins.

Right from the start, it was clear that Jenkins was not
ready to pitch. He walked two of the first three batters he
faced, and Boswell brought them both home with a double.
Two innings later, the Mets added another pair of runs when
Clendenon homered with a man on. Seaver, who had disposed of the first nine Cub batters, was reached for three hits
and a run in the fourth, but that was all. He allowed only two
more hits on the way to his twenty-first win, while the Mets
continued to peck away for three more runs and a 7–1 decision.

In the late innings, with the game secure and the Mets
about to find themselves within two percentage points of first
place, Met fans serenaded Durocher and his Cubs with a
chorus sung to the tune of "Good Night, Ladies." It went:

"Goodbye Leo, goodbye Leo, goodbye Leooo, we hate to see you go." On and on it went that way, and Tug McGraw recalls the emotional high.

"The fans were waving white handkerchiefs," he says, "and without any prompting, they began singing 'Goodbye Leo' in unison, as if Peter Nero were down there conducting. It was unbelievable. That was the same night that the black cat came down on the field and Ron Santo stopped clicking his heels."

Now, the Mets were within reaching distance of first place. They trailed the Cubs by half a game, but that was simply a matter of arithmetic. The Cubs were two games ahead in the win column, but they had lost one game more than the Mets. This meant that the Mets were in unfettered control of their own destiny. To take first place, to win the division title, all they had to do was keep winning; now it was the Cubs who needed help. The Mets' opportunity to take the lead came the very next night, September 10, when the Montreal Expos came in for a twi-night doubleheader. If the Mets swept the two games, the Cubs, whether they won or lost in Philadelphia, would forfeit the hold they had had on first place for the past 154 days.

The chance to climb to the top was entrusted to Jim McAndrew. McAndrew had been pitching exceptionally well for the past month, but he started the game shakily. He yielded leadoff triples in the first two innings, and both runners scored on errors. However, the Mets responded with single runs in the first and fifth, and McAndrew proceeded to pitch nine consecutive shutout innings. He allowed only one more hit, matching pitches with the Expos' Mike Wegener. In the top of the twelfth, Ron Taylor relieved McAndrew and almost lost the game. The four batters he faced all hit him hard. The first two drove the ball at Met fielders for outs, but then Angel Hermoso lined a solid single, and Kevin Collins (who had started the season with the Mets) singled to center. Agee fielded the ball and tried to catch the runner at third, but his throw skipped away, and Hermoso tried to score. Taylor, backing up the play, retrieved the ball and threw to the plate in time to get the out and end the threat. In the bottom of the inning, Bill Stoneman relieved Wegener, who had struck out fifteen Met batters, and with two out the Mets struck. Jones singled, Shamsky walked, and Boswell bounced a single up the middle for the winning run.

With the first game in hand, all eyes turned to the scoreboard, which showed that the Cubs and Phillies were tied 2 – 2 at the end of six. The scoreboard in Philadelphia was also being watched closely. At 8:47 P.M., when the Met win was posted, a roar went up that was followed by the cadenced chant of "Let's go, Mets." The Cubs, who had played before more than fifty thousand the night before, were now performing in front of just four thousand Philadelphians, but they clearly had not escaped the aura of the Mets. It was as if the Mets had become syndicated now, the shared property of fans in every city but Chicago. The Cubs had not won a pennant in twenty-five years, and the Phillies had been without one for nineteen, but it was the Mets who had captured the heart of the nation, and as the 1969 season headed for home, the Cubs would face hostile audiences whenever they were on the road.

At Shea, with the Mets trailing 1 – 0 in the bottom of the third, the scoreboard posted a run for the Phils. The crowd, at the edge of frenzy since the Mets won the opener, was now whooping and cheering without pause as attention shifted from the playing field to the scoreboard and back. No matter where one looked, there was cause for elation. The Mets were romping around the bases in the third inning, six of them scoring, while in Philadelphia, as the scoreboard testified, the Phillies were adding three more runs in the eighth. At 10:13 P.M., the final came in from Philly. The Cubs had lost, 6 to

2. In Shea, strangers embraced and danced in the aisles. The scoreboard flashed the message: "Look Who's No. 1."

It was certain now. Even if the Mets lost the second game, they would hold a percentage-point lead over the Cubs. But Nolan Ryan, holding a five-run lead, had no thoughts of losing. He was on his way to a three-hitter with eleven strike-outs, winning 7–1. The Mets had increased their lead to a full game. They were pulling away. In the clubhouse, there was champagne, thanks to the optimistic foresight of Mc-Graw, Kranepool, Swoboda, and Harrelson. Seaver, ever the pragmatist, had begun to assess the possibilities of the Mets' new, unaccustomed position. "I think being in first place will just make us tougher," he told the press. "I think it will help us." McAndrew, in his quiet, unassuming manner, was nonetheless exultant. He had, after all, been largely responsible for pitching the Mets into first place.

"That was my biggest game of the season," McAndrew says now. "The twenty-three consecutive shutout innings I pitched was more of an achievement, but that game with Montreal is what put us in first place, and that's what stands out for me personally, even though I didn't get the win. Taylor pitched the twelfth, and he was hit hard. He gave up two hits, and he got the last out when he threw a runner out of the plate. Seaver kidded him about it in the clubhouse after the game; he said that the throw to the plate was the only good pitch he made all inning.

"Actually, the whole middle part of the season stands out for me. My arm was live and I was in a good groove. I had what you call a comfortable fastball that was live when I kept it down. When I got it up in the strike zone I got in trouble, because the pitch straightened out and I didn't throw hard enough to just throw it by a hitter. I had a tough time early in the season. I tried to catch a one-hopper back up the middle with my bare hand and bruised the bone in my little finger. I soaked it in a whirlpool and that softened the skin and I developed a blister and was out for six weeks. I was literally unable to throw a baseball for a month, and when I came back I altered my delivery to compensate and injured my shoulder."

Having been forced to sit out much of the early part of the season, McAndrew was reluctant to tell Hodges about the injury to his shoulder. But Duffy Dyer knew about it, and he told the manager.

"Gil called me into his office," McAndrew recalls, "and he said, 'If you have a physical problem, I want to know about it. There's no pennant that's worth your career. I'm managing *you*. It's *you* that I'm responsible for and *you* that I care about.' That's the kind of man Hodges was. He cared about his people; he stood for his players with a total commitment. Gil was a manager of men, not just baseball players. I never realized how fortunate I was to be exposed to a man like that until years later. Ballplayers are basically blue-collar kids and they respect someone who's physical, and Gil was physical. But there was so much more to him than that. He had one set of rules for everyone, but he had the ability to interpret those rules individually. That's an art form as far as I'm concerned. He was a guy you wanted to play for. You respected his ability, his morality, his demeanor. He was able, somehow, to take you aside and talk to you and not say anything point-blank, but when the conversation was over you knew what he wanted of you and you wanted to work harder to achieve it than you did when you entered the room.

"As far as making a mistake was concerned . . . In 1968, shortly after I was called up to the Mets, I was given a start against Houston. I had two strikes on Jimmy Wynn and I threw him a half-speed, hanging curveball, and Wynn hit it out of the ballpark and beat me 1 to 0. I felt crushed. The next day, Gil took me aside and told me, 'Never throw an off-speed pitch in the strike zone to a power hitter with two strikes on him or it will cost you money.' But he didn't tell it to me after the game; he waited until I had settled down a little and could take it in a constructive manner."

McAndrew, who studied psychology at the University of Iowa, never put his training to professional use, but there is a reflectiveness about him that suggests that his major was no idle choice.

"I enjoyed reading that kind of material," he says. "I was undecided what vocation I wanted to pursue, and like all youngsters of that age I was trying to figure out who I was. But I never practiced psychology. I had enough trouble understanding myself, let alone pretending to understand others."

It is a remark that appears typical of McAndrew. Quietly thoughtful and unassuming, he speaks with the measured reserve of a man whose style is derived from the fundamental values of rural America. He was raised on a farm in Lost Nation, Iowa, a town of some five or six hundred people, and he didn't leave the area until he received his degree and began his career in professional baseball.

"Actually, basketball was my first love," says McAndrew, "and I received a scholarship to play both sports at the University of Iowa. But I tore my knees up playing basketball, and I lost my quickness and my cutting ability. After my second year, I concentrated exclusively on baseball."

When McAndrew was picked by the Mets in the eleventh round of the 1965 amateur draft, his first reaction was one of disappointment.

"No one with the Mets had ever spoken to me," he says, "and so I didn't expect to be drafted by them. One of my buddies from college was drafted by Minnesota, and of course the Twins were near the top at that time, and here I was drafted by the lowly Mets. But when I reflected later, I realized that with the Mets I would be given a real opportunity to compete and to travel to another part of the country. Until then, I had never been more than sixty or seventy miles from home."

After a brief visit to the Mets' rookie camp, McAndrew was shipped to Auburn for the balance of the 1965 season and all of 1966.

"I got knocked around pretty hard there," he says. "I was still naive, as far as baseball was concerned. Baseball is a minor sport in the Big Ten, and I never got much in the way of instruction, either there or at Auburn. I was a tall, skinny kid, around six-two, and I weighed only 150 pounds, so they wondered if I was physically strong enough to play the game. But after the 1966 season, I talked them into sending me to the instructional league in St. Petersburg, and there, under Whitey Herzog and Bob Scheffing, I received for the first time what I would call quality instruction. They taught me how to pitch. I had a good year with Williamsport, which was double-A, in '67, and then went to Jacksonville, which was triple-A, in '68. But in spring training that year I reinjured my arm. I had damaged my right elbow in my third year at college, and now it acted up again. I thought my career might be over. But as it turned out, what I had done was to tear the scar tissue that had formed in the elbow, and with the adhesions gone, my arm straightened out. I could extend it a full hundred and eighty degrees for the first time in years, and all of a sudden I went from what they called a cute double-A pitcher to a power pitcher. At Jacksonville, I struck out more than a batter an inning, and the Mets called me up in July of 1968."

McAndrew had a strong half-season with the Mets, though you would not necessarily know it from his record. He managed to lose seven of eleven decisions while allowing just a shade more than two earned runs a game. In the process, he began to acquire some of the discipline that was required of Met pitchers, the ability to work a game without the expectation of bountiful support.

"We knew we weren't going to get many runs to work with," McAndrew says. "In spring training of 1969, Rube Walker told us, 'Just pitch a shutout and pray for a tie.' We all laughed, but in the backs of our minds we felt that we couldn't afford to give up a run because we didn't want to lose. But that feeling helped make us pretty good competitors. Gentry was a great competitor, and I don't think there was any tougher competitor in baseball than Seaver. Of course he had the great arm to go with it and so did Koosman. I think Koosman had the best arm in baseball. Seaver pitched better, but I don't think anybody threw the ball better than Jerry Koosman in 1969. He was awesome at times. His ball was live, and he didn't even look like he was trying, but when he was on, he was scary.

"When you talk about competing, it's hard to say exactly what it takes to win. But you have to be scared enough, disciplined enough, and you have to stay within your ability; you have to know what you can do and what you can't. The whole team was that way, not just the pitchers. There was a good chemistry on that team. We were young and cliquey off the field. There were guys that ran together: Harrelson, Grote, Ryan, and Seaver; Koosman and Taylor; Kranepool, Swoboda, and McGraw. But once we got to the ballpark, we were a team. We had our leaders—Seaver and Clendenon, I guess, were the most vocal. Donn kept you loose. He was a veteran who had his head screwed on straight and he kept things in perspective. 'Clink' could sling it and he could take it too. Swoboda, of course, always had an opinion on everything and—I think he would say it about himself—he often put his foot in his mouth. But I think Ronnie was a great guy. He sounded off a lot, but he never meant any harm toward anyone. He was basically a very caring person, but he was outspoken. There were a lot of different types on the club, but we all pulled together, and Hodges was largely responsible for that."

McAndrew soon will be renewing acquaintances with his former teammates. He is in New York for the Mets' Old Timers' celebration, arriving a few days early from his home in Parker, Colorado, where he works as a regional sales manager for a coal company. It is mid-July and McAndrew is dressed for a New York summer, but even in white dress shorts and a blue sportshirt he effects the look of a man who is never careless about his appearance. There is about him the carriage and precision of a West Point cadet.

McAndrew is looking forward to the reunion. He has been out of baseball for eleven years, and he is eager to recapture the feel of the 1969 season, particularly the month of September, when the Mets were reaching an emotional peak and the Cubs were clearly beginning to buckle under the strain.

"That last month of the season," McAndrew says, "it seemed that the Cubs were more worried about us than what they themselves were doing. Ernie Banks was calling the clubhouse almost every night to find out what we had done, and we were just going out and playing ball. Most of our guys had the inner arrogance to feel that we could win each day. We were young enough and naive enough to go out there and do our thing without worrying about anyone else. We were just having fun and playing ball."

The day after the doubleheader sweep of Montreal, the first-place Mets continued having fun and playing ball in the same manner they had for the past week. Gary Gentry shut out the Expos 4–0, pitching a six-hitter and striking out nine. It was the Mets' seventh straight win, the eighth in their nine-game homestand. Meanwhile, before another sparse crowd in Philadelphia, the Cubs dropped their eighth in a row, blowing a late-inning lead to the Phillies.

The Cubs now trailed the Mets by two games and showed every sign of being a team at the edge of the abyss, ready to answer the call of the deep. On the night they surrendered first place to the Mets, Ken Holtzman saw fit to issue a warning, aimed most specifically at Koosman and Seaver. ". . . they act like they run the league," Holtzman said. "They think they can intimidate our guys. . . . I'll say one thing. If it's close when they come to Chicago, I better not hear anyone popping off. I can speak for Fergie and Hands, too. If they start coming close to our hitters in Chicago, their whole team better watch out."

That same night, when Hodges arrived at his home in Brooklyn, he found a sign hanging on the front door. It read, simply: "No. 1."

PART SEVEN

Late Summer Magic

16

Now, WITH FIRST PLACE FIRMLY in their grasp, the Mets faced the unfamiliar task of trying to hold it. A team accustomed only to pursuit was likely to be unprepared for the hazards of playing on the lead. There is a certain freedom, an abandon of purpose, that comes with making the chase. Having nothing to lose, one can turn a calculated recklessness into easy profit. A team in first place, however, risks a part of its collateral each time it takes the field. Day after day, it must carry the weight of its own expectations.

For the next week, the first-place Mets would defend their division lead on the road. Their first stop was Pittsburgh, where they would play four games over the weekend against the team that was arguably the most powerful in the division at that time. The Pirates had five .300 hitters—Roberto Clemente, Willie Stargell, Matty Alou, Richie Hebner, and Manny Sanguillen—in their starting lineup, and a rookie named Al Oliver who was just a few points under. The Mets, in turn, would be playing without three of their most potent bats. Cleon Jones was nursing a strained rib muscle in his lower back, Ken Boswell was away for the weekend on military duty, and Art Shamsky was sitting out the series in observance of Rosh Hashanah. With four right-handers scheduled to pitch for Pittsburgh and a first-place lead to protect, there was reason for Shamsky to ponder the alternatives.

"I was torn about what to do," he recalls. "I talked to some people about it and got their advice. With Cleon injured, it made the decision even tougher for me. But as much as I wanted to play, I felt it was not worth sacrificing my personal beliefs about what I thought was morally right. I remember sitting in the hotel that night, listening to the games. For me, that was one of the turning points of the season."

It was Friday night, September 12, and what Shamsky heard was the Mets winning both ends of a doubleheader by identical scores of 1 to 0, with the pitcher driving in the only run of each game. In the opener, Koosman pitched a three-hitter for his fourteenth victory, winning his own game with a single to right off Bob Moose in the fifth inning. It was his fourth hit in seventy times at bat that season. In the second game, Don Cardwell, who had not lost in more than a month, pitched eight shutout innings before yielding to McGraw in the ninth. He drove home his run with two out in the second, grounding a single through the left side of the infield off Doc Ellis. Cardwell remembers it clearly.

"My hit was a solid line drive to left," he says with a twinkle in his eye. "Koosy hit this little blooper that just fell in."

"That's not how he remembers it," Cardwell is told.

"What did he say?"

"He said you hit a little grounder that the shortstop couldn't reach, and he lined a shot off the right-field wall, and the only reason he was held to a single was that he stumbled coming out of the batter's box."

Cardwell responds with a good-natured laugh. His wife, Sylvia, laughs too. They are in especially good humor on a weekend visit to New York from their home in Clemmons, North Carolina. The next day, the Mets will celebrate their twenty-fifth anniversary, and the Cardwells are in town to mark the event. We are sitting in a corner on the mezzanine level of the Grand Hyatt Hotel. Cardwell has converted the space into a private interview area by hauling several easy chairs from their original locations and placing them around a small table. At six feet four and somewhat over his playing weight of 210, Cardwell lifts each of the large chairs by their arms and carries them as easily as he might heft the bat with which he got his game-winning hit. He insists that his hit, unlike Koosman's, was no fluke, that he was by far the better hitter. The record bears him out. Cardwell outhit Koosman that year, .049 to .048. But it was his arm, not his bat, that helped carry the Mets during August and September.

"I pitched super ball the second half of the year," he says. "In my last fourteen starts I never gave up more than two runs in a game and we won every one of them. I got the decision only five or six times, but the team won every ballgame."

It was far different from his first half of the year. Cardwell had pitched in the worst of luck early in the season, getting virtually no offensive support. It seemed that any run he allowed cost him the ballgame and that the best he could do with a shutout was no decision.

"There's nothing you can do about that kind of thing," Cardwell says. "You just don't know *what* in the world is happening. A couple of times we'd score a run and the guys would say to me, 'Okay, there's your run, now hold 'em.' Of course I'd been through those kind of streaks before, where you just pitch your heart out and you can't get any runs. But you can't let it get to you. You just have to keep pitching the way you were and wait for your luck to change."

That was the attitude of a veteran who had pitched for both contenders and also-rans during his thirteen years in the big leagues. In point of big-league service, Cardwell was the Mets' elder statesman. He broke in with the Phillies in 1957, when the Giants and the Dodgers were still in New York and the Phillies played their home games in a bandbox called Shibe Park. It was a period that helped prepare him for life with the Mets, for the Phils finished last two of the three seasons he spent with them. He moved up from eighth place to seventh when he was traded to the Cubs in 1960, but he found himself playing for a last-place team again a year after being traded to Pittsburgh, in 1963. However, the Pirates were a team that had taken aim on the future. They moved up a notch in 1964, then leaped to third place the following year, and by 1966 they were a legitimate contender, falling just three games shy of a pennant. That was Cardwell's last season with Pittsburgh.

He was playing golf at a course near his home early in December when the golf pro broke the news to him. "Guess what?" he said. "You've been traded to the Mets." As easy as that, Cardwell slipped from a contender to a ninth-place team, but he didn't mind at all.

"I wasn't used much in Pittsburgh in 1966," he says. "I don't know why, I wasn't pitching badly, but the last part of the season they just stopped using me. Now I knew the Mets needed pitching, and this was an opportunity for me to get back where I started. I was just about to turn thirty-one, and I felt I had some good years left, so I was pleased with the trade. As it turned out, I was the opening-day pitcher."

In 1967, the Mets were embarking upon their youth movement. Each year the pitching staff grew younger, and Cardwell became more of a veteran presence, prized as much for his composure as for his fastball in on the fists.

Jerry Grote, an unquestioned authority on the subject of Met pitching, singles out Cardwell for his settling influence on the rest of the staff. "The other pitchers liked him and they really looked up to him," Grote says. "In his own quiet way, he was a real leader. He'd go up to a guy and put his arm around him if he needed encouragement, or he'd chew his butt out if that's what he needed. He led by example, by going out and doing. 'Hey, boys, we gotta win a damn ballgame. Let me have the ball, let's go.' And he'd go out there and win a ballgame, and I mean big ones. He did the job for us."

Cardwell, however, was not aware of his role as a team leader.

"I never felt like a teacher or a tutor," he says. "But I had been in the league for quite a few years and I didn't get too excited out there, and maybe that helped to settle down some of the younger pitchers.

"There was a big change in attitude on the club between 1967 and 1968. The youngsters who were coming up from the minor league system had a more positive outlook. They had been winning in the minors, and they expected to win in the majors. But Hodges had more to do with that than anyone. The previous management had been too easygoing. Gil was strict; he had rules and you followed them no matter who you were. And with all the kids coming up, he was able to shape the team the way he wanted it. There were just enough veterans around to give the club stability, and by 1969 the chemistry on the team was really great.

"I was more than ten years older than a lot of those kids, but I never felt out of place going to dinner with them on the road. There was always a good feeling among us. There was no animosity between the guys who played every day and the ones who filled in. We were just a close-knit ballclub, on the field and off. I remember only one incident of friction, and I was involved in it. Some of the younger guys used to wear those love beads around their necks, and some of us older guys didn't take to that too much. We were on a flight from L.A. to Houston, and I kind of got on Swoboda's case. He was wearing love beads, and I snatched them off his neck and threw them in the trash can. Then I went back to my seat and strapped myself in. He came up to me and we exchanged some words. I started to take a swing at him, but I forgot I had my seatbelt on, and that was the end of it. Rocky's a good guy, though. He thought I was a southern redneck, and I thought he . . . I thought he was just a Rocky."

Cardwell laughs at the recollection. In his early fifties now, he appears to be somewhat more nostalgic about his playing days than some of his younger teammates. Cardwell retired after the 1970 season, while many of the other Mets still had their best years ahead of them. He followed their careers while working as a fleet manager for an automobile dealer in his native North Carolina. The memories of his time as a player therefore seem much more a part of the past, and he calls them up with that special reverence with which middle age looks back upon youth.

He isolates the moment when he first thought the Mets would win the division title. "We were in San Francisco in the middle of August," he says. "We were still pretty far behind, but we had started to win again after a dry spell. I was out having dinner with Bob Murphy [a Mets' broadcaster], and I said, 'You know, I think we're going to win it.' Bob said, 'Are you kiddin' me?' I said, 'No, I think we're gonna win it.' He said, 'Let me buy you a drink.'

"But I wasn't the only guy on the team who felt that way. When we started to make our move, we didn't think anyone could beat us. Gil would come into the clubhouse before the game and say, 'Let's go, let's go, let's go.' And we'd say, 'Okay, let's go. Here's another one. What's it gonna take to win this one?' We were getting super pitching and we weren't making mistakes. We weren't killing anybody, but we weren't beating ourselves. We made the plays when we had to, we got the base hits when we had to. We were on a roll.

We felt we were gonna win every ballgame when we walked out there. And from that time on, we didn't lose too many."

Indeed, from the start of that road trip, on August 16, to the two 1 – 0 victories over Pittsburgh, on September 12, the Mets won twenty-five of thirty-one ballgames. The next day, Saturday, they made it twenty-six of thirty-two and ten in a row. With Seaver looking for his twenty-second win, they were trailing 1 to 0 in the seventh when they pieced together the tying run on a walk, a single, and a groundout. Then in the eighth, with runners on second and third and one out, Pittsburgh pitcher Chuck Hartenstein elected to walk Clendenon intentionally and pitch to Ron Swoboda, who was batting .239 with only six home runs for the season. Swoboda promptly hit his seventh. With clusters of Met fans chanting "Let's go, Mets," he drove a Hartenstein fastball four hundred feet over the ivy-covered left-field wall in Forbes Field, and the Mets made it three straight over the Pirates.

They were beginning to look unbeatable. Seaver's victory was his seventh in a row, and when Pittsburgh scored in the third inning, it was the first run the Mets had surrendered in thirty-seven innings. Their pitchers had now gone eighteen consecutive games without allowing a home run. The Cubs, who were spending the weekend in St. Louis, not their favorite city, had reason to despair. On Friday night, they had snapped their eight-game losing streak by beating the Cardinals 5 – 1, but they still lost ground to the Mets. On Saturday, Ferguson Jenkins blew a lead in the eighth inning, and the Cubs slipped to three and a half games back. On Sunday, they had a chance to pick up a game when the Mets finally lost one to Pittsburgh, but Bob Gibson outlasted Ken Holtzman 2 – 1 in a tough, ten-inning struggle. The choice of Gibson to start the game on three days' rest instead of his customary four raised some eyebrows among Cub followers. The Cardinal manager, Red Schoendienst, explained that his intent was to give the pitcher a better opportunity to win twenty games, but Gibson was more direct. "If we can't win, I hope the Mets do," he was quoted as saying. "The Cubs . . . ran off at the mouth."

When the weekend was over, the Mets led the Cubs by three and a half games with sixteen left to play. It was not too soon to identify a "magic number." The number was thirteen. Any combination of Met wins and Cub losses totaling thirteen would clinch the division championship. The Mets would try to trim it further in St. Louis. Had Gibson not pitched out of turn, they would have been obliged to deal with him upon arrival. Instead they would face lefty Steve Carlton. Like Gibson, Carlton was on his way to a Hall of Fame career, but he was just getting started. It was only his third full season in the majors. Gibson, on the other hand, had won ninety-five games in the past five seasons and would have twenty more when 1969 was in the books. So the Mets appeared to be getting much the better of it.

Carlton, however, pitched like the last train was leaving. His fastball was swift and live, and his slider flashed with uncommon quickness. He struck out the side in the first two innings. But in the fourth, he walked Clendenon, and Swoboda followed with a home run that put the Mets ahead 2–1. The Cards scored twice off Gentry in the fifth to recapture the lead, and Carlton continued striking out Mets at a record-setting pace. In the sixth, he struck out Swoboda for the second time. But two innings later, again protecting a one-run lead, again with a man on first, and again with a 2–2 count on Swoboda, he fed Ron the same pitch he threw him in the fourth, and it ended up in precisely the same spot, in the left-field mezzanine. The Mets won the game, 4 to 3.

That Carlton struck out the side in the ninth for the fourth time in the game, that he set a new major-league record with nineteen strikeouts, that in doing so he surpassed the likes of Bob Feller and Sandy Koufax—all this only added to the irony. When Feller, Koufax, and the Houston Astros' Don Wilson struck out eighteen batters in a game, they each walked away with a victory. But nineteen strikeouts were not enough for Carlton against a Met team that seemed to have forgotten how to lose. As for Swoboda, he now had hit three home runs and accounted for eight of the Mets' nine runs in their last two victories. Mayo Smith, the manager of the Detroit Tigers, summed it up this way: "Swoboda," he said, "is what happens when a team wins a pennant."

"I had a good last month of the season," Swoboda says, "but the game against Carlton was the high point; it always will be. Here's a man who's still pitching seventeen years later. He was on his way to becoming a great pitcher then, and he was having the best day of his life. I came to bat four times that game, and he had two strikes on me all four times. He got me twice, and I got him twice. But what made it so big was that each home run put us ahead when we were behind a run.

"I knew I was swinging the bat well at the time. Ralph Kiner had been working with me in the batting cage, and I was in a good groove. But what I'm most proud of is that I came through in tough situations. Look at the number of runs I drove in against the number of hits I got [fifty-two RBIs with seventy-seven hits]. I never had consistency as a hitter, and I take responsibility for that. I just couldn't concentrate enough to arrive at a high degree of consistency. I was never smart enough to figure out technique and make adjustments in hitting. But I produced when we had a shot at it. I rose to those occasions somehow. I always had a problem with concentration, but in clutch situations it was not as hard to concentrate."

Swoboda discusses his flaws and his strengths with a studied candor. He imparts the sense that he has given much thought to these matters, that he has looked deeply within himself and fixed upon the need to be totally honest. He is, clearly, a man of complex drives and inclinations. Even as a young ballplayer, he seemed to mix a veneer of boyish innocence with an awareness of life's more profound subtleties. He is no quick study. At age forty-two, he appears to have spent more time than most in trying to resolve the contradictions imbedded in his moods.

It is a brutally hot June morning in Phoenix, Arizona. The temperature is near 110° and rising. In the two days I have spent in Phoenix, Swoboda is the first man I have seen wearing a dress shirt and necktie. When the interview is over, he will go to work at a local television station, where he serves as sports director and does the daily sports segment on the evening news. He is carefully groomed and trim, even leaner than in his playing days, and quite formal on first meeting. It is a meeting I had not planned in advance, for Swoboda had turned down my request for an interview when I called him from New York two months earlier. He had been at first cordially reluctant and then adamant about not meeting with me. But I tried him again when I got to Phoenix, after spending a congenial couple of hours with Gary Gentry, and this time he acceded. "Well, okay," he said, "why not?"

The next day, when we met at my hotel, Swoboda was cooperative, but he still seemed wary.

"I checked you out with Gentry," he told me.

"And I take it he gave me a good recommendation," I suggested.

"He said you were harmless."

Nonetheless, Swoboda appeared to be excessively cautious during the early part of the interview. He was not uneasy. He was, after all, a man grown accustomed to the systole and diastole of question-and-answer. As a player, he had been interviewed hundreds of times. Then, for the past fifteen years or more, he had worked on the other side of the microphone, in the brittle medium of television, in New York, Milwaukee, New Orleans, and now Phoenix. Still, he was tentative. Experience had taught him to guard against the impetuous response.

Looking back, Swoboda speculates that he might have been too quick to sign a professional contract, that his arrival in the major leagues may have been too hurried. He was nineteen years old and just beginning his sophomore year at the University of Maryland when he signed with the Mets in the fall of 1963.

"I had been telling everyone that I was going back to school," Swoboda says, "but Sterling Fowble, a birddog scout for the Mets, said they wanted to make me an offer. He and Wid Matthews, whose claim to fame was signing Stan Musial, came into my living room, and Matthews said, 'We're going to offer you $35,000, and there's no guarantee that this offer will be on the table tomorrow morning.' Now, you have to understand this in context. My mother and father were working people. Between the two of them, I don't think they earned thirteen thousand a year. I looked at them for advice, but they said, 'It's your decision.' Well, I didn't know shit from shinola about negotiating with people. Anyone with any business perspective would have known not to bite for that offer the first time out of the box, but I wasn't insulted by it either. So I jumped at the bait. They offered me a quick trip to the big leagues, which was true, but no kid should be in a hurry to get there. I got there before I was ready."

Swoboda started his career with the Buffalo Bisons at the triple-A level, but he lasted only three weeks.

"My first game," he recalls, "I went 3 for 5 with a home run, and I said, 'This shit's easy.' But the next night Mel Stottlemyre pitched and I struck out four straight times. My career pretty much followed that pattern."

Swoboda was sent down to Williamsport, where he completed the 1964 season, and the next year he was with the Mets. He joined Ed Kranepool and Cleon Jones, as Stengel's

Youth of America began to arrive on the scene. But Swoboda believes he was there on a pass.

"I didn't make the team," he is quick to point out. "I was just there. In those days they had what was called the first-year rule. If you played a full year in the minors and were not retained on the big-league roster or declared the one designated player that could be farmed out and protected, you could be drafted by another team. So I played the whole season with the Mets, but I had no business being in the big leagues. The first guy I batted against was Don Drysdale. It was opening day at Shea Stadium, and Casey sent me up to pinch hit. I didn't want to go up there. I just wanted to watch a big-league game from the bench. I kind of sat back so Casey wouldn't see me. I knew I didn't belong there and, shit, this was Don Drysdale, but he sent me up to hit. The first pitch Drysdale threw me was a fastball that I never saw and took for strike one. Then he threw me a fastball that I never saw and swung at for strike two. Then he threw me this lollipop of a breaking ball, and I hit a line drive to Jim Lefebvre at second base. It felt so good to hit the ball; I felt like a fish that had been dragged into the boat and somehow managed to flop back out."

But after that first appearance, Swoboda began swinging the bat as if each game were another round of batting practice. He hit four home runs in his next fifteen at-bats and had a total of fifteen by the All-Star break.

"I thought I was Superman," he says. "But the problem was that although the technique was there, I had no idea what the technique was. After the All-Star break it was never quite the same, but I didn't know why. No one there taught hitting technique, and I was just lost. The second half of the season was tough. Westrum took over for Stengel, and he didn't understand what his job was. Stengel understood his job: it was to be entertaining, to teach the writers to write funny about a team that was pathetic. Casey was a wonderful guy.

"But despite all the losing, those first few years were great. You were going to all these towns, with all these women ready to jump you, I couldn't believe it. You were not accountable for being proficient as a major leaguer, and you were at that age of innocence that only comes once. Hell, I was in New York, in the big leagues! It was great! But anything you're given without having to earn, you never look at as critically as you should. You just take it and go with it. I probably would have been better off if they had shipped me out after that first year. The big leagues is no place to learn how to play baseball."

Swoboda is speaking more readily now, the formality softened a bit, the chariness gone from his mood. At first I think that he has grown more comfortable with me; then it occurs to me that I have nothing to do with it, that what has happened is that he has shaped the interview in his own mind and is at ease with its content. He is like a man composing a piece at a typewriter: once the form is determined in the early going, the sentences begin to flow more freely. Clearly, Swoboda is one who invests his words with a certain weight. He appears to have that delicate, contradictory writer's sense that one must be prepared to tell everything without revealing too much.

He was, in a way, the quintessential Met. He inspired hopes that could not be achieved, then converted resignation and despair into ecstasies of triumph with feats that were no longer expected.

"No one in his right mind thought we could win it in 1969," he says. "Jerry Grote might say he thought so, but Jerry's prone to saying things like that. If he had that kind of prescience, he should have been in the stock market. Of course he certainly had his hands on a pitching staff. I don't know, maybe being the catcher of that staff he had reason to feel that way. But I certainly didn't think we could win it. I thought we could compete, that we could play with some people, but we had begun to feel that way in 1968. We had a system that was loaded with talent. Whitey Herzog was director of minor league operations, and he is as good a baseball man as there is. It was a good time for Hodges to be there too. That was the most amazing organization for talent I've ever seen except for the Yankee teams of the fifties and early sixties.

"So I wasn't surprised that we were able to compete, but I didn't start thinking pennant until late August, when we began moving on the Cubs and their weaknesses were starting to show. Most of that year I was thinking, 'Isn't this a bitch? We're going to start coming around as a team and we're going to finish second to the Cubs.' But late in the season the Cubs found that they were in a race with a faster horse. I mean we had depth, especially pitching depth, and the Cubs were getting tired. They played all those day games, and they used the same lineup every day. All season long, they were skinny on pitching, especially relief pitching, and they never really had a center fielder. They used that kid Don Young, and when he made a few bad plays Leo got on his case. Leo dragged his ass up there in the first place and threw him in the middle of a pennant race. You don't do that; that's a blueprint for failure. So the Cubs were getting weaker and we were getting stronger because we platooned, and our pitching staff took the pressure off everybody. It was around that time, during the latter part of August, that I first felt we would win it. Things really started happening for us then.

"You know, if you go back and look at the films of that season, you'll see that at almost every juncture where something could have gone our way, it went our way—about ninety-nine percent of the time. It didn't have to go our way, but it did. It wasn't destiny. I don't believe in destiny. What I believe is that you can get to a state where you are not interfering with the possibilities. We had no preconceptions. We had the innocence of someone who had never been there before. Hell, what did we have to lose? We had no thoughts of what happens if we don't get there. We were ingenues. We had that wonderful, clear-minded innocence of not having the responsibility of winning it, of not having to doubt ourselves if we stumbled, and that's a marvelous state to achieve. The trick in this whole world is to get to that point where you retain the same clarity of thought after you get there, after you've been through all the struggles; to control your emotions so that you can let the machine work for you. That was the state we achieved that year, and I was delighted to be part of it.

"New York and the New York fans were really great. They booed you sometimes, they booed me when I struck out five times against St. Louis, but they were never cruel. I related to them. I never felt above anyone who bought a ticket; I just had a different role than they did, but we were part of the same phenomenon. By 1969, they had earned the right to call themselves fans. I remember when they were there in 1965, and they sure as shit weren't seeing anything that resembled baseball. I mean, they should have put a disclaimer on the ticket to the effect that any resemblance to major league baseball was purely coincidental. But the fans came. There was something emotional there, some bonding, and I felt close to it. I felt fortunate to be a part of that transition from outhouse to penthouse."

That transition was now nearly complete. While Swoboda was taking the measure of Steve Carlton, the Cubs were being beaten by the Expos. They now had lost eleven of their last twelve games and trailed the Mets by four and a half.

With fifteen games left to play, the magic number stood at eleven. The following day, the Mets were rained out in St. Louis and the Cubs edged Montreal, 5 to 4. It didn't seem to matter.

CHAPTER

17

ON TUESDAY, SEPTEMBER 16, the Mets flew into Montreal. Exactly one month earlier they had arrived in San Diego with the look of a team that had left its season behind. They were in third place, nine and a half games in back of the Cubs. In the next thirty-one days they had made up fourteen games in the standings. Now they marched into Montreal as though they had the rest of the division by the throat and were going to shake until the neck snapped.

They were still the Mets, however. When they arrived at Jarry Park on Wednesday they discovered that they were without an essential piece of equipment. Their bats had been left on the chartered flight from St. Louis and wound up in Newark, New Jersey. So they started their game with the Expos using a reserve supply that was carried for emergencies. The stray bats, meanwhile, were airlifted from Newark to JFK Airport in New York and then to Montreal, rushed to the ballpark, and uncrated in the fourth inning. The Mets put them to good use immediately, scoring three quick runs off Gary Waslewski.

The Expos performed as if they had no bats at all, for they failed to score a run during the two-game series. Koosman pitched his second straight shutout for his fifteenth win of the season on Wednesday, and Seaver won his twenty-third game on Thursday. It was his eighth in a row, his sixth shutout and sixteenth complete game of the season. He and Koosman had now won fourteen of their last fifteen starts. Over the course of the year, the Met pitching staff had thrown twenty-four shutouts and forty-five complete games. They had not allowed a home run in their last twenty-two games, covering 207 innings. The team had won thirteen of its last fourteen and twenty-nine of its last thirty-six.

The Met bandwagon was rolling, and it was picking up an assortment of new passengers along the way. New York Mayor John V. Lindsay, a casual fan at best, had begun making visits to the Met clubhouse. He had been an unfamiliar figure at Shea during most of his four-year term, but now he was involved in a bitter (some thought hopeless) campaign for reelection, and perhaps he thought that a touch of Met magic might be contagious. U.S. Senator Jacob Javits dispatched a telegram describing the Mets as "a living symbol of the fact that success is within the grasp of the fighting underdog in New York City." City Council President Francis X. Smith credited the team with keeping New York peaceful during a summer of riot and conflict in other metropolitan centers. "The excitement generated by the Mets has kept the city cool," he said. Baseball Commissioner Bowie Kuhn, who attended the two games in Montreal, noted, "Everywhere I go, from coast to coast, the Mets have captured the people's interest. It's rising to a crescendo right now. Even the Customs men asked me, 'How about those Mets?'"

Those Mets returned to Shea Stadium Friday night to play five games over the weekend with the Pittsburgh Pirates. They were greeted by a crowd of 51,885, which established a season record for attendance. They were also greeted by a Pittsburgh power assault that scored eight runs in each game while sweeping a doubleheader. In the fourth inning of the second game, Willie Stargell sent a Jim McAndrew pitch deep into the right-field seats for the first home run off Met pitching in 221 innings.

No sooner had the second game ended than speculation began about whether the Mets were beginning to feel the pressure. Tom Seaver scoffed at the notion. "The game has never been so much fun," he said. "Where is the pressure? I don't know. How does pressure manifest itself? Maybe we're too inexperienced at winning in the major leagues to know what pressure is. Maybe this is pressure and we're mistaking it for excitement."

Bob Moose, a right-handed pitcher for Pittsburgh, believed it was pressure. "I think they must be a little nervous," he said. "They say they don't feel the pressure, but you can't help feel it some. . . . They were never in a pennant race before. They have to feel it."

Moose, a twenty-two-year-old youngster in only his second full major league season, had had little opportunity to learn about pressure, but he gave his viewpoint added weight on Saturday when he beat the Mets with a no-hitter. It was their third loss in just over twenty-four hours. But it did little harm to their cause, for during that same period the Cubs were losing two of three to the Cardinals. The magic number was down to six. The next day the Mets cut it to four, winning both ends of a Sunday doubleheader behind Koosman and Cardwell, who were becoming a formidable entry. It was nine days since they had parlayed a pair of 1–0 victories against the Pirates in Pittsburgh. For Cardwell, it was the one hundredth win of his career; a plaque commemorating the game still hangs above the bar in his den.

"Seaver was going to pitch the next day," Cardwell says, "and so he kept the chart of the game, keeping a record of all my pitches and what each batter did. Well, the only run I gave up was a home run to Stargell, and I mean he really tattooed it. If the wind wasn't blowing in, it would have cleared the scoreboard. Now Seaver, instead of drawing the line in Stargell's block on the chart, he drew the line across three blocks. The guys made the chart into a big plaque and presented it to me, and now when people come to the house they look at it and say, 'What's this big old line over here?' And I say, 'Well, Stargell hit one off me . . .' "

There were no long lines on the pitching chart the next day, as Seaver crafted a neat four-hitter to beat the Cardinals, 3 to 1. He walked no one, faced only thirty-one batters, and picked up his twenty-fourth win of the season. The magic number was now three. The race was over. The only question remaining was whether the Mets would clinch the division title at home or on the road. The two games to be played with the Cardinals, on Tuesday and Wednesday, were the last scheduled for Shea Stadium. If they won them both and the Cubs lost at least one of their two games with the Expos, the Mets would take to the road as division champions.

The Cubs cooperated, dropping Tuesday afternoon's game 7–3. When the Mets took the field that night, the magic number was two. Eleven innings later it was one. They edged Bob Gibson 3–2, with four shutout innings of relief from McGraw; a diving, tumbling, game-saving catch by Swoboda with the bases loaded in the top of the eighth; a score-tying single by Shamsky in the bottom of the eighth; and singles by Swoboda, Grote, and Harrelson in the eleventh. The Mets had clinched at least a tie.

A year earlier, to the day, they had clinched ninth place in Atlanta while Hodges was suffering a heart attack in the Met dugout. Now Hodges found a telegram waiting for him on his desk in the manager's office. It was from Dr. Linton H. Bishop, Jr., the Atlanta cardiologist who had treated him and had recommended that Hodges resume his activities in baseball. It read: "Happy to see you're No. 1. Hope your team does as well as your heart."

In the Met clubhouse, the team's travel itinerary for the

rest of the season was pinned to the bulletin board. It read this way: "New York to Philadelphia to New York (for the Mayor's Trophy game with the Yankees) to Chicago to Paradise." The final notation on the timetable indicated that the Mets would leave Chicago at 6:30 P.M. on Thursday, October 2, aboard a chartered flight. It concluded: "Destination Paradise—Site Unknown."

The first stop in Paradise would be a Western Division city. Atlanta had just squeezed by the Giants into first place. Cincinnati was three games behind. The Dodgers and Astros had slipped out of contention. But the Braves, in the midst of a ten-game winning streak, were the team with momentum. The Mets, for their part, were looking for their fifth straight win and their ninety-sixth of the season as they prepared to go for the clincher. The Cubs had clung to life by beating the Expos that afternoon. If they had lost, the Mets would have taken the field as champions. Now they had the opportunity to win it for themselves. It was Wednesday, September 24, and those with a feel for the moment could hear a new page turning.

The final home game of the season was traditionally Fan Appreciation Night at Shea. A key-chain bearing the Met logo was presented to each person entering the ballpark. On this night there were 54,928 of them, and not all of them had reached their seats when the Mets presented them with another gift. They scored five runs their first time up against Steve Carlton. Harrelson led off by looping a single to right. Agee walked. Jones, starting for the first time in almost two weeks, received a standing ovation before striking out. But Clendenon, batting cleanup, lined Carlton's next pitch 410 feet over the center-field wall for a three-run lead. Then Swoboda walked and Ed Charles drove his third home run of the year over the 396-foot sign in right-center. And that was all for Carlton, who had struck out nineteen Mets the last time he faced them. Dave Giusti replaced him and main-

tained order until the fifth, when Clendenon homered again
to stretch the lead to 6–0.

That was far more than Gary Gentry needed. He yielded
singles to Lou Brock in the fourth and Mike Shannon in the
fifth and was working on a two-hit shutout when the Cardinals came to bat in the ninth. With the crowd on its feet and
cheering every pitch, Brock and Vic Davilillo opened the inning with successive singles. Gentry struck out Vada Pinson.
The next batter was Joe Torre, the man the Mets had cov-
eted at the start of the season, whose niche had finally been
filled by Clendenon. The clock on the scoreboard read 9:07.
The game was barely two hours old. In less than four sec-
onds it would be over. Torre hit a sharp grounder to shortstop, a routine double-play ball. Harrelson fielded it and
flipped to Weis, who made a perfect relay to first. Torre was
out by plenty. It was over. Then came the deluge.

They came pouring over the walls and through the gates
like inmates sprung in a jailbreak. In one sudden burst, they
swept across the field in delirious celebration, snatching at
whatever would yield itself. The bases were torn loose, home
plate and the pitcher's slab were dug out of the dirt, slats
were ripped from the outfield fence, chunks of sod were
gouged from the field. Some fans scaled the walls and just
sat there, watching the scene unfold, while others remained
in the stands, bearing witness, it might be said, to an event
without precedent. The lid was being lifted from seven years
of unblinking frustration. Seven seasons of derision and scorn,
of failures beyond counting, were now dissolving in one un-
stinting tide of emotion. The need was to preserve the moment, to freeze it forever as a relic that was immune to the
slippage of time. What might justly have been termed van-
dalism on other occasions was here a quest for nothing less
than a totem of myth being shaped at its source.

Little heed was paid to personal safety. The first-aid room
at Shea was filled with casualties of the celebration waiting to

be treated for assorted injuries, not all of them minor. One teenager tried to scale the scoreboard and broke both legs when he fell twenty-five feet and landed outside the outfield fence. Six others suffered broken bones. The field itself did not fare much better. Gaping holes were left in the turf, where more than a thousand square feet of sod was ripped out. The wheels and the netting were taken from the batting cage. Pieces were hacked from the scoreboard. The matting was torn from the coaches' boxes. The pitcher's mound would have to be rebuilt. Only first base was left, somehow, intact.

After half an hour, the stadium lights dimmed and the parking lot became the focal point of a residual celebration. The exits leading out to the network of highways around the stadium were clogged with autos inching forward by increments. Pennants waved from the windows of cars. Huge, orange-colored plastic bugles that emitted the sound of foghorns echoed through the darkness. The chant of "We're number one" was set in counterpoint by the cadence of automobile horns—*beep-beep-ba-beep*, "We're number one"—all through the parking lot and out, finally, onto the Grand Central Parkway.

Inside the Met clubhouse, the scene was barely more restrained. Five cases of champagne were emptied quickly, with only small amounts of it used as intended. Seaver, standing atop a table in the middle of the room, poured a full bottle over the head of Gil Hodges while the manager was being interviewed for television by Ralph Kiner. Hodges was undaunted. "They're a great bunch of boys," he told the press. "They showed confidence, maturity, togetherness, and pitching. They proved it could be done." M. Donald Grant, the usually stolid chairman of the board, joined in the frolics. "Our team finally caught up with our fans," he said. "Our fans were winners long ago." Gary Gentry, whose four-hit shutout had triggered the revel, was reminded that his pregame wish had been answered by his teammates. "I hope it's an easy game," he had said, "that we get a lot of runs early." But even the five-run lead had not served to relax him completely. "I was nervous for the first four or five innings," he said after the game. "Then I was just more or less in a hurry to get the game over with so that everyone could enjoy what was happening."

Gentry also sensed that he was being given a rare opportunity to complete a game, something he had done only six times during the season. It was a circumstance that troubled him then and that, many years later, continues to rankle.

"I felt I was a victim of the relief syndrome," he says now. "Before I got to the majors, I was used to finishing my games, and I pitched with that in mind. My whole career, I felt if I could get past the first few innings I could complete the ballgame. But with the Mets, except for Seaver, you weren't allowed to pitch the last two, three innings unless you had a big lead. And most of our games were close. That's why I had so few decisions that year. Seaver and I each started thirty-five games, but he had thirty-two decisions and I had only twenty-five. It's hard to get the decision if you're not around at the end.

"When I negotiated my contracts in future seasons, I never talked won-and-lost record or ERA. I would say that I started so-many games and I lost so-many games; that means I did my job in the others. You can't control what happens when you come out of a game with the score tied. If you look at the record, you'll find there were not too many games that year in which I didn't pitch well. But the relief syndrome had taken over baseball in the sixties. The starting pitcher was just expected to get you to the seventh or eighth inning and keep you in the ballgame. Before that, if you started a game you were expected to complete it. That was my style of baseball. I always felt that I got to the majors ten years too late."

It is easy to believe that Gentry is earnest in his assessment. His direct, measured responses instill in the listener a sense that he will say what he thinks regardless of consequence. We are having a drink in a hotel bar in downtown Phoenix. Gentry has taken time from his job as a real estate developer to meet with me. It was not difficult to pick him out from among a group of unfamiliar faces in the lobby. Not quite forty years old, he looks like he might still be playing ball. At perhaps a shade over six feet, he is lean and wiry, and he walks with the easy, certain gait of the marshal whose presence brings order to a small town in the Old West. A full mustache, added since his playing days, reinforces the image. Gentry exudes the same quiet confidence he displayed as a rookie in 1969.

"There was no question in my mind that spring that I would make the starting rotation," he says. "They had Seaver and Koosman, and I think McAndrew had been brought up during the '68 season, but the Mets used a five-man rotation, and I had no doubt I could break into it. As it turned out, I became the number-three starter."

Gentry's self-assurance had been nourished throughout his baseball career, as an amateur and as a pro.

"I never played on a team that didn't expect to win," he says, "so what happened in 1969 was a natural transition for me. I was accustomed to winning. In 1965, in junior college, we won the national championship; in '66, we got there again but lost in the finals; in '67, at Arizona State, we won the NCAA championship; that same year I spent the last two months of the season with Williamsport and we won the league title; and in '68, when I was with Jacksonville, we won the championship there too. So when I came up with the Mets in '69, I never thought about anything except winning. I didn't know that much about the team's history. I just knew that I was going to pitch in the big leagues, and I expected to win.

"When I got to the Mets, I found that major league baseball was exactly what I expected it to be," he says. "Rookies were rookies then. You ate last, you fetched beer for the veterans, things like that. It's different now; even in my later years it was different. Now, rookies feel that you owe them a living. It wasn't like that then. There was a good attitude on the Mets when I got there. We had a good mix of people, old and young, and we were all very much into playing baseball. We knew we had to play together to win, and we hung together both on the field and off.

"Hodges had a lot to do with that. He was a wonderful guy to play for but a tough guy to get to know. I got to know him pretty well, because we had similar personalities. One of his traits was his silence. He didn't miss anything, and I mean *anything*, but he didn't come right out and talk to you unless he had something he wanted you to know. He could just look at you and you'd know something was wrong; he never had to tell you. When he came to tell you something, you knew it was pretty serious. He wasn't very open, but he knew what he wanted, and he kept the team working together.

"The pitchers were especially close. My locker was between Seaver's and Koosman's, and we helped one another and learned from watching each other. You can sometimes learn more by watching than by asking questions. I learned a lot from Seaver about preparing mentally for a game. He understood a lot about the psychology of pitching. He was able to get away with making a number of bad pitches in a game because the batters were never expecting him to make a mistake. They would go up to the plate thinking Seaver wouldn't give them a good pitch to hit. If they got a good pitch, they thought they would never see another one, and they weren't ready when it came. After I was traded to Atlanta, I told the hitters that Seaver would eventually give them a good pitch to hit if they were patient, but they wouldn't believe me."

Gentry was traded to Atlanta at the end of the 1972 season. At the time, he found the prospect of a change agreeable. It was an opportunity to rejuvenate a career that had begun to stagnate. He was still only twenty-six years old.

"Actually, I felt pretty good about it," he says. "I was going to a team with a lot of hitters, and I was probably going to be their number-one starter. Besides, I was a little irked with the way the Mets had handled me. I had hurt my arm in 1970, but I didn't know how serious it was. I was getting shots and taking pills to ease the pain, and I asked the Mets to send me to a specialist but they refused. I missed part of the season, then had a pretty good year in '71, but '72 was a disaster. There was still something wrong with my arm.

"When I was traded to Atlanta, I got a call welcoming me to the team, and they didn't even know I was hurt. But I had a great spring and started the season well. Then, two months into the season, I couldn't throw the ball. They sent me to all the good doctors, and when they got my original X-rays from New York they found a bone chip in the elbow. For three years it had been grinding away in there, and all the vacant spots were filling up with pieces of bone. The doctor told me that if I had had a fifteen-minute operation in 1970, all I would have needed was a three-week recovery period and I probably would have been all right. Now they said they were going to perform the same operation, but they couldn't be sure of the results. So I missed the rest of that season. In '74 I came back and had another good spring, but a month into the season I couldn't throw again. This time I needed a two-hour operation, and that was the end of the season for me.

"The next year I felt like Superman, but I never really got a chance to pitch. They had developed a set rotation without me, and at the end of spring training they said they thought it would be better for me to work out of the bullpen for a while. I told them it didn't make sense, that coming off an arm operation it's better to pitch on a regular schedule. But the manager, Clyde King, who had already proven that he couldn't manage in the big leagues, and the pitching coach, Herm Starrette, insisted on using me in relief. I had a couple of good outings, and then one bad one when I was brought in in a mop-up situation after throwing five warmup pitches, and the next day I was released. Eddie Robinson, the general manager, called me into his office and said, 'It looks like your arm still hurts.' I said, 'I don't have any pain in my arm,' but he said, 'We're going to release you and give some of our younger guys a chance.' Younger guys? I was twenty-eight!

"So I went back home and did probably the most foolish thing I've ever done; I did nothing. I didn't work out, I just did nothing. About a month later, I got a call from Rube Walker. He said the Mets could use another starting pitcher. He said, 'Go to Jackson, Mississippi, and show that you can pitch and we'll bring you right up.' But I hadn't thrown a ball in a month and I tried to rush it. I threw about a hundred pitches warming up for my first start and I felt fine. But the second pitch I threw in the game, I heard a rip and I knew I tore something in the arm. I tried another pitch and I heard the rip again, and that was it. I went to the doctor and he looked at my arm and said, 'You tore this muscle, and you tore this muscle, and you broke this bone. How did you do that?' I said, 'Throwing a baseball.' He said, 'I've never seen anything like that.' And I never pitched again. I went home to Phoenix and started learning the real estate business from the bottom up."

Gentry's foreshortened career, in which he won only forty-six games over four full seasons and three fragments, was nonetheless studded with moments of brilliance. Almost twenty percent of his victories were shutouts, and an unusually large number of them seemed to come in critical games. His won-and-lost record, however, was never better than one game over .500. His six-hit shutout in the clincher, which brought him even at 12 and 12, was of course his biggest win of the '69 season, and the efforts to commemorate it were immediate and diverse.

The following day, Mayor Lindsay proclaimed the week of September 28, the last of the regular season, as New York Mets Week. City Council President Smith went Lindsay one step better. He introduced a resolution that would make all of October "Mets Month."

The poet Ogden Nash composed a verse for the occasion that placed the Mets' triumph in historical perspective. It appeared in *The New York Times* under the unassuming title, "A Poem." It read:

> Whenst camest thou, Mrs. Payson, dear?
> Out of the nowhere into the here.
> At last thy patient loyal clients
> Can forget the Dodgers and the Giants.
> Then what about O'Malley & Stoneham?
> *De mortuis nihil nisi bonum.*

PART EIGHT

Pennant

C H A P T E R

18

LOSERS ARE RARELY REMEM-
bered. Only champions remain engraved in memory. Run-
ners-up are sometimes recalled, either for the gallantry of
their effort or for the unexpected ease with which they succumbed. All others fade into an undefined mass, no matter
how great the merit of their quest. It has always been that
way, and no degree of tampering with the system has changed
it. During the sixties, basketball and football introduced increasingly complex playoff structures to determine their
champions. Four teams, eight, as many as sixteen teams qual-
ified to compete for a league championship. But only the fi-
nalists were ever touched by glory. Divisional winners were
forgotten as quickly as yesterday's lunch.

Now, in 1969, baseball was pioneering its own, restrained version of playoff competition. The teams had played
a 162-game tournament to select the four that would vie for
the National and American League pennants. There was room,
therefore, to wonder just how much importance history would
invest in divisional championships. What measure of respect
had the Mets earned with their season-long heroics? They
had not, after all, won a pennant. They had outdistanced
only half the teams in the National League. If they failed

to win the best-of-five pennant playoff, would the future still honor their triumph? The leagues, at that time, had devised no plan for recognizing a division title. Officially, it would seem, the Mets had not won anything of lasting significance.

But the last week of September was no time to muse upon such abstract considerations. The Mets still had five games to play in the regular season—three in Philadelphia and two in Chicago—and those games would be used to prepare the team, particularly the pitching rotation, for its Western Division opponent. Three teams were still in the running in the West, but Atlanta had begun to open ground with a late-season rush. First Cincinnati fell from contention; then, three days before the season's end, the Giants were eliminated. The Braves wrapped up their division title by winning seventeen of twenty games, the last ten in a row.

The Mets, meanwhile, took a five-game winning streak into Philadelphia and ran it to eight straight with three successive shutouts. Koosman opened with a four-hitter; then Seaver allowed only three; and in the third game Gentry, Ryan, and Taylor yielded a total of four. Hodges had elected to use his bullpen in that game only because the relief corps had been on a virtual sabbatical for the better part of a week. When they finished in Philadelphia, Met pitchers had not allowed a run in forty-two consecutive innings. The team had won thirty-six of its last forty-six games, fifteen of them by shutout.

On Wednesday, October 1, the Mets moved into Chicago for the last two games of the season. The series that both teams had looked to as critical just a few weeks earlier now held as little drama as a pair of preseason warmups. Ken Holtzman pitched the first game for the Cubs, but there was no beanball duel this time. The teams played a passive twelve innings, with the Mets finally winning 6–5. It was their one hundredth victory of the season and their ninth in a row.

When they lost to the Cubs the next day, it was of little consequence.

The Mets had ended their season with a record of 100–62, a twenty-seven-game improvement over 1968. Since August 15, when they trailed the Cubs by nine and a half games, they had won thirty-eight and lost eleven. They had gained seventeen and a half games in the standings in little more than six weeks and finished a full eight lengths ahead of the Cubs. Now they were on their way to Atlanta.

At the start of the season, the Braves were almost as prohibitive a long shot as the Mets. They had been, after all, no better than a .500 team in 1968, finishing in fifth place, sixteen games behind the Cardinals and only eight games ahead of the Mets. In '69, however, they survived a season-long tug-of-war in the West with the same kind of surge that had carried the Mets to the top. On August 19, just three days after the Mets stirred to wakefulness, the Braves were in fifth place in their division. But they won twenty-seven of their next thirty-seven games and swept past the other four contenders. They finished the season with ninety-three victories, good enough for a three-game margin over the Giants and four games over the Reds. What the Mets had done with pitching, the Braves had achieved with power. That, anyway, was the story line that had been adopted for the league's first pennant playoff. But the contrast between the two teams was not as sharp as some had drawn it.

Atlanta's pitching was far more than adequate. Phil Niekro had won twenty-three games with his knuckleball, while Ron Reed, the towering right-hander, had won eighteen. For the Mets, Seaver had twenty-five victories and Koosman seventeen. Pat Jarvis and Gary Gentry, who would match up in the third game, each had thirteen wins. The fourth and fifth starters for the Braves, George Stone and Milt Pappas, had combined for five more victories than Cardwell and McAndrew. The biggest difference was in the bullpen, where

Cecil Upshaw was the Braves' only reliable reliever, recording twenty-seven of the team's thirty-two saves. The Mets' saves,
by contrast, were distributed among Taylor with thirteen,
McGraw with twelve, and Koonce with seven.

As for power, the Braves had hit thirty-two more home
runs than the Mets, but most of that difference was provided
by Hank Aaron, whose forty-four homers were only one short
of Willie McCovey's league-leading total. The rest of the Braves'
power came chiefly from Orlando Cepeda, the first baseman, and Rico Carty, recently recovered from tuberculosis,
who had been sharing outfield time with Tony Gonzalez and
Felipe Alou. The infield of Felix Millan at second, Sonny
Jackson at short, and Clete Boyer at third contributed more
to defense than to run production; and the starting catcher,
Bob Didier, had failed to hit a home run in 352 times at bat.

Direct comparisons, however, could not be as readily
trusted in 1969 as in previous seasons. Since the teams played
in separate divisions, their schedules were far from identical.
An examination of their head-to-head meetings might prove
more instructive than seasonal records, and here the Mets
had the clear edge. They had beaten the Braves eight of twelve
times, winning four at home and four in Atlanta. Perhaps
even more revealing was the fact that the Mets had won six
of the last seven games between the teams, and two of the
last three were by shutouts. But the professional handi-
cappers were not impressed. They installed the Braves as 11−
10 favorites, or even−6 in the argot of the betting parlors.

The format of the playoffs dictated that the first two
games would be played in Atlanta and as many of the next
three as would be necessary in New York. All of the games
were scheduled to be played in daylight, beginning on October 4. The starting pitchers, to no one's surprise, were Phil
Niekro and Tom Seaver. They made for an interesting contrast. Niekro, who was thirty years old and in his sixth major
league season, relied almost exclusively on a knuckleball that

fluttered and darted towards the plate on a trajectory as unpredictable as a football thrown end over end. Seaver, who was not yet twenty-five, was the incarnation of the power pitcher, his fastball propelled at better than ninety miles an hour from a compact motion driven so hard by his right leg that his knee brushed the dirt of the mound after every pitch. The only trait they shared, it would be discovered, was a gift for longevity. Sixteen years later, in 1985, each would win his three hundredth game, and eighteen years later, Niekro would still be pitching in the big leagues. But in 1969, the statistic that interested observers most was the record each pitcher had posted against the opposing team. Seaver was 3–0 against the Braves, while Niekro was 0–3 against the Mets.

Neither was very effective in the first playoff game in National League history. It was a game that belonged to the hitters, each team taking its turn on the lead. The Mets opened the scoring in the second when Shamsky led off with a single to right, Boswell walked on four pitches, and Grote lined an opposite-field hit to score a run. Harrelson struck out, but the third strike eluded Bob Didier, the Braves' twenty-year-old rookie catcher, and Boswell brought home the second run of the inning.

Seaver, however, was unable to protect the lead. In the home half of the second, Rico Carty hit a long double, went to third when Boswell was unable to handle Cepeda's grounder, and scored on Clete Boyer's sacrifice fly to the left-field wall. In the next inning, Atlanta took a 3–2 lead on successive doubles by Felix Millan, Tony Gonzalez, and Hank Aaron. In the fourth, it was the Mets' turn again. With two out, Kranepool singled off Millan's glove, Grote walked, and Harrelson bounced a triple that split the distance between Cepeda's glove and the first-base line.

The game had effected a give-and-take pattern now. In the fifth, the lead was erased for the third time in as many innings when Gonzalez homered deep into the right-field seats to tie the score at 4–4. Two innings later, Hank Aaron, who had hit five home runs in twelve regular-season games against the Mets, made it an even half-dozen, and the Braves were back in front. But not for long.

The Mets, who contended that they never felt they were out of a ballgame, now showed why. In the top of the eighth, Garrett doubled inside the third-base line, and Jones looped a single to left to bring the Mets even for the third time. Shamsky singled for his third hit of the game. Then came the first of three plays that tilted the game in the Mets' favor. Boswell, trying to move the runners up, missed a bunt attempt and Didier fired the ball to second. But Jones, who appeared to be picked off, never looked back and cruised easily into third before a play could be made. After Boswell bounced into a forceout, with Jones holding at third, the Braves committed their second misplay of the inning. Kranepool grounded to Cepeda, whose throw to the plate had Jones beaten by a wide margin, but the ball kicked into the dirt and rolled past Didier, and the Mets edged back in front 6–5. Grote advanced both runners with a ground ball, and Harrelson was walked intentionally to load the bases and bring Seaver to bat. Hodges, however, had anticipated the situation and had Taylor warming up in the bullpen. J. C. Martin, the ten-year veteran catcher, batted for Seaver and lined a clean single to center. Now came the inning's third pivotal play. Gonzalez charged the ball hard, hoping to make a play at the plate, but the ball got by him. It rolled to the wall while all three runners scored, and the Mets handed Taylor a 9–5 lead which he safeguarded for the last two innings. For Martin, it was perhaps his most critical hit of the season—but not his only one, as he is quick to point out.

"I had a number of big hits that season," Martin recalls, "and some of them won important ballgames. I remember hitting a home run off Fergie Jenkins that helped beat the

Cubs right here in Chicago. That was fairly early in the season, but it was a big win for us at the time. Not many people remember it because we weren't considered a real contender then."

Martin himself did not think of the Mets as a legitimate contender until much later in the year.

"Around the middle of the summer," he says, "I asked Al Weis if he wanted to go to the World Series in Chicago. We were roommates and we both lived in the Chicago area. We were nine, nine and a half games back then, and I thought the Cubs were going to win it. Al said, 'Sure, let's go.' So we made arrangements with some of the Cub players to get tickets for the Series."

Martin smiles now when he considers the turn of events that made him a participant in the Series rather than a spectator. He still resides in Wheaton, a Chicago suburb, where he has worked in the construction business and in a local nursery since retiring from baseball in 1972. It is a warm night in early summer. Outside, a clock with a baritone register tolls nine times. Martin is a big, affable man with hands that seem large and strong enough to squeeze the pulp out of a baseball. He has waited at home for me patiently and with good humor as I made my way along unfamiliar roads from Weis's house in nearby Elmhurst. When Weis phoned to tell him I would be a bit late, the two former roommates had made plans to fly to New York together for the Old Timers' celebration the following month. They have remained friends over the years, each having returned to the town he lived in before being traded to the Mets.

Martin had spent more than ten years in the White Sox organization. After playing four seasons in their minor league system, he was brought up for the last three weeks of 1959, just in time to find out what it was like to be with a team when it clinches a pennant. That was the year of the Go-Go Sox of Nellie Fox and Luis Aparicio and Jim Rivera, a team that won with speed, pitching, and defense while hitting fewer home runs than any other club in the major leagues. Martin, however, was added to the roster too late to take part in the World Series.

"They didn't even give me tickets to the Series," he says. "I stayed home and watched it on television."

But he remained with the White Sox for most of the next eight seasons, and although the team never won another pennant, Martin learned what it took to play for a contender.

"We were always in the running, usually chasing the Yankees," he says, "but we were never far out of it. During one stretch, we finished second three years in a row. So when I was traded to the Mets at the end of the 1967 season, I didn't like it at all. I was going from a team that had never been in the second division to one that had never been out of the cellar. What can you think? I thought my career was over, and shucks, it had just begun. Shows how much *I* knew.

"But when I got there in '68, I saw that there was a tremendous amount of young talent on the ballclub, and they were just learning how to play. A lot of the players had never been on a winner, and they didn't know what it took to win. But once we started putting it together, we had real good chemistry on that club—good defense, some speed, and guys that could really throw hard. It was great to get behind the plate and watch those guys throw. They had all the talent in the world, and I watched them develop from raw throwers into real good pitchers. I had caught a pretty good staff in Chicago for seven years—guys like Billy Pierce and Early Wynn—so I knew pitching when I saw it.

"Ryan, Koosman, and Seaver all had great talent, and they could all throw hard. Koosman didn't throw as hard as Seaver did, but he had a better command of his pitches and better control. He also mixed his pitches up better than Tom did. Tom was just a power pitcher in 1968. Nolan threw harder than either of them, but he didn't have as good command as the other two. It took him time to learn to get his pitches down. He used to rush too much and his arm would stay high and that kept his pitches up, so he had a tough time in the National League. The best thing for him was being traded to the American League, where he was able to get the high strike. The thing about Tom was that he always had a good knowledge of what he wanted to do, but it was a question of his learning how to pitch. He had to learn that you pitch differently in different situations: you pitch one way early in the game and another way late in the game; you pitch differently when you have runs than when you don't. Tom learned all that in the big leagues, and he learned it quickly. You only had to tell him once."

Martin, of course, played no small part in hastening the maturity of the pitching staff. He had handled some of the best pitchers in the game when he was with the White Sox, and he knew what it meant to play under pennant pressure.

"I didn't have to *act* the part of the elder statesman," he says, "it was pure fact. Some of the younger players would come up to me and say, 'What do you think, J.?' I was able to help the pitchers in situations they had never faced before. The important thing was just to keep them calm and ease the pressure."

Martin, who had little hope of overtaking the Cubs in mid-August, saw the pressure begin to take effect on the Cubs in September when the Mets began to close in. By the middle of the month, he had become a believer.

"I began to feel we could win it after that doubleheader in Pittsburgh when we won both games 1 to 0," he says. "We went into Pittsburgh, and nobody liked playing in Forbes Field. It was like an airport, 460 feet to center field, it was just an awesome place. We had to go in and play those guys, and every one of them could hit; they had great hitters. But we shut them out both games, and our pitchers drove in the only runs. After that, I said, 'Hey, this club is gonna win, I mean we have a great shot.' Then we went into St. Louis and beat Steve Carlton in a game where he struck out nineteen batters. After that game, I said to Al, 'Hey, we might not need those tickets for the World Series.' "

Martin believes that handling late-season pressure is the key to winning a pennant race, and he credits Hodges with keeping the Mets on an even keel.

"He had cold water running in his veins," Martin says. "He'd come out to the mound in a tight situation when one run's gonna beat you and a kid's out there pitching, and he'd have his hands in his hip pockets and he'd be talking so low you could hardly hear him. Never once did I see Gil Hodges react in a way to cause panic. Never once! I don't care what happened. We could pull the dumbest play in the world, but he'd never show panic. And he instilled that in his players. You got the feeling, 'Just do what Gil says and don't panic.'

"That was the big difference between the Mets and the Cubs. I found that out when I was traded to the Cubs just before the 1970 season. Leo was the type of manager to cause panic and confusion among his players. If you went up to pinch hit and took a strike, he'd throw a towel out of the dugout. Most of their players couldn't stand that type of pressure. I think Gil would have won with the Cubs in '69. I think it was the manager that made the difference."

Martin was initially optimistic when he was told he was going to the Cubs. He thought it might be a chance for him to play on a second straight pennant-winner.

"It was Easter Sunday morning in 1970," Martin says. "I went to the ballpark and Gil was waiting for me. He asked me to come into his office. He said, 'I have some bad news and some good news, and I'll give you the good news first. I'm trading you back home.' I said, 'To the White Sox?' He said, 'No, to the Cubs. We need a young catcher in the or-ganization and we're trading you for Randy Bobb.' The bad news, of course, was that I was leaving the Mets. But I thought the Cubs had a real good chance of winning. They had tremendous talent over there. They had great pitching, a good bullpen, and All-Star candidates at almost every position. But I found there was one thing they could not do: they could not play in the seventh, eighth, and ninth innings, and that's when you win ballgames. They were so tight and so wound up that they could not perform in the late innings, and that's why the Cubs weren't able to win.

"It was different with the Mets in '69. Hodges kept us believing that we were never out of a game. No matter what the situation was in the late innings, we'd be saying, 'All we need is one break; if we get one break we're gonna win it.' Then when we got the break it was like we expected it, and we just took off from there. That's what it takes to have a pennant-winner."

And that was precisely the script the Mets followed in winning the opening game of the playoffs. They stayed close, and when the breaks came they cashed them in for five eighth-inning runs. The victory, however, did not disguise Seaver's disappointing effort. After the game, he analyzed his own performance.

"I was more nervous than usual," he said, "and my mental state led me to rush my motion. My hips were more open when I was throwing the ball, and my arm dropped lower. The crux of the whole thing, though, was that I just felt more nervous than usual. The anxiety never eased."

The next day, Koosman betrayed no signs of anxiety early in the ballgame. In fact, he did not surrender a hit until the fourth inning, and by that time the Mets had an 8–0 lead. Ron Reed, who had beaten the Mets twice during the season and had allowed them only four runs in twenty-eight innings, fell behind quickly. Agee led off the game with a single, Garrett and Jones walked, and Kranepool put the Mets ahead with a bad-hop single off Millan's glove. The Mets mounted a more serious assault in the second. Koosman walked, Agee homered, Jones doubled, and Shamsky singled. The Mets led 4 to 0. They did not let up. In the third, after Cepeda's error put a runner on first, Harrelson doubled him home and then scored on Garrett's single to make the score 6–0. The Mets were relentless. In the fourth, Shamsky singled and Boswell hit a home run off Milt Pappas. Now it was 8 to 0. The Braves finally broke through against Koosman in the bottom of the inning when Carty doubled and Cepeda singled, but the Mets got the run right back and led 9–1 when the Braves came to bat in the fifth.

Koosman got the first two batters, but then he made three mistakes and never finished the inning. His first mistake was breaking late to cover first base on a ground ball by Millan. His second was walking Gonzalez with Hank Aaron on deck. His third mistake was hit by Aaron for a three-run homer. Now Koosman unraveled. He walked Carty, Cepeda doubled, and Boyer scored them both with a hit up the middle. Taylor was rushed in from the bullpen to get the last out, but the Braves had already scored five times and now trailed by only three, 9–6.

In the top of the seventh, the Mets scored twice more when Jones homered with Agee on third. It was a shaken Agee who crossed the plate, for two pitches earlier he nearly had his head taken off by a line drive off Jones's bat. With two out, Agee had decided to try to steal home. He was more than halfway to the plate and just about to slide when Jones swung. The drive, barely foul, missed Agee's head by inches. Agee retreated to third gingerly, Jones took a pitch, and then both men took the easy route home.

McGraw came in to start the seventh and, as he recalls it, "the adrenalin was really pumping. That game was a milestone for me," he says. "I always used to rely on my catcher to call the game. I hadn't developed the confidence to call my own pitches, and with Grote I was half-scared to shake him off. He was kind of ornery, and if you shook him off he might fire the ball back and take your hand off. Hell, he could throw harder than I could, and I was a little intimidated. But by the time we got to the playoffs, I was getting a pretty good feel of how to use my pitches. I still rarely shook Grote off, because he was great at setting up hitters. But Aaron had been hitting us hard and when he started walking up to the plate, I flashed on a sequence of pitches that I thought could get him out. Grote had a different sequence in mind."

It should be noted that when he came to bat against McGraw, Aaron had already hit Met pitching for two home runs and a double, and had five RBIs. After the game, he told reporters that he had guessed correctly on both hits he had gotten off Seaver the day before. "I was guessing curveball when I hit the home run, and I got it," he said. "If he'd thrown me a fastball, I'd probably have struck out." So McGraw's determination to stick to his own sequence was not necessarily capricious. Still, Grote did not take to it easily.

"I kept shaking him off, and he was really getting pissed," McGraw recalls. "He started snapping his fingers down to give the sign. He wanted me to go after Aaron with the screwball, but I thought he'd be looking for the screwball, and he was. I threw him two fastballs for strikes. Then I wasted a screwball outside for a ball and froze him with a fastball on the inside corner for strike three. It went exactly as I had planned it."

The rest of the game went just as neatly for McGraw. He shut the Braves out for three innings, and the Mets took a two-game lead back to New York. They needed one more victory to clinch the National League pennant, and they had three days in which to get it.

C H A P T E R

19

IT WAS MONDAY, OCTOBER 6.
The first playoff game at Shea was to start at 1 P.M. No day
had been set aside for travel. In all likelihood, the Braves
could have used one. A team that has lost the first two games
of a short series on its home field is already in a badly com-
promised position. Survival now depended on winning three
straight games on the road. Even more demoralizing for the
Braves was the awareness that they had delivered as expected
but still lost twice. They were a team that won with hitting,
and they had hit the Mets' two best pitchers hard. They had
scored eleven runs and made nineteen hits, three of them
home runs. They had mistreated Seaver and manhandled
Koosman, and they had nothing to show for it.

The difference in each game had been defense and relief pitching. Atlanta had committed five errors, most of which
were converted to runs. The Mets, by contrast, were making
the Braves earn what they got, and the bullpen was giving
up nothing. McGraw's three shutout innings had saved the
win for Taylor, who now had a win and a save in the Mets'
first two playoff games. Taylor, in fact, was becoming something of a specialist in pitching shutout relief in postseason
play. In the 1964 World Series, while with the Cardinals, he

had pitched four and two-thirds hitless innings against the Yankees.

"That was a great day for me," Taylor recalls. "We were down two games to one in the Series. The day before, Mantle had hit that home run off Barney Schultz in the ninth to win it for the Yanks. Now this was on Sunday, and we were behind 3 – 0, and then Kenny Boyer hit a grand slam in the top of the fifth to put us ahead, and I came in to pitch the sixth, seventh, eighth, and ninth against the Yankees, and I shut them out without a hit. That was quite a thrill because it was the old Yankee Stadium, and they had Mantle, Maris, and all the boys. That game tied the Series and we went on to win it in seven."

Nineteen sixty-four was Taylor's first year as a relief pitcher. He had been a starter for six seasons in the minors and had a 4 – 2 record in a starting role with the Cardinals in 1963.

"We had finished second to the Dodgers that year," Taylor says, "and in 1964 we thought we had a good chance to win it, but we needed a right-handed relief pitcher. Howie Pollet, the pitching coach, asked me to try it. I had a pretty good year, and I remained a reliever."

Despite Taylor's good year in 1964, he was traded to Houston the following season, and he did not fare well in the Dome. He spent part of 1966 on the Oklahoma City roster, and in the spring of 1967 he learned that the Astros were ready to turn him loose.

"I got a call from one of the team's officials who said they had given Bing Devine permission to talk to me. Bing phoned and said, 'How do you feel about coming over to our organization?' I said, 'Sure, just get me out of Houston.' So I drove across Florida from Coco Beach to St. Petersburg. I had a good spring, and I went north with the Mets. They were just beginning to put a good team together then," he says. "By 1968, we had a solid core of players, but we lost a lot of games by one run. The following year, we added some maturity and started winning some of those close games. We went from a competitive team at the end of '68 and the beginning of '69 to a contender by midseason to a winner by the end of the season.

"I think the turning point came just before the All-Star break. We went into Chicago and lost the first game, then came back and won the next two. From that point on, the feeling grew that we could beat the Cubs. Hodges did one of the greatest jobs of managing in the history of the game. He defined everyone's job at the start of the season and made very few changes. There wasn't much grumbling on the team, because everyone knew what was expected of him. We were given what amounted to job descriptions, just like in industry."

Taylor was the only member of the '69 Mets who already knew the feel of playing for a championship team, but even for him, the Mets' ascent had a meaning of its own.

"There was something special about winning in New York," he says, "particularly with the Mets. It was such a big thing for the city. I wasn't aware of it until afterwards, but they say that the crime rate actually dropped that summer. During the season, I was more worried about a line drive coming back at me than the crime rate in New York, so I didn't realize what effect the Mets were having on the city until the season was over. It was a very different experience for the fans than it was for the players. We could feel the team maturing and becoming a contender during the course of the season, but the fans couldn't, and so we became known as the Amazing Mets. I never really thought we were that amazing. We had a pretty good team, especially the pitching staff. There were four guys on that staff—Seaver, Ryan, Koosman, and McGraw—who had pretty long careers. But I never minded being called the Amazing Mets as much as I did the Miracle Mets. It was no miracle that we won; we were just a good ballclub."

As he speaks, Taylor is watching a television monitor that carries a broadcast of a game between the Blue Jays and the White Sox. The game is being played not far from where we sit in the cafeteria of Toronto's Exhibition Stadium. Taylor—*Doctor* Taylor since 1977—is the team physician for the Blue Jays, and he is on call when the team plays at home. Now, suddenly, he breaks off in midsentence and is up on his feet. A Toronto player has been shaken up in a play at second base and is picking himself up slowly. Taylor is halfway to the door when the player dusts himself off, tests his leg, and moves back to his position. Satisfied that his services are not needed, Taylor returns to the table, where we resume the interview.

Taylor is congenial, more than accommodating, but it is clear that he is straining. It is a Friday evening in late May, and he is winding his way down toward the end of a sixty-hour work week. His job with the Blue Jays is little more than an interlude in his weekly routine. He also runs a private practice and is director of the S. C. Cooper Sports Medicine Clinic at Mount Sinai Hospital in his native Toronto. The clinic, which he founded in 1980, is now one of the largest in Canada. It treats more than twelve thousand patients a year, all of them walk-in victims of sports injuries.

The practice of medicine is Taylor's third career. His first was professional baseball, which he commenced in 1958 at the age of eighteen. His second, begun five years later, was engineering.

"I had quit school after Grade 12 to play baseball in the Cleveland Indians' organization," he says. "But I wanted to continue my education, so I went to the Cleveland farm director and got permission to skip spring training and join the team at the end of the academic year. I did that for five years. I completed Grade 13 and four years of engineering school at the University of Toronto while advancing from Class D to triple-A in the Indians' chain. Baseball was like a summer job to me. I played from May to September. Then, after receiving my degree in electrical engineering, I worked as a design engineer during the baseball off-season. But I always had medicine in the back of my mind, and I began to think about it more seriously after the 1969 season when I made a tour of the Vietnam war zone with some other players. It was my second trip there. I had gone on a hospital tour with Arthur Richman, the Mets' road secretary, in 1968, and it had a big effect on my life."

The point of decision, however, did not come until several years later, when Taylor sensed that his career was reaching its end.

"As a ballplayer, you live your life in microcosm," he says. "You never think you're going to be finished. Then, all of a sudden, you find it's over. You reach male menopause at an early age when you're an athlete. For me, it happened at thirty-four. I was sold to San Diego in 1972, and I knew I didn't have it anymore. Buzzy Bavasi, the general manager, wanted to send me to Hawaii, but I didn't want to go. I did a lot of serious thinking. I asked myself, 'What am I going to do with the rest of my life?' I had an engineering degree, but when I sat down and thought about it I knew that what I really wanted was to be a competent physician. The trips to Vietnam had a major influence on me. They were probably two of the most significant occurrences that gave my life direction."

After taking courses in organic chemistry, biology, embryology, and physical chemistry, Taylor was admitted to the University of Toronto Medical School. He completed his residency in 1979, at the age of forty-one, and began his new career with the Blue Jays. He is now in his eighth season as team physician and has apparently mastered the technique of following the progress of a game while focusing his attention elsewhere.

"I always set aside Friday night for doing interviews with people writing books," he says.

We watch the final few innings of the game from the press box; then Taylor heads for the trainer's room to see that all in need are tended to. It is almost eleven o'clock when we leave the ballpark. Despite the late hour, he has invited me to his home to meet his wife, Rona, and have a drink.

The three of us talk casually for a while, and then Taylor asks if I would like to see a videotape of highlights from the 1969 season. And there it is, all happening again—the key hits, the acrobatic catches, Ron Taylor himself, seventeen years younger, striding in to the mound with runners on base. Even now, there seems to be an element of freshness in it as Taylor watches the film, as if the reality of that season requires confirmation from time to time.

"It all happened so fast," he says. "It was difficult to grasp it at the time. Everything seemed to be happening so suddenly. Now, whenever I show a friend the videotape, I look at it and I say, 'That was really something.' "

If the 1969 season had a dreamlike quality for Taylor, it was fast becoming a nightmare for the Braves. Faced with the unhappy prospect of being swept in their league's first playoff series, they took to the attack promptly against Gary Gentry. They had scored two runs before many of the 53,195 patrons found their way to their seats. With one out, Tony Gonzalez singled and Hank Aaron hit his third home run in as many days—a long, arching drive off the center-field flagpole. The Mets tried to respond in their first turn at bat, but a promising start was squashed abruptly. Agee led off with a double into the left-field corner, and Garrett followed with a line drive that appeared headed for center field. But Pat Jarvis, the Braves' pitcher, speared the ball and threw to second before Agee could get back to the base.

In the third, Gonzalez and Aaron were back at Gentry's throat with a single and a double to open the inning. The next batter was Rico Carty. Gentry worked the count on him to a ball and two strikes but then was asked to leave the game. The problem was the second strike, which Carty lined, just foul, high off the left-field wall. Hodges started for the mound immediately, and Gentry, who was celebrating his twenty-third birthday that day, was not happy to see him coming. There appeared to be a brief but unpleasant exchange between the manager and the pitcher, and even now Gentry recalls the incident with unconcealed resentment.

"All year long you're pitching in back of Seaver and Koosman," he says, "and you know you're as good as they are. There's no reason not to say it if you believe it," he adds parenthetically. "Now, we go into Atlanta and Seaver and Koosman get their butts kicked in the first two games, but we still win. We go back to New York, and I feel that I have a chance to prove myself. Our two big guys got hit hard and we still lead the series 2 to 0, so I go out there feeling that I have nothing to lose. I make a mistake to Aaron in the first inning, and in the third Carty knocks me out of the game with a foul ball. I only gave up two runs."

Gentry's disappointment became Nolan Ryan's opportunity. His first pitch out of the bullpen was a sizzling fastball that Carty watched for strike three. Ryan walked Cepeda intentionally to fill the bases, then struck out Clete Boyer and got Didier on a fly ball to end the threat.

The Mets then took the initiative. Agee hit Jarvis's first third-inning pitch over the right-center-field fence to make the score 2 to 1, and an inning later the Mets grabbed the lead. Shamsky singled for his seventh hit of the playoffs, and Boswell homered into the Met bullpen. The Mets led 3 to 2.

The Braves, however, would not go easily. With two out in the fifth, they recaptured the lead when Carty walked and Cepeda cracked a Ryan fastball over the wall in center. But the Braves did not have long to savor their advantage. In the bottom of the fifth, Ryan, who had only three hits during the regular season, bounced a single between first and second. Agee flied to left. Then Wayne Garrett, who had not hit a home run since May, drove one into the loge seats just inside the right-field foulpole to climax what had become a home-run derby. Home runs had accounted for all the scoring in the game thus far; the Mets had three of the five homers and five of the nine runs.

Now the Mets showed that they knew how to score without benefit of the long ball. Jones followed Garrett's home run with a double, and Boswell looped a sinking line drive to right to give the Mets their first two-run margin of the game, 6 to 4. They added another run in the sixth, then relaxed for the final three innings while Ryan held the Braves harmless. He allowed two baserunners in the eighth, but Felipe Alou lined to Harrelson for the third out. In the ninth, pitching to the crowd's chant of "Let's go, Mets," Ryan dispatched the side in order. In seven innings of relief, he had allowed two runs on three hits, walked two batters, and struck out seven. It was a performance that crowned his season.

"It made winning the pennant a little more special to me than just being on the ballclub," Ryan says now. "To feel that you contributed to winning it gives it more meaning."

Ryan discusses the '69 Mets dispassionately. His recollections of that season seem to lack the fervor with which others recall a championship year. He sometimes speaks of the team in the third person, as if he weren't really a part of it.

"It was a young ballclub that didn't know what its limitations were and really played the game day to day and enjoyed it," he says. "Things fell into place for us and we were in the right place at the right time. It was definitely a team effort."

Of course Ryan's perspective on that season is necessarily different from those of his former teammates. At the time, he had not yet begun to fashion the substance of his career. His Hall of Fame credentials—the strikeout records, the five no-hitters, the All-Star appearances—would be established over the next two decades, with other teams. In 1969 he was viewed as little more than a young, quick gun out of Texas with an arm that might make a claim upon legend. He could throw a baseball, they said, faster than any man alive, at better than a hundred miles an hour. But he had little else to work with. His breaking ball was an impostor, and the direction his heated fastball might take was always subject to conjecture. Only time would reveal whether he would be the second coming of Bob Feller or the reincarnation of Rex Barney.

He had been drafted by the Mets out of a small-town Texas high school in 1965. He was only eighteen years old then, but scout Red Murff saw him pitch a high-school game and phoned New York to say he had found a kid who could throw harder than Sandy Koufax. Ryan pitched in two games for the Mets in 1966 and joined the team full time two seasons later, pitching both in relief and as a spot starter. But while the velocity of his fastball continued to attract attention, he became as well known for his inconsistency as for his ability to strike out batters at the rate of almost one an inning. Ryan had other problems as well. His fastball raised blisters on his fingers, and he soaked his hand in pickle brine to toughen the skin. But the pickle brine did not serve to heighten his performance. In his four years with the Mets, he won only twenty-nine games and lost thirty-eight.

At the end of the 1971 season, the Mets gave up on him. In a trade that would be remembered as a landmark for the imbalance of talent exchanged, the Mets sent Ryan to the California Angels for Jim Fregosi, a third baseman who would play one undistinguished season for the Mets before being sold for cash to the Texas Rangers. What is seldom recalled about that trade is that Ryan was not valued highly enough to bring Fregosi to New York in a one-for-one swap. The Mets packaged three minor league players to go with him. Bob Scheffing, the general manager who engineered the deal for the Mets, said that although Ryan was "a hell of a prospect, he hadn't done it for us. How long can you wait?"

The Angels did not have to wait very long. In his first three seasons in California, Ryan won sixty-two games, pitched three no-hitters, led the majors in strikeouts every year, and in 1973 recorded 383 strikeouts to break Sandy Koufax's single-season record. Ryan gives much of the credit for his rapid improvement to the Angels' pitching coach, Tom Morgan.

"Morgan helped me a lot with my mechanics," he says, "and he helped me to develop my curveball. You can't win regularly in the majors with just a fastball, no matter how hard you throw it. Also, I got to pitch on a regular basis, every fourth day, for the Angels. That's important for a power pitcher. That's why I didn't mind being traded in '72. I was happy to go to another organization and pitch regularly for a club that was in the building process rather than one that was trying to duplicate a World Series victory. I was getting frustrated over here."

When Ryan says "over here," he is referring to New York, more particularly to Shea Stadium, for that is where we are speaking. He is wearing the uniform of the Houston Astros, and we are seated in the visitors' dugout less than an hour before an early-season game with the Mets. It is only the fourth week of the 1986 season, but both the Astros and the Mets are leading their divisions, and they are about to engage in a preview of what in October would be a memorable playoff series. Later that evening, Dwight Gooden would beat the Astros with a two-hitter. The following night, Ryan would be driven from the mound in the fifth inning.

It is a cold night in Shea Stadium, and rain is on the way. I have been waiting to speak with Ryan for more than an hour. By arrangement with the Astros' public relations director, I had met him in the clubhouse shortly after 5 P.M., hoping to interview him there. But I found him surrounded by a cluster of friends, autographing baseballs and making plans for dinner. He said he would not be able to speak with me until after batting practice, which began at six o'clock and lasted for forty minutes. So I waited in the dugout while Ryan roamed the outfield, bagging loose baseballs, until batting practice ended. Then, when he returned to the dugout, there were two other writers waiting for him, each with his own menu of questions, and so the interview was conducted in the form of a press conference, each of us taking turns in pursuit of our own story lines.

Just a few nights earlier, Roger Clemens of the Boston Red Sox had struck out twenty batters in a game, breaking by one the record Ryan shared with three others, and the lifetime strikeout leader was much in demand for comment.

"I always thought that record would be broken," he says. "Records like that are easier to break than the endurance type. All it takes is one phenomenal outing against a certain type of ballclub—a free-swinging team, not a bunch of contact hitters. Will someone break Clemens's record? It's a possibility, but it might also stand for fifty years."

Ryan seems more at ease with such questions than the kind I wish to pose. The craft of pitching and the longevity of strikeout records are subjects that he treats with the cool detachment of the connoisseur. He appears less comfortable when asked to dip into himself, to reconstruct old feelings and attitudes that have been reshaped by the passing of the years. He betrays little nostalgia for the past or anticipation of the future. There is in his manner a tranquility as light and serene as his soft Texas drawl. The heat of competitive intensity, so quickly brought to a boil in interviews with other players, seems to be tempered in Ryan. Despite having spent the past two decades—virtually all of his adult life—under the relentless gaze of public scrutiny, he gives the impression of being a man who would sooner have passed those years working on his ranch in Alvin, Texas, than toiling beneath the glare of big-league cities.

Unlike most youngsters who are able to work their way to the majors, Ryan did not harbor such dreams of glory in his youth. His aspirations did not include a life in professional baseball. It was as if he had discovered one day that he had been graced with a facility that few men could equal, and such being the case, he was obliged to put it to use. So Nolan Ryan, who conceivably was able to throw a baseball as hard as any man who ever lived, became a professional pitcher. But it took years for him to acquire the subtle skills of his trade; and they were, in many respects, hard years.

"I had as good an arm as there was," he says, "but I came out of Texas with no prior pitching background except that I could go out and throw the ball hard. When I got to the major leagues, I still had to learn how to pitch. I had to learn to throw a curveball, and I had to develop control. I learned how to pitch in the majors."

The twenty-two-year-old Ryan had barely begun his education when he pitched the Mets to the National League pennant. The final out was a ground ball to third by Tony Gonzalez. Garrett's throw had hardly reached first base when, for the second time in less than two weeks, a riotous celebration erupted at Shea Stadium. It was a virtual replay of the one on September 24, when the Mets clinched the division championship. The playing field was again attacked and shredded. Again, champagne was spewed all over the clubhouse. This time, it was not just the principals who were doused. New York's besieged mayor was the object of a cascade poured by Tom Seaver and Rod Gaspar. Lindsay, now pretty much a regular at Met games, displayed the politician's finely honed instinct for being in the right place at the right time. The following day, a photo of the mayor, champagne running down his well-chiseled features, appeared prominently in local newspapers. It was, some would say, his first real step toward reelection.

Many of the players, however, thought this second celebration was a bit strained, a poor imitation of the earlier one, which was spawned without benefit of rehearsal.

"It seemed a little forced," Seaver said. "The other time it was more spontaneous."

"The main difference," said Shamsky, "is that the first time we had done something nobody believed we could do."

Hodges was nonetheless appreciative. "This is the championship of the whole league," he said, "not just one division. As I said then, you go one step, and then you go another step, and this step is further than the other one. And the next one would be bigger still."

In the losing clubhouse, some of the Braves voiced their own reaction.

"They beat the hell out of us," said manager Luman Harris.

Hank Aaron, who batted .357 with three home runs, two doubles, and seven RBIs in the three games, said simply, "They *are* amazing."

PART NINE

World Champions

CHAPTER

20

THE WORLD SERIES IS IMBUED
with an aura of mystery that is absent from other sports events.
For it brings together contestants that are fundamentally unknown to one another. They have not met during the regular season and have played no common opponents. Baseball
alone isolates its leagues completely. Each batter who steps to
the plate will be facing a pitcher he knows only by reputation. Every runner looking to take the extra base will be cal-
culating the strength of an arm he has never tested. There
are, of course, occasional exceptions: players who have been
traded from one league to the other, teams that have met in
a previous World Series or in the casual climate of a preseason game. But for the most part, the teams vying for a world
championship have no past to draw upon, and the freshness
of their confrontation lends to the World Series the stimulat-
ing sense of primal combat.

The team that the Mets were preparing to meet was the
Baltimore Orioles, a club that many believed (with some jus-
tification, it turned out) had just crossed the threshold that
opened onto a dynasty. The Orioles were being heralded
widely, if a bit prematurely, as a reincarnation of the Yankee
teams of the early sixties. They had, after all, won 109 games

during the regular season, finishing nineteen games ahead of second-place Detroit, and then polished off the Minnesota Twins three straight in the playoffs. It was a team of exceptional balance that had the tools to win in any manner required of them. They hit for average, and they hit for power. As a team, the Orioles batted .265, compared with the Mets' .242. When it came to the long ball, the contrast was even sharper: Baltimore had hit 175 home runs; the Mets, 109. Tommie Agee had led New York with twenty-six home runs; the next-highest total was Art Shamsky's fourteen. For the Orioles, Boog Powell had thirty-seven; Frank Robinson, thirty-two; Paul Blair, twenty-six; and Brooks Robinson, twenty-three. In all, Baltimore had scored 157 more runs than the Mets, an average of almost a full run a game. So much for the offense.

An analysis of the teams' defense and pitching proved equally discouraging for the Mets. The Orioles fielded what was likely the best defensive team in either league. With an infield anchored by Brooks Robinson at third, Mark Belanger at short, and Davey Johnson at second, and an outfield covered by Paul Blair in center with Don Buford and Frank Robinson on the flanks, the Orioles had made fewer errors than any team in baseball. And if it was an edge in pitching that the Mets would look to for balance, they would find none. Baltimore's pitchers were the stingiest in the majors, having yielded the fewest runs and combining for the lowest earned run average, 2.83, as opposed to the Mets' 2.99. Their three top starters—Mike Cuellar, Dave McNally, and Jim Palmer—had a cumulative won-lost record of 59 and 22. Seaver, Koosman, and Gentry had done no better than 55 and 28. If there was any condition that might lend hope to the Mets' chances, it could be found nowhere in the closely kept ledgers of baseball's arithmetic. The oddsmakers made the Orioles 8-to-5 favorites.

Of course, the Mets were accustomed to the underdog's

role. Odds of 8 to 5 were paltry compared to the 100 to 1 that had been laid against them at the start of the year. The Mets, it was argued in the New York press, had destiny on their side. They were plugged into circuits of mystical origin. All season long, chance seemed to be banked in their favor, full fields of magic were summoned from hidden currents whenever help was needed. The mere logic of baseball was as nothing when arrayed against such forces.

The Orioles bristled at the suggestion that the Mets were charmed.

"I don't believe in that team of destiny business," said Brooks Robinson. ". . . In 1966 [when the Orioles took four straight from the Los Angeles Dodgers], we beat those two guys [Koufax and Drysdale], and these guys [Seaver and Koosman] can't be as good as them. . . . We're here to prove there is no Santa Claus."

Manager Earl Weaver offered his own analysis of the Mets. They had, he said, "two pitchers, some slap hitters, and a little speed. They say the Mets have desire. The Orioles have just as much desire and a lot more talent. That's what I think, anyway."

And there was a light-hearted exchange between Frank Robinson and Merv Rettenmund, a utility outfielder for the Orioles, that was widely quoted and would turn out to be ironically prophetic. They had watched on television in the clubhouse as the Mets celebrated their victory over Atlanta, and they heard Rod Gaspar, of all people, forecast a four-game sweep of the Orioles.

"Bring on Ron Gaspar," Robinson shouted derisively.

"Not Ron, *Rod*, stupid," Rettenmund said.

"Okay," said Robinson, "bring on Rod Stupid."

Boog Powell took a realistic, if skeptical, approach. "We still don't know if they're for real," he said, "but we'll find out."

They would begin finding out in Baltimore on Saturday, October 11.

The Mets were ushered off with the full attention of local politicians basking in the team's new image. Governor Nelson Rockefeller hosted a cocktail party for the Mets on Wednesday in his Fifth Avenue apartment; standing on a marble coffee table, he proclaimed that the Mets' victory was "better than the moon landing." Mayor Lindsay, ever hopeful of tapping the source of Met-magic, was at LaGuardia Airport for the team's departure on Thursday. Wearing a button that proclaimed "We're No. 1," he read a composition of his own creation that parodied Ernest L. Thayer's "Casey at the Bat."

However, with the first game barely underway beneath bright October sunshine, it was not Casey but Don Buford who was at bat for Baltimore, and he did not strike out. The squat left-fielder drove Seaver's second pitch of the game over the right-field wall, just beyond the leaping grasp of Ron Swoboda. Swoboda, who was raised in Baltimore and had played a high-school game at Memorial Stadium, said later that he should have caught the ball but had timed his leap poorly. As a member of Hodges's right-handed-hitting platoon, he had not played for the past eight days, since the end of the regular season; and now, he said, "It was like starting all over again. I was nervous, not coordinated, kind of real stiff. I should catch that ball."

Buford's home run, aside from giving the Orioles a sudden 1–0 lead, had no visible effect on Seaver, who regained his composure quickly and pitched his way through the rugged Baltimore lineup. Then, with two out in the fourth, he ran into difficulty with the bottom part of the batting order. Elrod Hendricks singled to right, Johnson walked, and Belanger bounced one through the right side of the infield for a 2–0 lead. Mike Cuellar, the pitcher, looped a soft pop fly into center for another run, and Buford lined a double on one bounce to the right-field wall. Now the Orioles led 4 – 0, and Cuellar, who had won twenty-three games during the regular season, was handling the Mets' right-handed hitters with little effort.

He had his first brush with trouble in the seventh, when singles by Clendenon and Grote and a walk to Swoboda loaded the bases with one out. After Al Weis got a run home with a sacrifice fly, Rod Gaspar was sent up to hit for Cardwell, who had replaced Seaver in the sixth. Gaspar, who represented the tying run, tapped a slow roller in the direction of third base, and what unfolded was a tableau that was becoming as familiar as the picture of Willie Mays racing out from under his cap in pursuit of a fly ball. Brooks Robinson swooped in with his bare hand extended, snatched the ball from the grass, and with a twisting, overhand motion, threw to first base in time to get the fleet Gaspar.

Still trailing 4 – 1, the Mets had one more chance in the ninth, but with two on and two out, pinch hitter Art Shamsky grounded weakly to second base.

"I had a chance to be a hero," Shamsky says now, "but it didn't work out that way. No one likes to make the last out in a World Series game." Shamsky, who also recalls making the final out of Bob Moose's no-hitter, would not get many more chances in the Series.

Having platooned half of his starting lineup throughout the late stages of the season and the playoffs, Hodges was determined to follow that same pattern during the Series. It could not have been the easiest decision for him to make. Against Atlanta, the left-handed platoon of Kranepool, Boswell, Garrett, and Shamsky had batted .396 with ten runs batted in. Now Hodges was, in effect, sitting nineteen hits on the bench against two of Baltimore's three starters and going instead with Clendenon, Weis, Charles, and Swoboda. Of the four, only Weis had made an appearance in the playoffs, being used as a late-inning defensive replacement for Boswell in the third game and going hitless in one time at bat. But Hodges never wavered. His two-pronged lineup had won twelve of its last thirteen games going into the Series, and he would win it or lose it with the system that had gotten him there.

If Hodges had any grounds for concern, it might have been his pitching. Seaver had now suffered through two shaky postseason starts, giving up nine runs in twelve innings. He was nursing a tender calf muscle, strained while shagging flies during batting practice in Atlanta, and he had started the first game of the World Series feeling he could not go the distance.

"When I strained my leg, I didn't run for four days," Seaver said after the game, "and I have to run to be effective. In the fourth inning, I realized I was running out of gas. My legs seemed to be getting tired, and I started to drop out of the strike zone. I figured that would happen, but I thought it would be in the seventh or eighth inning, not the fourth."

Now, almost two decades later, Seaver looks back and considers that Baltimore's opening-game victory might have provided the Mets with a psychological edge for the balance of the Series.

"When the game was over," he says, "the Orioles were jubilant. They were jumping up and down and slapping each other on the back, and we didn't expect them to react that way. We thought they were an overpowering team that would take winning for granted, like the old Yankee teams. So the feeling began to spread among us that the Orioles were not as sure of themselves as their comments had indicated. Clendenon remarked on that in the clubhouse. He said they looked elated, even surprised, that they won the game. We began to feel that this was no superteam after all. The Orioles showed us that they felt we belonged on the same field with them. Their reaction helped us."

"It also helped to get the opening-game tension out of the way. I was a little nervous before the game," Seaver recalls, "but not like against Atlanta. This time the tension eased when the game started. Buford's homer didn't concern me much. It's only one run. You can't think of those things in symbolic terms. A starter's job is to keep his team in the game, and I didn't think one run would be enough to win it."

However, Frank Robinson believed the leadoff home run had more of an impact. He said he was surprised by the Mets' lack of enthusiasm, noting that there was so little cheering from the bench during their seventh-inning rally. "More than likely," Robinson said, "the home run by Buford took the heart right out of them." Bud Harrelson remembers it differently.

"When Buford got to second base, he says to me, 'You guys ain't seen nothin' yet,'" Harrelson recalls. "Well, I didn't say anything to him, I just let him go. He crosses the plate and everyone congratulates him, but before the next guy got up, I said to myself, 'Obviously *they* haven't seen nothin' yet, either. We've only been to bat one time.' You couldn't let that stuff affect you, let it distract you. But we weren't distracted. We were young and naive for the most part. We were in the World Series, and we were happy to be there. Pressure? What pressure? We had everything to gain and nothing to lose. There was no pressure on us. No one expected anything from us. I remember after some games that year saying, 'Those guys are playing like we used to play.' A team would have us by the throat, they'd be beating us by two runs in the eighth inning, and then they'd make a mistake and we'd kill them. That's the way it was with us all year.

"Now, when a team comes from way behind and pulls an upset, people say, 'Just like the '69 Mets.' The '69 Mets came to epitomize what an underdog can accomplish. At the

end of the movie *Oh, God,* George Burns says, 'My last miracle was the '69 Mets.' These guys here are sick of hearing
about it."

The "guys here" of whom Harrelson speaks are the Mets
of 1986, already heirs-apparent to the '69 team even though
the season is barely two weeks old. They had finished a close
second to the Cardinals a year earlier and were installed as
preseason favorites to win their division title. They are off to
a good start, and now, on a raw, wet afternoon in April, they
are milling about the Shea Stadium clubhouse before a night
game with the Pittsburgh Pirates. Batting practice has been
canceled because of the wet weather, and the players are
dressing slowly, filling the extra time as their tastes would
have it. Dwight Gooden, the Cy Young Award–winner, is
part of a four-handed card game. Ron Darling, wearing a
leather jacket over his street clothes, is sitting in front of his
locker, working the *Times* crossword puzzle. Bill Robinson,
the first-base coach and batting instructor, is looking over the
pitching chart of the previous day's game.

Harrelson and I are seated in a quiet corner of the clubhouse, recalling earlier glories, measuring the past against the
present. As the third-base coach for the champions-to-be, he
recognizes the differences in mood and attitude between the
two teams.

"The big thing is that this team is expected to win," Harrelson says, "and that's what creates pressure. In '69, if someone screwed up, no one made anything of it. Now, if someone
screws up, it's a big deal. People ask questions, you're expected to explain why it happened. That's the big difference
between the two teams. This one is playing under pressure
that we never really understood in '69. But I wouldn't try to
compare the quality of the teams. They're from different eras,
and the players don't care about making those comparisons.
Let me tell you a story:

"Last year, we were out in L.A., and Tommy Davis and

Orlando Cepeda were there. They came up to me and said they wanted to meet Dwight. So I called Dwight out of the dugout and said, 'I'd like you to meet a couple of guys I played with,' and I introduced them both by name. Well, I spoke to Dwight later, and he told me he'd never heard of either one of them. So people like to compare the present with the past, but the players don't really give a rap."

Harrelson runs his fingers through a shock of wavy red hair that has surrendered nothing to the years. He appears as sprightly and nearly as lean as the hyper young shortstop who always managed to muster more strength than seemed possible from his spare, boyish frame. He is not the only bridge that connects the Mets of '86 to 1969. The manager of the current team is the same Davey Johnson who played second base for the Baltimore Orioles seventeen years earlier. Their experience of that season, however, was vastly different. The Orioles, loaded with power and pitching, were favored by many to unseat the Detroit Tigers as American League champions. The Mets, of course, were never thought to be a contender.

"No way we thought we had a chance at the start of that season," Harrelson says. "We just wanted to be better than we were in 1968. In spring training, Hodges told each pitcher: 'Just win at least one more than you lose. That way I know we'll finish no worse than ten games above .500.' He spoke to the other players too. There were a few that he thought didn't really have their heads in the game. He told them they could become better ballplayers if they became thinking ballplayers. He began to set the stage for a change in attitude. He told us that we lost about thirty-six one-run ballgames the previous year. 'Those games can go either way,' he said. 'Let's win some of them.' What he did was get us thinking, 'Hey, it isn't fate that we lose those close games; we can just as easily win them.' He changed the view we had that if you get blown out one day and lose 6 to 5 the next that you can be satisfied with the improvement, that it's okay to play just good enough to lose. The idea, he said, was to play just good enough to win, and in 1969 we won most of those one-run games.

"Gil was a very positive manager. He just didn't let negatives enter into your thinking. In spring training, he approached me and said, 'You're the strongest player I've ever seen at 147 pounds.' Shit, my chest stuck out. Here he had a guy in spring training weighing in at 147 pounds, and he could have said, 'You're going to have to go on a weight program and build yourself up a little.' But instead he was positive, and he made me feel strong. That's the way he was. He looked at everything from the positive side, and he made us think positive too.

"But even with that attitude, none of us expected to do it in '69. We knew we had a moving organization; we knew we were getting good draft choices; we knew we had young, strong pitching. So we were optimistic about improving, but we didn't have any great expectations."

Harrelson's expectations began to increase in early June, however, when the Mets completed their eleven-game winning streak. A glimmer of hope began to take the form of revelation.

"We had always had trouble with the West Coast teams, particularly out there," he recalls. "But we beat all three of them at Shea and then went out to the Coast and beat them all again. At that point I think we began saying, 'Hey, we're not doing this with mirrors, we're not doing this with miracles. We're playing good baseball, we can win; we can beat anybody if we play our game. Then, a week or so later, we got Clendenon, and he made a big difference. He added some power and he also helped solidify our young guys. We didn't have any one leader on the club—that was Hodges's role. But Clendenon led by example, and guys like him and Charles did a lot to help steady our younger players.

"So by the middle of June, things started to come to-

gether. We began to develop a positive attitude and a looseness that carried us right through the season. By the time we
got to the World Series, we felt we could beat anyone."

The Mets needed every bit of that confidence, that psychological "looseness," for when they arrived in Baltimore for
the start of the Series, they discovered that they were being
given little chance by the locals.

"I picked up the paper in Baltimore," Harrelson says,
"and they had one of those damn World Series analyses, player
by player. Harrelson against Belanger, Baltimore plus one;
Charles and Brooks Robinson, plus two, Baltimore; Blair ver-
sus Agee, toss-up. They won almost every position. If we went
by that analysis, we should have flown out of Baltimore and
just gone home. We were beat on paper. They were a domi-
nant ballclub with experience, and they supposedly should
have blown us out. But shit, we didn't care, we didn't believe
that. Hah! Big deal! We're here and we're happy to be here,
you know?"

On Sunday, the Mets defied the analysis. They evened
the series in a tense, well-played game that featured defense
and pitching. The pitching was provided by Jerry Koosman
and Dave McNally, each of whom had earned reputations as
big-game pitchers. McNally, in fact, entered the game with a
string of twenty consecutive scoreless innings in postseason
play. He had shut out Minnesota in the second playoff game,
giving up only three hits in eleven innings; and in the 1966
World Series he had beaten Don Drysdale with a four-hitter.
He won both games by scores of 1 to 0.

Now, on another sparkling fall afternoon, McNally added
three more shutout innings to his total before Clendenon sliced
a drive to right field that just cleared the fence to give the
Mets a 1−0 lead, their first of the Series. Koosman, meanwhile, was giving the Orioles nothing at all. He took a no-
hitter into the seventh inning, but Paul Blair ended it with a

line-drive single to left. Then, with two out, Blair stole second and scored the tying run when Brooks Robinson bounced a single through the middle of the infield.

When the game went to the ninth inning, still tied at 1–1, Koosman was working on a two-hitter, and McNally had allowed only three. Brooks Robinson had deprived the Mets of two hits with exceptional plays in the fourth and eighth, and the two shortstops—Harrelson and Belanger—had also turned difficult chances into outs. McNally had no trouble with the first two Met batters in the ninth, but Ed Charles managed to get a ground ball past Robinson at third. Then, with the count 2 and 2 on Grote, Charles broke for second. It was what Hodges later described as a run-and-hit play: the baserunner moves, but the batter swings only if the pitch is to his liking. Grote chose to swing, and he grounded the ball past Belanger; Charles, given a head start, made it all the way to third. It turned out to be a critical maneuver, because Al Weis lined McNally's next pitch sharply to left, on one bounce to Buford, and it is unlikely that Charles would have been able to score from second. But he made it easily from third, and the Mets had a one-run lead to nurse in the bottom of the ninth.

Baltimore's turn started innocuously enough. Buford hit a routine fly ball to Swoboda in right, and Blair bounced out to short. That brought to the plate Frank Robinson, perhaps the last Oriole batter Koosman would have chosen to face in that situation. Robinson was in his fourteenth big-league season, with a guaranteed place in the Hall of Fame. He had won Most Valuable Player awards in both leagues and was closing in on five hundred home runs. At age thirty-four, Robinson was by no means past his peak. He had finished the 1969 season with thirty-two home runs, 100 runs batted in, and a batting average of .308. It was, however, a physically diminished Frank Robinson that started the World Series. Two days before the Series opened, he developed a virus that left him six pounds lighter and in weakened condition. He went 0 for 4 and struck out twice in the first game. Then, taking batting practice before the second game, he fouled a ball off his left instep and played in pain for the full nine innings. He was hitless in three times up when he came to bat in the ninth, but he was no less an intimidating presence.

Hodges, looking to prevent an extra-base hit, sent Weis from second base to the left-field corner, employing the same shift he had used during the season against Richie Allen and Willie McCovey. But Koosman, pitching carefully, walked Robinson on a 3–2 pitch and did the same with Boog Powell, the power-hitting first baseman. Now Hodges chose to play the percentages. With the right-handed-batting Brooks Robinson due up, he replaced Koosman with Ron Taylor, who had pitched two spotless innings against the Orioles in the first game, striking out three of the six batters he faced. Hodges, in his direct but understated way, handed Taylor the ball and said simply, "You've got to get one man out."

Taylor did it, but it wasn't easy. With the count full, Robinson hit a sharp grounder in back of third. Charles fielded the ball cleanly and started toward third base for the force-out. But Rettenmund, who was running for Frank Robinson, clearly had Charles beaten to the base. Seeing he had no play at third, Charles wheeled and threw low to first, where Clendenon scooped the ball out of the dirt for the third out.

So the Mets had their first World Series victory. Koosman had handled Baltimore's hitters effortlessly. He had thrown only 103 pitches, twenty-two of them in the ninth inning. Perhaps more significantly, Met pitching had done well in neutralizing the power segment of Baltimore's batting order throughout the first two games. Blair, Powell, and the two Robinsons had managed just two singles among them. For the Mets' part, their right-handed platoon had batted .308 while scoring and driving in all three New York runs. The surprise had been the utility infielder, Al Weis, who drove home the Mets' only run in the first game and the winning run in the second. A .215 hitter for the season, .219 lifetime, he was on his way to becoming one of the hitting stars of the World Series.

"You never know why things like that happen," Weis says when asked about his sudden emergence as a hitter. "In six seasons with the White Sox I hit three home runs, then I hit two in two days at Wrigley Field. It's hard to explain those things. But part of it is that Hodges gave me confidence. All through the season he let me hit in a lot of situations where other managers would have taken me out. I played for two managers in Chicago—Al Lopez and Eddie Stanky—and they were both good managers, but I think they would have pinch hit for me a lot of times when Gil let me bat. He gave a lot of players confidence, especially players like myself, utility men. When the Mets traded for me and Agee, Gil told me he would not have made the trade if I wasn't included. And when he released me in 1971, he said it was one of the toughest decisions he ever made. Things like that give you confidence.

"You know, I started four of the five World Series games, and I got into the fifth game as a defensive replacement. I would have considered myself lucky to have played in even one game. Think of all the really great players who never got into a World Series, guys like Ernie Banks and Billy Williams. I was lucky just to get the chance, and then I was fortunate enough to perform well."

Weis recalls the 1969 season with a wistful nostalgia that is sometimes solemn. He is, by all measure, a modest man, one who treasures his success like an unexpected gift that might as easily have fallen to another. He knows, of course, that his achievements were earned, but he is aware too that the opportunity to earn them was awarded by chance, and he is grateful for the favor.

Born in Franklin Square, Long Island, not much more

than a long throw from where Shea Stadium now stands, Weis lived in the New York metropolitan area until he enlisted in the navy at the age of seventeen. It was while in the service, playing for the naval base team at Norfolk, Virginia, that he attracted the notice of big-league scouts. Los Angeles offered him a tryout, but the Chicago White Sox tendered a contract, and he signed it. After three years in Chicago's minor league system, Weis joined the White Sox in 1962. For the next six seasons, he earned his keep playing second, short, and third— all on a part-time basis—for a team that was always a contender but never a champion.

By 1967, he had settled in the Chicago area. He was married, he had a family, and he owned a home in the nearby suburb of Elmhurst. During the summer, he played baseball for the White Sox. In the off-season, he and J. C. Martin worked for the White Sox public-relations department, selling season tickets to companies in the Chicago area. More than ten years passed since he'd left New York. Then, on an afternoon in mid-December, he learned he was on his way back.

"I came home from work about four o'clock," he says, "and my wife told me that Johnny Murphy of the Mets had called. When I called back, Murphy said, 'I'd like to welcome you to the New York Mets.' My reaction was, 'Oh, no.' After all these years with a contending team, I was going to a last-place club. It's the ambition of every player to play in a World Series; now I figured that was the end of that dream."

Weis remembers his debut with the Mets as being anything but auspicious.

"We opened the 1968 season on the road," he says, "and I didn't get to play in the first few series. But Buddy [Harrelson] wasn't able to play the third game in Houston, so I started at shortstop, and the game went twenty-four innings. I played the whole game, went about 1 for 10, and in the twenty-fourth inning I made an error that lost the game for us. I let a ball go right through my legs. We left Houston around three or four in the morning and flew to New York. The next day was an off-day, then we opened our home schedule against the Giants. I was starting again, and when I was introduced and trotted onto the field I heard quite a few boos from the fans. But Juan Marichal was pitching that day, and I got two hits off him and drove in a few runs and all was forgotten. I was a hero."

That was the beginning of Weis's career as the Mets' "supersub." It was a role he accepted readily and filled well.

"I think the job I had was one of the toughest in baseball," he says. "You play one day and then sit out two or three. It throws your timing off. You're called off the bench in the late innings to go in for defensive purposes; you're not warmed up and the game is on the line. But I adjusted to it. I got to know Gil and anticipate when he was going to call on me. When it got down to the sixth or seventh inning and we were ahead, I'd start to get myself ready. In Shea, there was a runway from the dugout to the clubhouse, and I would jog a little there and try to get myself loosened up. It's a tough job, especially in cold weather, but that was my role on the club, and I filled it the best way I could."

In speaking with Weis, it becomes quickly apparent that he is, by temperament, ideally suited for such a role. He describes himself as a journeyman ballplayer, knowing as he does that it is not a term of deprecation, that while only a handful of players are capable of lifting a team and carrying it beyond its own expectations, it is the journeymen who, day by day, keep it close enough to matter.

We are seated in the backyard of the Weis home, the house in suburban Elmhurst that the family never relinquished. It is a soft early-summer evening. Al's wife, Barbara, has served their guest some iced tea while we discuss the project at hand. Weis, who had a reputation for being taciturn during his playing days, now requires little prompting. Each memory revives another, and he summons them freely. It is nearly dusk when the interview is over.

I am due shortly at J. C. Martin's home, a drive of about thirty minutes if one knows his way. But the Weises are eager to show a visitor their home—particularly the basement, which is a treasure house of baseball memorabilia. Al hauls out and hefts the bat he used to hammer out critical hits in the World Series. He tries on his old mitt. The walls are adorned with photos, some of the young Al Weis, a tad trimmer than the gray-haired, mustachioed gent now nearing fifty. He points proudly to one wall that is completely covered with a montage of black-and-white photographs—scores of uniformed ballplayers interlocked in an artful pattern that appears to support the wall itself. In a way, it does.

"All of those pictures have been cut and shaped and pasted right onto the wall," Weis says. "They can never be removed. Whoever buys the house, buys the photos with it. They will be there as long as the house is standing."

CHAPTER

21

On Monday, the teams rested. It was a day set aside for travel from Baltimore to New York, even though the cities were no more than an hour apart by air. Both teams no doubt welcomed the extra day, for it allowed them to adhere to a three-man pitching rotation. The opening-game starters would be able to pitch again in Wednesday's fourth game. The match-ups thus would remain the same throughout the Series—unless weather forced a cancellation.

Tuesday came up cool and overcast, with rain a distinct threat. Hodges announced that if the game were postponed, he would bypass Gentry and come back with Seaver in the third game. Weaver, on the other hand, said he would stay with Jim Palmer. Indeed, he believed the scheduled Palmer-Gentry matchup was the one most favorable to the Orioles.

Palmer, though only a year older than Gentry, was already in his fifth big-league season. His World Series experience had been brief but impressive. In 1966, at the age of twenty-one, he outpitched Sandy Koufax with a four-hit shutout in the second game of Baltimore's sweep of the Dodgers. As for the season just ended, he had compiled a record of 16–4, the highest winning percentage in either league, and an earned run average of 2.34, second best in the American League. In the playoffs, he had allowed Minnesota only two runs while winning the third and deciding game. Gentry's numbers were far less imposing. He concluded his rookie season with thirteen victories, only one more than he lost, and an ERA of 3.43, more than a run higher than Palmer's. In his playoff start against Atlanta, he did not get past the third inning.

"I was over-relaxed when I pitched against Atlanta," Gentry said the day before he was scheduled to face the Orioles. "I wasn't psyched up enough . . . because we had won the first two games and all we had to do was win one of the next three."

Mental preparation was not likely to be the problem on Tuesday, however. With the Series even at a game apiece, conventional wisdom suggested that the Mets would need to win at least two of the three games to be played at home. So the first of those games was pivotal, and it was special for other reasons as well. It would be the first World Series game ever played at Shea Stadium and the first in New York since 1964. Five years might not appear to be an oppressively long stretch for a city to go without a World Series—not if one lived in Chicago or Philadelphia—but New York had developed a proprietary claim on the annual event. Only once before, during the period from 1906 to 1910, had there been a drought of comparable duration. From that point on, over the next six decades, New York had hosted the World Series thirty-seven times, thirteen times with representatives from both leagues. Its return, then, was an occasion worthy of note. Every seat in the stadium was, of course, accounted for, and the usual quota of once-a-season attendees was on hand.

Except for a heavyweight title fight, no sporting event attracts the uninitiate in such numbers as the World Series, especially when it is played in New York in an election year. Along with some of the show-business crowd and professional celebrities like Jacqueline Kennedy Onassis, most every politician running for public office put in an appearance at Shea that dreary afternoon. Mayor Lindsay had made attendance *de rigueur*. During the late stages of the season, Lindsay had managed to tie his fortunes to those of the Mets. His cause, it seemed to most political observers, was as futile, his prospects as barren, as the Mets' had been for the last seven years. Elected as a Republican in 1965, he was defeated in the party's primary four years later. Now, opposed by both Republican and Democratic candidates, he was seeking re-election as an Independent-Liberal. He was given little chance in November's election.

But Lindsay was politician enough to perceive that the prevailing climate offered the hope of benediction. The mood of the city, of the country, had been sullen in recent years, but it seemed to have been leavened a bit by the events of summer. "Miracles" of varying dimensions were apparently the vogue in 1969, and the mayor was a man who could sense the hint of a new one in the making. If men can walk on the moon, if the Mets can win the pennant, might not a forlorn mayor, renounced by his own party, be returned to office by an electorate with a freshened taste for the lost and abandoned?

So with less than a month remaining until election day, Lindsay (who was still, after all, the reigning Mayor of New York) was very much in evidence for the third game of the World Series. Also present was Mario Procaccino, the Democratic candidate, who was said to be miffed at the manner in which Lindsay had been making capital of the Mets' success but was too wary of provoking the fans' ire to say so. Both were vocal in their support of the Mets, but there was room to wonder whether the Democratic challenger might not discern that a Baltimore victory could hardly damage his chances. Whatever his preference, Procaccino had little choice

but to cheer with the crowd, and the cheers that afternoon
came early and often.

Tommie Agee hit Palmer's fourth pitch of the game on
a whistling line to center field, deep enough to clear the fence,
and it was 1 – 0, Mets. An inning later, with two out, Grote
walked, Harrelson singled, and Gentry drove a double over
the head of Blair and Robinson to make it 3 – 0. It was Gentry's first hit in his last twenty-eight times at bat, and the two
runs batted in doubled his season's total.

He proved to be as effective on the mound as he was at
the plate. He held the Orioles hitless until the fourth, when
Frank Robinson's drive to left was trapped by Jones just inches
short of a catch. Powell followed with a clean single to right,
moving Robinson to third, and Gentry struck out Brooks
Robinson with a high fastball for the second out. That brought
to the plate Elrod Hendricks, the left-handed-hitting catcher
who was Baltimore's only platoon player. Hendricks lashed a
twisting drive toward the green fence in left-center field. With
two out, the runners were moving and so was Agee. Robinson had already crossed the plate and Powell was heading for
third when Agee, still in full flight, stretched his gloved hand
out across his body, lunged slightly, and clamped the webbing of the glove around the ball just as he hit the fence at
the 396-foot sign. He bounced lightly off the wall and held
his gloved hand out, palm up. There, for all to see, was the
white of the ball peeping out beyond the webbing's topmost
edge. Agee trotted in across the field that way, the ball cra-
dled in the pocket of his glove, gently, like a wounded bird
in the shelter of its nest. The crowd stood and cheered as he
crossed the first-base line, casually flipped the ball to umpire
Shag Crawford, and disappeared into the dugout.

"I haven't hit a ball that hard to left field in two years,"
Hendricks said later. "I didn't see him catch it, but then I
look up and see the white of the ball in his glove, so I figure

he still might drop it. Then he holds the glove up and I just say, 'Damn!' "

The Mets increased their lead to 4−0 in the sixth when Grote doubled home Boswell. But with a four-hitter going into the top of the seventh, Gentry showed signs of weakening. The first two batters, Hendricks and Johnson, hit long drives that backed up Agee in center, and the next three batters walked. Paul Blair represented the tying run when he came to the plate, and Hodges, recollections of the third game against Atlanta still fresh in memory, called for Ryan. A week earlier, Ryan had rescued Gentry by striking out Rico Carty for the third out. It looked as if he might duplicate that effort when he whipped his first two pitches by Blair for strikes. But Blair lined his third pitch deep into the gap in right-center, and Agee was off and running again, this time to his left but still in the direction of the fence. Just when it appeared that he might lose his race with the ball, he launched himself in a headlong dive, snatched the ball as it was about to hit the grass, and skidded halfway across the warning track.

Now the cheers from Shea Stadium seemed to carry as far as the Belmont Park racetrack, about five miles to the south, where the second-smallest crowd in the track's history was following the game with ears cocked to portable radios. Jockey Eddie Belmonte rode four winners that day, but Steve Cady, racing writer for *The New York Times*, reported that Agee's seventh-inning catch elicited the day's lustiest roar.

At Shea, the Mets were obliged to weather one more brief crisis. Kranepool's eighth-inning home run had given them a 5−0 margin, but in their final turn at bat the Orioles loaded the bases with two out, and once again Blair was the batter. This time, Ryan was taking no chances. He reached back for his best fastball and threw three of them past Blair, who watched the last one go by for the game's final out.

Most of the talk after the game concerned the two plays by Agee. Inevitably, comparisons were made with Willie Mays's stunning catch of a drive by Vic Wertz in the 1954 World Series at the Polo Grounds. Hodges called Agee's second play the best Series catch he had ever seen. Agee disagreed. "The second one was easier," he said, "because it was on my glove side and I didn't have as far to go. I thought I might get it without diving, but the wind dropped the ball straight down, and I had to hit the dirt."

In the Baltimore clubhouse, the Orioles fielded questions of a different sort. "Do you feel the Mets are a team of destiny?" Weaver was asked, not for the first time. "No," he said, "I believe they are a team with some fine outfielders."

Frank Robinson had something to say on the same subject. "The writers want to make it look like someone's watching over them," he said, "but there's nothing to that. They're making the plays. They probably made them all during the season. . . . The Mets aren't pulling any strings."

The Mets had arrived at a juncture where whatever strings they might or might not pull were firmly in their own grasp. Seaver and Koosman were ready to pitch the next two games at Shea. If the Series returned to Baltimore and stretched its full length, Seaver would be ready again for the seventh game. Met pitching appeared to be very much in control. "Just beware when these guys bust loose," Weaver said before the third game. "If they get hot, they can tear it wide open." But the Orioles showed no signs of getting hot, having scored just one run in their last twenty-two innings. In the twenty-six innings they had played thus far, they were held scoreless in twenty-three and hitless in twenty. Their only home run was Buford's, leading off the first game of the Series; the supposedly anemic Mets had hit three.

Still, most observers doubted that Baltimore's bats would remain quiet. Although trailing two games to one, the Orioles were still slight favorites to win the Series. They were the clear choice to win the fourth game, which would match Seaver and Cuellar again. It was a game critical to both teams, and it would be played on a crystal-cool afternoon, as perfect a day as autumn could offer. But the Mets, incredibly enough, would be obliged to share the heart of New York that day, for the conscience of the city lay elsewhere, and it was bitterly divided.

Wednesday, October 15, had been designated as Moratorium Day, a national day of protest against the war in Vietnam and of mourning for the thirty-eight thousand Americans who had died there. Rallies were scheduled in every part of the city—in Wall Street and Central Park, at United Nations Plaza and in front of St. Patrick's Cathedral. Those backing the moratorium wore blue-and-white peace buttons in their lapels, and some had black mourning bands wrapped around their arms.

But the day was not theirs alone. Sentiments were still fairly evenly divided in 1969, and those who supported the war effort also chose to make their presence felt. They wore American-flag pins in their own lapels and, by prearrangement, drove that day with their headlights on. Neither group was at pain to conceal its distaste for the other. The hostility that for the past two or three years had been subliminal was drawn to the surface by the visible emblems of identification. Scuffles broke out on stolid streets normally given over to the conduct of business. Angry words were exchanged in the lobbies of office buildings. Police, on foot and in squad cars, were within view from any street corner, and at rallying points they were present in regimental numbers.

On a day when the city appeared to be under siege, Shea Stadium itself was no island of tranquility. Outside the ballpark, scores of college-age youngsters carrying placards and banners handed out antiwar literature. Atop the stadium, flags were hoisted from half-staff to full by edict of Commissioner Bowie Kuhn. Mayor Lindsay, who supported the moratorium, had ordered that flags on all city-owned buildings (of which Shea Stadium was one) be lowered in the traditional gesture of mourning. However, a military color guard consisting of 225 veterans wounded in Vietnam said they would boycott the stadium unless flags were flown at full-staff. Kuhn said his decision was intended to "promote the greatest amount of respect and quiet in the Stadium."

The pregame ceremonies were even quieter than Kuhn had intended. The Maritime Academy marching band, which was to play the national anthem, chose not to get involved in public controversy, so Gordon MacRae stood at home plate and sang the anthem without accompaniment. There was also a last-minute change in the pregame pitcher. Evangelist Billy Graham had been scheduled to throw out the first ball, but Graham was a personal friend of President Nixon's and a supporter of his Vietnam policy; before he could even warm up his right arm, he was replaced by a left-hander of unknown political persuasion—Casey Stengel.

Of perhaps greater consequence, the Mets' starting pitcher that day found himself caught up in the turmoil before he could enter the ballpark. As he made his way from the parking lot to the player entrance, Tom Seaver was handed a pamphlet with his own picture on the front page and a story quoting him as saying that the United States should pull out of Vietnam. Some days earlier, Seaver had been approached by members of the moratorium committee and asked if he would object to an advertisement saying, "If the Mets can win the pennant, why can't we end the war?" Seaver said he would not object, but he did not count on his acquiescence being used as it was. In the clubhouse, before dressing for the game, he told reporters that he resented it. "I'm a ballplayer, not a politician," he said. "I did not give them permission to use me. I have certain feelings about Vietnam, and I will express them as a U.S. citizen after the Series is over."

If Seaver was at all distracted by the currents of political activity that preceded the game, he was all concentration when he got to the mound. For the first eight innings, he shut the Orioles out and permitted only two hits, a pair of third-inning singles by the eighth- and ninth-place hitters in the batting order. He had been provided with a one-run lead in the second, courtesy of a home run by Clendenon, and in the third he had to work hard to protect it. Belanger opened the inning with an opposite-field single. With the Mets looking for a bunt, Cuellar looped a hit into short left-field. With the Mets still playing for the bunt, Buford chopped a high bouncer that appeared headed over first, but Clendenon stretched the length of his six feet four inches to snare it and turn it into a force play at second. Then Blair, an excellent bunter, tried to squeeze home the tying run. But Seaver threw him a high fastball, and Blair popped the ball in the air between the mound and home plate. Hoping to turn a double play, Seaver let the ball fall; but his only play was to first, where he got the second out while the runner held at third. Then Frank Robinson popped out to end the threat.

For the next five innings, neither team stirred. Seaver, in fact, did not allow another hit and had retired nineteen of twenty batters when, with one out in the ninth, Frank Robinson lined a single to left and Powell sent him to third with a ground ball through the right side of the infield. Brooks Robinson then sliced a sinking line drive to right-center field. It was the kind of hit that challenges an outfielder's instincts: play it safe and concede the single, or gamble on making the catch against the possibility of extra bases? Swoboda never considered letting the ball drop. He headed straight into the gap, cutting a precise angle between his own path and the flight of the ball; then he dove to his right, his body parallel to the ground, caught the ball backhanded, and landed hard, belly-whopper style, while Frank Robinson tagged up and scored the tying run.

The Mets put two runners on base in the bottom of the ninth but were unable to score, and the Orioles squandered a similar opportunity in the top of the tenth. The bottom third of the Mets' order was due up in their half of the inning, and a fresh Baltimore pitcher, six-foot-six Dick Hall, was brought in to try to keep the game even. He had hardly warmed up when he found himself in trouble not of his own making. Grote, the leadoff batter, hit a routine fly ball to medium-deep left field. Buford broke back on the ball, reversed himself and started racing in toward the infield, and then lost sight of the ball entirely against the brightness of the sky. Belanger, from his position at shortstop, almost made an over-the-shoulder catch, but the ball fell between them for a double.

"I thought the ball was hit harder than it was," Buford said later. "Then when I started in, I didn't pick it up right away because of the glare."

The tainted hit nonetheless put the winning run in scoring position and initiated a succession of strategic moves by the two managers. For the past seven innings, Baltimore had been managed not by Earl Weaver but by third-base coach Billy Hunter. The volatile Weaver had earned the distinction of becoming the first manager in thirty-four years to be ejected from a World Series game when he was ousted for questioning Shag Crawford's judgment on balls and strikes. So now it was Hunter trading critical maneuvers with Hodges. The Met manager made the first move when he sent Rod Gaspar to second to run for Grote. Hunter then ordered an intentional walk for Al Weis, who had reached base seven times in three games. Hodges sent up J. C. Martin, a left-handed hitter, to bat for Seaver. Hunter brought in Pete Richert, a left-hander, to pitch to Martin. Martin surprised no one by bunting Richert's first pitch toward first base. Hendricks sprang from behind the plate, but Richert beat him to the ball, spun, and fired to Davey Johnson covering first. The throw appeared to have the runner beaten, but it struck Martin on the left wrist and bounded across the infield dirt. Gaspar, who was Rod Stupid to some of the Orioles, was smart enough to turn third and head for home and careful enough to jump on the plate with both feet planted squarely.

"Eddie Yost [the third-base coach] was yelling, 'go, go, go,'" Gaspar recalls, "but I couldn't hear him. I just heard the fans cheering, and when I rounded third I looked over my shoulder and saw the ball rolling toward second base, so I took off for home instinctively."

The play that sent Gaspar home with the winning run soon became the subject of a lively though informal inquiry. That evening, news photographs clearly showed that Martin had one foot in fair territory when the ball hit him. Rule (605)k states that a baserunner must remain outside the baseline when a play is being made at first base. If he is in fair territory, as Martin was, he is to be declared out for interfering with the throw. The rules also state, however, that any protest must be lodged before the teams leave the field, and Billy Hunter raised no objection.

"From the bench, I was sure he was in foul territory," Hunter said when questioned about the play. It was nonetheless interesting to speculate how Weaver might have seen it had he been on the Baltimore bench.

Hendricks saw it as a play that should have been made by the catcher, who, with the field in front of him, would not have had to pivot to make the throw. He said he had called for the ball but that Richert could not hear him above the din of the crowd. "I don't think it was that good a bunt," he said. "Actually, it should have been a routine play."

Martin believes his getting hit with the throw was "just a coincidence," but he acknowledges having done what he could to allow circumstance its best opportunity. "You try to do everything you possibly can," Martin says, recreating the play many years later. "You know from experience that if you run close to the first-base line, the throwing angle is very narrow, particularly if the pitcher is left-handed and has to turn to make the throw. So you run as close as you can. I wasn't thinking about getting hit or anything, I was just looking to shield the ball from the man covering first. As it turned out, the ball happened to hit me on the left wrist. But there was no argument at the time. All the controversy was in the media the next day."

The controversy was active enough to prompt umpire Crawford to issue a statement the following day. Crawford said he believed that Martin's foot had touched the inside of the baseline, and therefore he should not have been called out. But the debate was of no real consequence. No matter what the photographs indicated, the play was one that turned on the judgment of the umpire rather than an interpretation of the rules, and no protest would have served to reverse the call. So the play finally was deposited in the storehouse of baseball lore—to be summoned periodically as evidence documenting the legend of the Mets' inevitability. They were now, after all, just one victory away from an upset of substantial dimensions.

Hodges, however, was still circumspect. Asked how he liked his team's chances, he replied tersely: "Better than yesterday."

Brooks Robinson was more direct when he analyzed Baltimore's situation: "We can't afford to lose until next spring," he said.

CHAPTER

22

IT WAS THURSDAY, OCTOBER 16, and the city was tranquil again. The cool morning was lit with bright sunshine, and the shadows that split the streets were deep and sharply drawn. Early that afternoon, New York would host its last baseball game of the season. The improbable tale that had begun to unfold more than six months ago was near its end now.

The Mets were in an enviable position. They would have three chances, if they needed them, to win the World Series. But they had no taste to return to Baltimore. Dramatically, the story would lose a bit of its edge if they did not win it at home. Practically, the Orioles could not be trusted to remain dormant for too long. Until they scored in the ninth inning of the fourth game, they had been shut out for nineteen consecutive innings; they had scored only twice in the last thirty-two. Buford's double in the fourth inning of the opener had been their last extra-base hit. Since then, they had managed only twelve singles. If the Oriole hitters found their rhythm at Shea, two games in Baltimore could become a perilous piece of work. It would be prudent therefore to end it as soon as possible, and that task fell to Jerry Koosman.

Koosman, who had suffered recurrent arm problems during the first half of the season, recovered fully and had been at the peak of his form for the last two months. He had limited the Orioles to a pair of singles in the second game, enhancing his growing reputation as a big-game pitcher. Indeed, years later, a number of his teammates allowed that for a single game they would have chosen Koosman to start ahead of Seaver. With his flawless mechanics and his exhaustive knowledge of the fundamentals of pitching, Seaver was an ode to consistency, but Koosman was a pitcher whose effectiveness seemed to increase as the stakes mounted. He had, of course, played co-star to Seaver's lead for the past two seasons. But it was a role to which the unassuming Koosman was well suited.

"I was comfortable with my position on the team," he says now. "Tom liked taking a leadership role, and he was capable of handling it. I wasn't one who wanted very much publicity. I came from a small town in Minnesota and I found New York intimidating, scary. It took a lot of getting used to and a lot of adjustments. There were always media people around, and they sometimes put words in your mouth and then used them as quotes. I didn't appreciate that much at first, but later I got to learn what the writers were about and what they wanted to accomplish and I tended to understand them better. Tom was always comfortable with the press, though. He knew just how to handle them."

During his first two years in New York, Koosman was regularly described in the local papers as a soybean farmer from Appleton, Minnesota. But he had never really worked as a farmer, not professionally.

"My family had a farm," Koosman says, "and my two brothers and I helped out when school wasn't in session, but I never earned my living as a farmer. I went to an agricultural high school, where classes were held from October 1 to the end of March. Then, during the spring and summer, I would help out at home, but I also played baseball."

Koosman played for the town team in what was known locally as the "beer leagues," since the stake in most games was a case of beer. He was a thirteen-year-old outfielder in a league where most of the players were in their twenties and thirties, but he was physically mature for a teenager and he could throw the ball hard. By the time he turned fifteen, he had won a place in the pitching rotation and began to think he might be good enough to play professional baseball.

Two years later, while pitching for the army team at Fort Bliss, Texas, he received all the confirmation he needed. In his first season, he won twenty games and lost three, averaged eighteen strikeouts a game, and in one game struck out twenty-three batters. The first big-league scouts to come courting were Andy and Sid Cohen of the El Paso Sun Kings, a double-A farm club in the San Francisco Giants' organization. Koosman treated them to a shutout that included twenty strikeouts, and, although Andy Cohen described him as being "as green as a young clover field," he was invited to pitch batting practice for El Paso. Next on the scene was the Mets' Red Murff, who made two visits.

"The story made the rounds that the Mets discovered me through a tip from a Shea Stadium usher," Koosman says, "but that's not exactly true. Murff had already been to scout me once. Then my catcher on the Fort Bliss team, John Lucchese, wrote a letter to his dad, who was an usher at Shea, saying that the Mets ought to send a scout to see this young left-handed pitcher, and Murff came to see me again. This time, he offered me a contract. The Minnesota club also offered me a contract, and the Giants were still interested, but I decided to sign with the Mets. Actually, the Twins offered me a bigger bonus, and they were my home club, but they were building a pennant-winner in 1964, and I felt that if I could make it to the big leagues earlier with the Mets I would more than make up the difference in the bonus money."

It worked out as Koosman expected. After spending most of the next three seasons in the minors, he broke into the Mets' starting rotation in 1968. It was the start of a long, sometimes distinguished career that spanned eighteen seasons and eventually led him back to Minnesota, then to the Chicago White Sox, and finally, for two seasons, to the Phillies.

Now, as we speak, he is spending his first season in more than two decades outside of professional baseball. We are in the branch offices of an overnight courier company in Mendota Heights, a suburb of Minneapolis. Koosman is working as president of the newly formed agency, but it is an affiliation that will be short-lived. He already has thoughts of returning to baseball, but not as a manager.

"That's a pressure situation," he says, "and it takes the right kind of person to deal with it. I think I could do it, but I don't think it would be the right line for me. If I did go back into baseball, I would feel more comfortable as a coach, maybe a pitching coach."

There is about Koosman a plain-folks, homespun manner that calls to mind the young Jimmy Stewart. He is neighborly in a small-town way; speaking to him for the first time, one gets the sense of having met him before.

My schedule is tight on the day of our appointment: I had been in Chicago the previous day and need to return that same afternoon. Koosman readily offers to meet my early-morning flight to Minneapolis and get me back to the airport for my return flight to O'Hare. We drive to his office in his black-and-white van, he puts up a fresh pot of coffee, and we talk for the better part of two hours while Koosman autographs stacks of baseball cards on which he is shown wearing the uniform of the Minnesota Twins.

He is, clearly, still preoccupied with baseball. His career had been brought to an end by a knee injury that never had time to heal, and he finished his last season on the disabled list.

"I was operated on in May," he says, "but I tried to come back too soon, and I just couldn't pitch on the knee. The Phillies invited me back to spring training this year but I decided it was time to hang it up. I wasn't sure I made the right decision at first, but seeing what happened to Steve Carlton today. . . . I just didn't want to end up that way. I didn't want to have that year when they tell you, 'Hey, we don't need you anymore.' "

We had both learned that morning that Carlton, a twenty-two-year veteran, had been given his unconditional release by the Phillies and was looking to catch on with another team. Koosman preferred to cut away cleanly. He did not wish to tarnish the memories of a career that had glittered with success right from the start. In his first full season with the Mets, he had won nineteen games, more than any pitcher in the team's history, and the best of it was still a year away.

"That first year, 1968, was a beautiful, fun year," Koosman says. "It was Hodges's first season with the Mets. We had heard how strict he was and what a tough disciplinarian, and it didn't sound good for us. But he turned out to be the opposite of everything we heard. He clowned around and joined in the fun, and it was unbelievable after what we expected. But the next year, he became the Gil Hodges we had heard about; everything was business.

"Looking back, I could see what he was doing. In '68, he was just letting the ball roll and seeing how everyone handled different situations—who was mature enough and who reacted how. The next year, he put all that knowledge to use. He knew each player's abilities, both mental and physical. He never let anyone get in over his head, never asked anyone to do something he wasn't capable of doing. He molded us into one smooth-running machine."

As the Mets approached Game 5, that smooth-running

machine was poised on the brink of winning a world championship, and Koosman was looking to achieve a long-standing goal that had eluded him in the first game.

"I had always believed that you should set a goal that you have to strive for but that isn't too easy to reach," Koosman says. "So one of the goals I set for myself was to pitch a no-hitter in a World Series game, and in the first game I pitched I had one going into the seventh inning. My other goal was to get a hit every time up in a World Series game; no pitcher had ever done that, but I came a lot closer to the first goal than the second."

In his next try, Koosman came closer to achieving his second goal. His no-hitter was already gone when Belanger led off the third with a looping single over first base and Dave McNally hit the next pitch into the Orioles' bullpen for a 2–0 lead. It was Baltimore's first extra-base hit in the last thirty-five innings, and two outs later they added another when Frank Robinson hit a towering drive into the parking lot beyond the center-field fence. The three-run inning exceeded by one the Orioles' total output over the previous three games and, at least temporarily, stilled a Shea Stadium crowd that had come to the park with the scent of blood in its nostrils. The Mets stirred briefly in the third when Koosman, who had only four hits in eighty-four times up during the regular season, opened the inning with a double past third base. But the top of the order failed to advance him, and both sides remained quiet for the next two innings.

In the sixth, there occurred two plays—one in each half of the inning—that suggested the turn of the game and, in a way, were synoptic of the Mets' whole season. In the top of the sixth, with one out, Frank Robinson was struck in the right thigh by a Koosman fastball. There was no doubt that the ball hit him, but plate umpire Lou DiMuro ruled that the pitch had first glanced off Robinson's bat for strike two. The call brought Earl Weaver out of the Baltimore dugout while Robinson, who had already started for first base, returned to the dugout and disappeared into the runway, where the trainer sprayed his thigh with ethyl chloride. A full five minutes passed before Robinson emerged and, before a backdrop of waving handkerchiefs, took a called third strike. Boog Powell followed with a single (which would have put two runners on base with one out if DiMuro had seen the previous play differently), and Brooks Robinson flied out to end the inning.

Then came the second controversial play, a mirror image of the first. Jones, leading off the Mets' half of the sixth, skipped away from a breaking ball that was low and inside and that caromed, off something, in the direction of the Mets' dugout. DiMuro called the pitch a ball, but Jones, pointing to his right instep, claimed the ball had struck him on the foot. A new argument ensued, and Jones had the benefit of expert counsel. Clendenon, who was studying for the bar in the off-season, moved up to the plate from the on-deck circle to plead the case in Jones's behalf. What he needed was a solid piece of evidence, and it was soon forthcoming. Out of the Met dugout came Gil Hodges, whose subdued but firm demeanor suggested the surprise witness whose testimony would be irrefutable and whose character was beyond reproach. Hodges strode to the plate slowly, serenely, his huge right hand enveloping a baseball with a black smudge on its surface. He offered the ball to DiMuro. The black smudge was definitely shoe polish, but was the ball the same one that McNally had thrown to Jones? Yes, it was, said DiMuro, he had seen it roll into the dugout. He motioned Jones to first base.

Clendenon, the counselor-in-training, then stepped to the plate and lined a 2-and-2 pitch off the auxiliary scoreboard in left field for his third home run of the Series, bringing the Mets within one run of the Orioles. An inning later, they drew even. Al Weis, whose only two home runs of the season had helped the Mets win a series from the Cubs at Wrigley Field, drove McNally's second pitch of the inning over the 371-foot sign in left-center field. It was Weis's first home run at Shea Stadium and only the seventh in his eight big-league seasons, but it came as no surprise to his six-year-old son, Daniel.

"Jerry Grote's wife drove my family to the ballpark that day," Weis remembers. "It was Dan's birthday, October 16, and on the way there he said, 'My dad's gonna hit a home run for me for my birthday today.' They didn't tell me about it until after the game. I don't know how to explain it; call it circumstance, fate, whatever, but I hit one that day. My mother and father were at the game too, but my dad missed the homer. He was getting some beers and he heard the crowd cheering and he said, 'What happened?' My mother said, 'Your son just hit a home run.' "

So the score stood deadlocked at 3 – 3 after seven. Koosman made short work of the Orioles in the top of the eighth, and McNally, who had not lost a decision since August 3, departed before he could lose this one. With the Mets' right-handed platoon due up in the home half, Eddie Watt, a right-handed relief specialist who had led the Orioles in saves, was brought in to start the inning. Jones welcomed him with a 395-foot double off the center-field wall. That left Hodges with some difficult decisions to make. Clendenon, Swoboda, and Charles—all platoon players—were due to bat in succession, and Kranepool, Shamsky, and Garrett—the left-handed-hitting squadron—were on the bench. Hodges chose to ignore the percentages. Clendenon was asked to sacrifice Jones to third, but after fouling off two bunt attempts, he grounded to Brooks Robinson, and Jones remained at second. The next move was up to Weaver. With first base open, he might have elected to walk Swoboda intentionally to set up a double play that would end the inning. But he decided to deal with the batter at hand, and he soon regretted it. Swoboda lined Watt's second pitch down the left-field line, where Buford tried for a backhand catch but could do no better than trap the ball on a short hop. Swoboda had a double, and Jones scored to give the Mets their first lead of the game, 4 to 3. The tumult in the stands began to echo through the city—in taverns and restaurants, in offices and schoolrooms, on street corners and avenues—where televisions and radios carried the news to a widening audience. The din subsided briefly as Charles flew out to left but rose again when Grote sliced a low line drive to first. Powell bobbled the ball, then recovered and threw to Watt covering the base, but the pitcher could not control the throw. He juggled the ball and dropped it while Swoboda steamed around third and scored before Watt could make a play at the plate. It was 5 to 3, Mets, and the Orioles were down to their last turn at bat.

Koosman, who had allowed only one single since the third inning and had retired sixteen of the last seventeen batters, started the ninth by walking Frank Robinson. Now each succeeding batter would represent the tying run, and Koosman could not afford another mistake. He induced Powell to ground to second for a forceout. A crescendo was building in Shea Stadium, and it swelled an increment when Brooks Robinson flied to Swoboda in right. Davey Johnson was the batter now. The crowd was on its feet, the roar so loud that it muffled the sound of bat meeting ball and sending it on an arc into left-center field. It was hit fairly deep, but high, and Jones was tracking it to his left, gliding along the edge of the warning track. Then he stopped and waited as the ball fell toward his glove. He caught it with both hands high above his head and clutched it tight, then brought his hands down with a quick, sure motion as he crouched toward the ground, his right knee almost brushing the grass in a gesture at once humble and triumphant.

It was 3:17 P.M. on Thursday, October 16, 1969. The New York Mets were champions of the world.

For the third time in as many weeks, Shea Stadium was the scene of a rowdy, jubilant rampage. Yet again, the field was plundered and stripped of its markings. Whatever could pass for a souvenir was carried away. Somehow, the pitching rubber was salvaged to be presented to the city with the inscription: "To the greatest city, with the greatest fans, from the greatest team."

The Met clubhouse was appropriately raucous. There were the customary champagne showers, the embraces, the interviews with the media, the statements seeking definition of an event that could not quite be defined.

"This is the summit," said Ed Charles. "We're number one in the world and you just can't get any bigger than this."

Swoboda agreed. "It's the first and the sweetest," he shouted, "and because it's the first, nothing can ever be that sweet again."

"There is no most valuable on this team," said Clendenon, who had just been named the Series' Most Valuable Player.

Cleon Jones addressed the credibility issue. "Some people still might not believe in us," he said, "but then, some people still think the world is flat."

Mayor Lindsay, who had announced that a ticker-tape parade would mark Monday, October 20, as Mets Day, was understandably eager to invest the Mets' championship with a touch of the miraculous.

"On Monday," he said, "the number-one city in the world will honor the number-one baseball team in the world. Our city will be honoring a modern miracle—a miracle in which every New Yorker found pride and joy."

Hodges, who may or may not have heard the mayor's pronouncement, said simply, "There's nothing miraculous about us."

Not surprisingly, it was Casey Stengel, the original manager of the original Mets, whose analysis cut closest to the

304 · A MAGIC SUMMER

bone: "You can't be lucky every day," Casey said, "but you can if you get good pitching."

If one was in search of a miracle, the place to look was out in the streets. In the gray canyons of midtown Manhattan, downtown in the financial district, uptown in Harlem, on the East Side and West Side, in the neighborhoods of the boroughs, spontaneous celebrations broke out on a cue no more calculated than the sudden, grateful impulse to display in public a joy that was now the common coin of the city.

The streets and avenues were clogged with people dancing and singing and chanting "We're number one." Strangers embraced and kissed and champagne corks popped, and from the windows of offices high above the ground, cascades of paper floated downward. Tons of paper of every variety wafted to the streets—pages torn from bookkeeping ledgers, IBM punch cards, printouts from computers and data-processing machines, yellow sheets torn from legal pads, hundreds of feet of glossy black film, thin strips from adding machines, rolls of toilet paper, and shredded copies of magazines and newspapers. A bra sailed lazily in the breeze. The debris was already ankle-deep, but whenever the flow ebbed the cry rose from the street, "More-more-more," and down it came again.

Not twenty-four hours earlier, these same streets had curdled with the sullen bitterness of political division. Police faced off against angry demonstrators. Nightsticks were swung to impart order. Street fights broke out among hostile partisans. Now, these streets bounced to a different beat. Groups joined hands and danced the hora while others formed wider circles and clapped to the rhythm—men in suits and ties, blue-jeaned mailroom clerks and miniskirted secretaries, the clean-shaven and the hirsute, uniformed police and sandal-shod hippies, even hawks and doves, for who now was asking?

It was late in the afternoon. The celebration had been going on for more than an hour, and its numbers continued to grow as offices closed for the day. The start of rush-hour traffic inched by cautiously in single file, and the motorists joined in the festivities. They sounded their horns—*beep-beep-ba-beep,* "We're number one"—and those in the street kept the cadence by thumping the hood and roof of each car as it passed. "Blow-your-horn, blow-your-horn," came the chant as each car went by, and the horns blew back, and so did the horns of the buses. "No fares," one bus driver announced. "Everyone rides free today." "Tell-us-why, tell-us-why," the cry came, and he waved his index finger and answered, "We're number one," and again the cry went up. A cadre of police approached and the crowd booed, but then one of the cops raised a finger over his head and led the chant himself. The pavement was now piled high and gusting with litter and still it poured down.

The following day, John Lindsay would be out in the streets exhorting sanitation workers to sweep them clean. The City Sanitation Department, which keeps records of such things, reported that more than one thousand tons of paper had been dropped on New York to mark the Mets' victory. It exceeded the shower that was heaped upon the Apollo 11 crew earlier that summer, though it was not quite up to those delivered in honor of Charles Lindbergh and General Douglas MacArthur. But those displays had been held on signal, part of ticker-tape parades that had been planned for weeks. The outpouring that honored the Mets needed no orchestration, and it was the largest of its kind since V-J Day ended World War II.

On Monday, the Mets would have their own ticker-tape parade. The motorcade would move from the Battery to City Hall to Bryant Park and then to Gracie Mansion, the home of the mayor. Each Met player would be presented with a tie clip and cuff links engraved with the seal of the city and a blue-and-gold tie sprinkled with small city emblems. Mayor Lindsay, who thanked the team "for giving us a summer of joy," received his own reward a few weeks later when he defeated both the Democratic and Republican candidates and was reelected in what some political analysts described as an upset of a magnitude nearly equal to that of the Mets.

By the time the day ended, several million New Yorkers had turned out to watch, cheer, and pay tribute. There was no way, of course, to put a number on how many rejoiced in spontaneous wonder on the afternoon and evening of the Mets' day of triumph, for the celebration was bounded by neither geography nor time. It simply erupted, and it went on.

The sun had fallen behind the buildings, and the deepening shadows of early fall were coming into the streets. And still they danced. It was more than three hours since the game had ended, and what was happening now could no longer be described as a celebration of victory; it had become a rite of renewal. They held hands and danced because something had occurred that day that restored a long-ago vision. Yes, they knew now, the tales of rebirth and vindication that had filled the days of their childhood were as real as the dreams of one's youth. It was not too late after all. One day, the glass slipper might fit any of these dancing feet; even the humblest among them might be found to be the fairest in the land. If you believed hard enough, and endured long enough, and reached far enough, it was still all possible. The story could be written anew. And now they knew at least how it started. It went:

Once upon a time. . . .

ACKNOWLEDGMENTS

A BOOK OF THIS TYPE INVARI-
ably owes much to many people, and I wish to express my
gratitude to all those who helped me during the eighteen
months it took to research and write it.

A special thanks is owed, of course, to the twenty-three
members of the '69 Mets who graciously gave their time and
shared their recollections with me: Ken Boswell, Don Cardwell, Ed Charles, Jack DiLauro, Duffy Dyer, Wayne Garrett,
Rod Gaspar, Gary Gentry, Jerry Grote, Bud Harrelson, Cleon
Jones, Cal Koonce, Jerry Koosman, Ed Kranepool, J. C. Martin, Jim McAndrew, Tug McGraw, Nolan Ryan, Tom Seaver,
Art Shamsky, Ron Swoboda, Ron Taylor, and Al Weis.

My editor, John Radziewicz, merits no small nod of appreciation. He worked with me closely from conception to
completion, offering needed guidance along the way, and often
persuading me to curb the literary excesses to which I am
inclined. My agent, Clyde Taylor, directed John to me at the
outset and communicated his confidence that, despite other
commitments, I would bring the manuscript in ahead of
schedule.

Jay Horwitz, the Mets' public relations director, and his
assistant, Dennis D'Agostino, helped me locate some of the

players and offered me the hospitality of Shea Stadium's clubhouse on more than one occasion. Paul Jensen and Tim Clodjeaux, of the White Sox public-relations department, set up my interview with Tom Seaver; Rob Matwick and Chuck Poole, of the Houston Astros, did the same for me with Nolan Ryan; and Howard Starkman, the Toronto Blue Jays' publicist, led me to Ron Taylor.

Arthur Pincus, executive editor of *Sports inc.: The Sports Business Weekly* and previously a sports editor with *The New York Times,* provided me with background information and clips from the morgue as promptly as I requested them. I wish, too, to acknowledge two other members of the *Times* sports staff, Joseph Durso and George Vecsey, whose splendid coverage of the 1969 season provided me with an enlightened and accurate account of the Mets' day-by-day progress. For background material, I also drew upon their books—Durso's *Amazing: The Miracle of the Mets* (Houghton Mifflin Company, 1970) and Vecsey's *Joy in Mudville* (McCall Publishing Co., 1970)—as well as Leonard Koppett's *The New York Mets* (Macmillan Publishing Co., 1970 and 1974). Another book I found useful was *The Mets from Mobile: Cleon Jones and Tommie Agee,* by A.S. (Doc) Young (Harcourt, Brace and World, 1970).

Among those who supplied me with other bits of information, source material, and leads were Steven (First) Cohen, my son's friend and namesake; Pat Lynn; Dick Rasmussen; and Sonny Jackson.

Finally, I would like to offer my appreciation to my family. Writing a book of this length while working at a full-time job is never a painless proposition. Its completion is aided or impeded by those with claims upon one's attention and time. I am indebted, therefore, to my wife, Betty, who was obliged to decline invitations and forgo vacation trips or make them alone while I adhered to my work schedule; my daughter and son-in-law, Linda and Eddie, who were always protective of my writing time; my son, Steve, who tracked my progress as I tracked his through law school; and my grandson, Michael, who arrived midbook and whose interruptions were always inspirational rather than distracting.

S. C.

S T A T I S T I C S

1969 NATIONAL LEAGUE STANDINGS

	W	L	PCT	GB	BA	ERA
EAST						
New York	100	62	.617	—	.242	2.99
Chicago	92	70	.568	8	.253	3.34
Pittsburgh	88	74	.543	12	.277	3.61
St. Louis	87	75	.537	13	.253	2.94
Philadelphia	63	99	.389	37	.241	4.17
Montreal	52	110	.321	48	.240	4.33
WEST						
Atlanta	93	69	.574	—	.258	3.53
San Francisco	90	72	.556	3	.242	3.25
Cincinnati	89	73	.549	4	.277	4.13
Los Angeles	85	77	.525	8	.254	3.09
Houston	81	81	.500	12	.240	3.60
San Diego	52	110	.321	41	.225	4.24

1969 METS

BATTING

	POS	G	AB	H	2B	3B	HR	R	RBI	BB	SO	SB	BA
Tommie Agee	CF	149	565	153	23	4	26	97	76	59	137	12	.271
Ken Boswell	2B	102	362	101	14	7	3	48	32	36	47	7	.279
Ed Charles	3B	61	169	35	8	1	3	21	18	18	31	4	.207
Donn Clendenon	1B	72	202	51	5	0	12	31	37	19	62	3	.252
Kevin Collins	3B	16	40	6	3	0	1	1	2	3	10	0	.150
Duffy Dyer	C	29	74	19	3	1	3	5	12	4	22	0	.257
Wayne Garrett	3B	124	400	87	11	3	1	38	39	40	75	4	.218
Rod Gaspar	OF	118	213	49	6	1	1	26	14	25	19	7	.228
Jim Gosger	OF	10	15	2	2	0	0	0	1	1	6	0	.133
Jerry Grote	C	113	365	92	12	3	6	38	40	32	59	2	.252
Bud Harrelson	SS	123	395	98	11	6	0	42	24	54	54	1	.248
Bob Heise	SS	4	10	3	1	0	0	1	0	3	2	0	.300
Cleon Jones	LF	137	483	164	25	4	12	92	75	64	60	16	.340
Ed Kranepool	1B	112	353	84	9	2	11	36	49	37	32	3	.238
J. C. Martin	C	66	177	37	5	1	4	12	21	12	32	0	.209
Amos Otis	OF	48	93	14	3	1	0	6	4	6	27	1	.151
Bobby Pfeil	IF	62	211	49	9	0	0	20	10	7	27	0	.232
Art Shamsky	RF	100	303	91	9	3	14	42	47	36	32	1	.300
Ron Swoboda	RF	109	327	77	10	2	9	38	52	43	90	1	.235
Al Weis	IF	103	247	53	9	2	2	20	23	15	51	3	.215
Team Total			5427	1311	184	41	109	632	598	527	1089	176	.242

PITCHING

	W	L	PCT	ERA	SV	G	GS	CG	IP	BB	SO
Don Cardwell	8	10	.444	3.01	0	30	21	4	152.1	47	60
Jack DiLauro	1	4	.200	2.40	1	23	4	0	63.2	18	27
Danny Frisella	0	0	—	7.71	0	3	0	0	4.2	3	5
Gary Gentry	13	12	.520	3.43	0	35	35	6	233.2	81	154
Jessie Hudson	0	0	—	4.50	0	1	0	0	2	2	3
Al Jackson	0	0	—	10.64	0	9	0	0	11	4	10
Bob Johnson	0	0	—	0.00	1	2	0	0	1.2	1	1
Cal Koonce	6	3	.667	4.99	7	40	0	0	83	42	48
Jerry Koosman	17	9	.654	2.88	0	32	32	16	241	68	180
Jim McAndrew	6	7	.462	3.47	0	27	21	4	135	44	90
Tug McGraw	9	3	.750	2.24	12	42	4	1	100.1	47	92
Les Rohr	0	0	—	20.25	0	1	0	0	1.1	1	0
Nolan Ryan	6	3	.667	3.53	1	25	10	2	89.1	53	92
Tom Seaver	25	7	.781	2.21	0	36	35	18	273.1	82	208
Ron Taylor	9	4	.692	2.72	13	59	0	0	76	24	42
Team Total	100	62	.617	2.99	35	365	162	51	1468.1	572	1012

1969 NATIONAL LEAGUE CHAMPIONSHIP SERIES

	R	H	E	PITCHERS (innings pitched; winner and loser in **bold**)

GAME 1 - OCTOBER 4

| New York | 9 | 10 | 1 | **Tom Seaver** (7), Ron Taylor (2) SV |
| Atlanta | 5 | 10 | 2 | **Phil Niekro** (8), Cecil Upshaw (1) |

GAME 2 - OCTOBER 5

| New York | 11 | 13 | 1 | Jerry Koosman (4.2), **Ron Taylor** (1.1), Tug McGraw (3) SV |
| Atlanta | 6 | 9 | 3 | **Ron Reed** (1.2), Paul Doyle (1), Milt Pappas (2.1), Jim Britton (0.1), Cecil Upshaw (2.2), Gary Neibauer (1) |

GAME 3 - OCTOBER 6

| Atlanta | 4 | 8 | 1 | **Pat Jarvis** (4.1), George Stone (1), Cecil Upshaw (2.2) |
| New York | 7 | 14 | 0 | Gary Gentry (2), **Nolan Ryan** (7) |

1969 WORLD SERIES

	R	H	E	PITCHERS (innings pitched; winner and loser in **bold**)

GAME 1 - OCTOBER 11

| New York | 1 | 6 | 1 | **Tom Seaver** (5), Don Cardwell (1), Ron Taylor (2) |
| Baltimore | 4 | 6 | 0 | **Mike Cuellar** (9) |

GAME 2 - OCTOBER 12

| New York | 2 | 6 | 0 | **Jerry Koosman** (8.2), Ron Taylor (0.1) SV |
| Baltimore | 1 | 2 | 0 | **Dave McNally** (9) |

GAME 3 - OCTOBER 14

| Baltimore | 0 | 4 | 1 | **Jim Palmer** (6), Dave Leonhard (2) |
| New York | 5 | 6 | 0 | **Gary Gentry** (6.2), Nolan Ryan (2.1) SV |

GAME 4 - OCTOBER 15

| Baltimore | 1 | 6 | 1 | Mike Cuellar (7), E. Watt (2), **Dick Hall** (0), Pete Richert (0) |
| New York | 2 | 10 | 1 | **Tom Seaver** (10) |

GAME 5 - OCTOBER 16

| Baltimore | 3 | 5 | 2 | Dave McNally (7), **E. Watt** (1) |
| New York | 5 | 7 | 0 | **Jerry Koosman** (9) |

WORLD SERIES TEAM TOTALS

	W	AB	H	2B	3B	HR	R	RBI	BA	BB	SO	ERA
New York	4	159	35	8	0	6	15	13	.220	15	35	1.80
Baltimore	1	157	23	1	0	3	9	9	.146	15	28	2.72

WORLD SERIES BATTING

New York

	POS	AB	H	2B	3B	HR	R	RBI	BA
Jerry Grote	C	19	4	2	0	0	1	1	.211
Cleon Jones	OF	19	3	1	0	0	2	0	.158
Tommie Agee	OF	18	3	0	0	1	1	1	.167
Bud Harrelson	SS	17	3	0	0	0	1	0	.176
Ron Swoboda	OF	15	6	1	0	0	1	1	.400
Ed Charles	3B	15	2	1	0	0	1	0	.133
Donn Clendenon	1B	14	5	1	0	3	4	4	.357
Al Weis	2B	11	5	0	0	1	1	3	.455
Jerry Koosman	P	7	1	1	0	0	0	0	.143
Art Shamsky	OF	6	0	0	0	0	0	0	.000
Tom Seaver	P	4	0	0	0	0	0	0	.000
Ed Kranepool	1B	4	1	0	0	1	1	1	.250
Ken Boswell	2B	3	1	0	0	0	1	0	.333
Gary Gentry	P	3	1	1	0	0	0	2	.333
Rod Gaspar	OF	2	0	0	0	0	1	0	.000
Duffy Dyer	C	1	0	0	0	0	0	0	.000
Wayne Garrett	3B	1	0	0	0	0	0	0	.000
J. C. Martin	3B	0	0	0	0	0	0	0	.000

Stolen bases: Tommie Agee

Baltimore

	POS	AB	H	2B	3B	HR	R	RBI	BA
Don Buford	OF	20	2	1	0	1	1	2	.100
Paul Blair	OF	20	2	0	0	0	1	0	.100
Brooks Robinson	3B	19	1	0	0	0	0	2	.053
Boog Powell	1B	19	5	0	0	0	0	0	.263
Davey Johnson	2B	16	1	0	0	0	1	0	.063
Frank Robinson	OF	16	3	0	0	1	2	1	.188
Mark Belanger	SS	15	3	0	0	0	2	1	.200
Elrod Hendricks	C	10	1	0	0	0	1	0	.100
Andy Etchebarren	C	6	0	0	0	0	0	0	.000
Mike Cuellar	P	5	2	0	0	0	0	1	.400
Dave McNally	P	5	1	0	0	1	1	2	.200
Jim Palmer	P	2	0	0	0	0	0	0	.000
Clay Dalrymple		2	2	0	0	0	0	0	1.000
Curt Motton		1	0	0	0	0	0	0	.000
Dave May		1	0	0	0	0	0	0	.000
Merv Rettenmund		0	0	0	0	0	0	0	—
Chico Salmon		0	0	0	0	0	0	0	—

Stolen bases: Paul Blair

1969 METS REGULAR SEASON

Game No.	Date	Opponent	W-L	Score	Record	Position
1	4/8	Montreal	L	11–10	0–1	4(T)
2	4/9	Montreal	W	9–5	1–1	3(T)
3	4/10	Montreal	W	4–2	2–1	3
4	4/11	St. Louis	L	6–5	2–2	3
5	4/12	St. Louis	L	1–0	2–3	3(T)
6	4/13	St. Louis	L	3–1	2–4	4(T)
7	4/14	At Philadelphia	L	5–1	2–5	5(T)
8	4/15	At Philadelphia	W	6–3	3–5	4(T)
9	4/16	At Pittsburgh	L	11–3	3–6	5
10	4/17	At Pittsburgh	L	4–0	3–7	5
11	4/19	At St. Louis	W	2–1	4–7	4(T)
12	4/20	At St. Louis	W	11–3	5–7	3(T)
13	4/21	Philadelphia	L	2–1(11)	5–8	3(T)
14	4/23	Pittsburgh	W	2–0	6–8	3(T)
15	4/25	Chicago	L	3–1	6–9	4
16	4/26	Chicago	L	9–3	6–10	4(T)
17	4/27(1)	Chicago	L	8–6	6–11	
18	4/27(2)	Chicago	W	3–0	7–11	4(T)
19	4/29	At Montreal	W	2–0	8–11	3(T)
20	4/30	At Montreal	W	2–1	9–11	3
21	5/1	At Montreal	L	3–2	9–12	4
22	5/2	At Chicago	L	6–4	9–13	5
23	5/3	At Chicago	L	3–2	9–14	5
24	5/4(1)	At Chicago	W	3–2	10–14	
25	5/4(2)	At Chicago	W	3–2	11–14	4
26	5/6	Cincinnati	W	8–1	12–14	4
27	5/7	Cincinnati	L	3–0	12–15	4
28	5/10	Houston	W	3–1	13–15	3
29	5/11(1)	Houston	L	4–1	13–16	
30	5/11(2)	Houston	W	11–7	14–16	3
31	5/13	Atlanta	L	4–3	14–17	3
32	5/14	Atlanta	W	9–3	15–17	3
33	5/15	Atlanta	L	6–5	15–18	3
34	5/16	At Cincinnati	W	10–9	16–18	3
35	5/17	At Cincinnati	W	11–3	17–18	3
36	5/21	At Atlanta	W	5–0	18–18	3
37	5/22	At Atlanta	L	15–3	18–19	3
38	5/23	At Houston	L	7–0	18–20	4
39	5/24	At Houston	L	5–1	18–21	4
40	5/25	At Houston	L	6–3	18–22	4
41	5/27	San Diego	L	3–2	18–23	4
42	5/28	San Diego	W	1–0(11)	19–23	4
43	5/30	San Francisco	W	4–3	20–23	4

Game No.	Date	Opponent	W-L	Score	Record	Position
44	5/31	San Francisco	W	4–2	21–23	3
45	6/1	San Francisco	W	5–4	22–23	3
46	6/2	Los Angeles	W	2–1	23–23	3
47	6/3	Los Angeles	W	5–2	24–23	2
48	6/4	Los Angeles	W	1–0(15)	25–23	2
49	6/6	At San Diego	W	5–3	26–23	2
50	6/7	At San Diego	W	4–1	27–23	2
51	6/8	At San Diego	W	3–2	28–23	2
52	6/10	At San Francisco	W	9–4	29–23	2
53	6/11	At San Francisco	L	7–2	29–24	2
54	6/13	At Los Angeles	L	1–0	29–25	2
55	6/14	At Los Angeles	W	3–1	30–25	2
56	6/15	At Los Angeles	L	3–2	30–26	2
57	6/17(1)	At Philadelphia	W	1–0	31–26	
58	6/17(2)	At Philadelphia	L	7–3	31–27	2
59	6/18	At Philadelphia	W	2–0	32–27	2
60	6/19	At Philadelphia	W	6–5	33–27	2
61	6/20	St. Louis	W	4–3	34–27	2
62	6/21	St. Louis	L	5–3	34–28	2
63	6/22(1)	St. Louis	W	5–1	35–28	
64	6/22(2)	St. Louis	W	1–0	36–28	2
65	6/24(1)	Philadelphia	W	2–1	37–28	
66	6/24(2)	Philadelphia	W	5–0	38–28	2
67	6/25	Philadelphia	L	6–5(10)	38–29	2
68	6/26	Philadelphia	L	2–0	38–30	2
69	6/27	Pittsburgh	L	3–1	38–31	2
70	6/28	Pittsburgh	L	7–4	38–32	2
71	6/29	Pittsburgh	W	7–3	39–32	2
72	6/30	At St. Louis	W	10–2	40–32	2
73	7/1(1)	At St. Louis	L	4–1	40–33	
74	7/1(2)	At St. Louis	L	8–5	40–34	2
75	7/2	At St. Louis	W	6–4(14)	41–34	2
76	7/3	At St. Louis	W	8–1	42–34	2
77	7/4(1)	At Pittsburgh	W	11–6	43–34	
78	7/4(2)	At Pittsburgh	W	9–2	44–34	2
79	7/6	At Pittsburgh	W	8–7	45–34	2
80	7/8	Chicago	W	4–3	46–34	2
81	7/9	Chicago	W	4–0	47–34	2
82	7/10	Chicago	L	6–2	47–35	2
83	7/11	Montreal	L	11–4	47–36	2
84	7/13(1)	Montreal	W	4–3	48–36	
85	7/13(2)	Montreal	W	9–7	49–36	2
86	7/14	At Chicago	L	1–0	49–37	2
87	7/15	At Chicago	W	5–4	50–37	2
88	7/16	At Chicago	W	9–5	51–37	2

Game No.	Date	Opponent	W-L	Score	Record	Position
89	7/18	At Montreal	W	5–2	52–37	2
90	7/19	At Montreal	L	5–4	52–38	2
91	7/20(1)	At Montreal	L	3–2	52–39	
92	7/20(2)	At Montreal	W	4–3(10)	53–39	2
93	7/24	Cincinnati	L	4–3(12)	53–40	2
94	7/25	Cincinnati	W	4–3	54–40	2
95	7/26	Cincinnati	W	3–2	55–40	2
96	7/27	Cincinnati	L	6–3	55–41	2
97	7/30(1)	Houston	L	16–3	55–42	
98	7/30(2)	Houston	L	11–5	55–43	2
99	7/31	Houston	L	2–0	55–44	2
100	8/1	Atlanta	W	5–4	56–44	2
101	8/2	Atlanta	W	1–0	57–44	2
102	8/3	Atlanta	W	6–5(11)	58–44	2
103	8/4	At Cincinnati	L	1–0	58–45	2
104	8/5(1)	At Cincinnati	L	8–5	58–46	
105	8/5(2)	At Cincinnati	W	10–1	59–46	2
106	8/6	At Cincinnati	L	3–2	59–47	2
107	8/8(1)	At Atlanta	W	4–1	60–47	
108	8/8(2)	At Atlanta	L	1–0(10)	60–48	2
109	8/9	At Atlanta	W	5–3	61–48	2
110	8/10	At Atlanta	W	3–0	62–48	2
111	8/11	At Houston	L	3–0	62–49	2
112	8/12	At Houston	L	8–7	62–50	2
113	8/13	At Houston	L	8–2	62–51	3
114	8/16(1)	San Diego	W	2–0	63–51	
115	8/16(2)	San Diego	W	2–1	64–51	2
116	8/17(1)	San Diego	W	3–2	65–51	
117	8/17(2)	San Diego	W	3–2	66–51	2
118	8/19	San Francisco	W	1–0(14)	67–51	2
119	8/20	San Francisco	W	6–0	68–51	2
120	8/21	San Francisco	L	7–6(11)	68–52	2
121	8/22	Los Angeles	W	5–3	69–52	2
122	8/23	Los Angeles	W	3–2	70–52	2
123	8/24	Los Angeles	W	7–4	71–52	2
124	8/26(1)	At San Diego	W	8–4	72–52	
125	8/26(2)	At San Diego	W	3–0	73–52	2
126	8/27	At San Diego	W	4–1	74–52	2
127	8/29	At San Francisco	L	5–0	74–53	2
128	8/30	At San Francisco	W	3–2(10)	75–53	2
129	8/31(1)	At San Francisco	W	8–0	76–53	
130	8/31(2)	At San Francisco	L	3–2(11)	76–54	2
131	9/1	At Los Angeles	L	10–6	76–55	2
132	9/2	At Los Angeles	W	5–4	77–55	2
133	9/3	At Los Angeles	L	5–4	77–56	2

Game No.	Date	Opponent	W-L	Score	Record	Position
134	9/5(1)	Philadelphia	W	5–1	78–56	
135	9/5(2)	Philadelphia	L	4–2	78–57	2
136	9/6	Philadelphia	W	3–0	79–57	2
137	9/7	Philadelphia	W	9–3	80–57	2
138	9/8	Chicago	W	3–2	81–57	2
139	9/9	Chicago	W	7–1	82–57	2
140	9/10(1)	Montreal	W	3–2(12)	83–57	
141	9/10(2)	Montreal	W	7–1	84–57	1
142	9/11	Montreal	W	4–0	85–57	1
143	9/12(1)	At Pittsburgh	W	1–0	86–57	
144	9/12(2)	At Pittsburgh	W	1–0	87–57	1
145	9/13	At Pittsburgh	W	5–2	88–57	1
146	9/14	At Pittsburgh	L	5–3	88–58	1
147	9/15	At St. Louis	W	4–3	89–58	1
148	9/17	At Montreal	W	5–0	90–58	1
149	9/18	At Montreal	W	2–0	91–58	1
150	9/19(1)	Pittsburgh	L	8–2	91–59	
151	9/19(2)	Pittsburgh	L	8–0	91–60	1
152	9/20	Pittsburgh	L	4–0	91–61	1
153	9/21(1)	Pittsburgh	W	5–3	92–61	
154	9/21(2)	Pittsburgh	W	6–1	93–61	1
155	9/22	St. Louis	W	3–1	94–61	1
156	9/23	St. Louis	W	3–2(11)	95–61	1
157	9/24	St. Louis	W	6–0	96–61	1
158	9/26	At Philadelphia	W	5–0	97–61	1
159	9/27	At Philadelphia	W	1–0	98–61	1
160	9/28	At Philadelphia	W	2–0	99–61	1
161	10/1	At Chicago	W	6–5(12)	100–61	1
162	10/2	At Chicago	L	5–3	100–62	1